IMAGES
of America

AROUND SYLVAN BEACH

On the cover: In 1916, a Har-Phel farm truck with a load of kids on the back was a common sight. Jessie Raut, the girl with the straw hat, caught meningitis and passed when she was 14. The boy that is saluting was born with a hole in his heart, but he lived to the age of 92. The past is an interesting mix of achievements and failures. (Author's collection.)

IMAGES
of America

AROUND SYLVAN BEACH

Brandy Ann

ARCADIA
PUBLISHING

ISBN 978-0-7385-5656-7

Published by Arcadia Publishing
Charleston, South Carolina

Printed in the United States of America

Library of Congress Catalog Card Number: 2007942116

For all general information contact Arcadia Publishing at:
Telephone 843-853-2070
Fax 843-853-0044
E-mail sales@arcadiapublishing.com
For customer service and orders:
Toll-Free 1-888-313-2665

Visit us on the Internet at www.arcadiapublishing.com

I asked God for everything;
That I might enjoy life.
He gave me life;
That I might enjoy everything.

In memory
of
Richard
His light continues to shine

CONTENTS

ACKNOWLEDGMENTS

The list of people that have helped my endeavor to save a part of Sylvan Beach's history is long, and words cannot reveal the deep gratitude I feel. I will simply list their names. Thanks go to Canal Village Archives in Rome, Lisa Brave; Sylvan Beach Historical Archives, Nanette Jackson, historian; Joe Benedict, Sylvan Beach administrator and public works superintendent; Robert Montross, historian; Jim Van Winkle, publisher of the *Queen Central News*; John Taibi, author; author Robert Hemmings, Pottery in North Bay; Skip Sable; April Staring; Rita Fern; Nancy Fusco; Bob Pickard; Arlene Pifer; Nicole Pilcher; and Gurney Jones.

Last but not least, I want to thank Garry R. White, a fellow author and close friend. He is my contributing editor and manager; without him, this work would have been a lot harder to do and taken a lot longer.

INTRODUCTION

The Erie Canal was one of the early achievements that influenced the development of the area. When completed in 1825 at a cost of $7.15 million, it was the longest canal in the world, built in the least amount of time at the least expense and with less construction experience. It was accomplished to a large extent by men earning around $3 a week; they used shovels and pick axes, working 10 hours a day, six days a week. Benjamin Wright, a chief engineer, earned $36 a week, and his assistant, James Geddes, a surveyor, earned $24. Stretching from the Hudson River in the east all the way to Lake Erie in the west, the canal opened the western territory for settlement and commerce.

The building of the Erie Canal was just one link in the long chain of events that led to the development of Sylvan Beach. For many years before Sylvan Beach existed, the entire area was simply known as Fish Creek. To be more specific, some sections received nicknames from locals, such as McClanathanville, named for a 600-acre family farm on the shores of Fish Creek.

Fish Creek was settled by George Haskins in the early 1800s. Later brothers George and William Covell joined him, and the area flourished with the addition of the only railway station available for shipping produce and passenger service. Lumber was transported to the station from as far away as Williamstown in Oswego County and Osceola in Lewis County. During those early years, it was not uncommon to see 15 to 20 wagon teams following one another into the station. As much as two million board feet of lumber a year was transported from Fish Creek by Durham boats and the railroad.

When Sylvan Beach began to draw vacationers, the Fish Creek railway station played an important role. The station was just a 15-minute walk from the "Coney Island of Central New York," or one could take a pleasant two-mile ride down Wood River.

Up the road, North Bay was a booming town, alive with trade and commerce. In 1871, Sandy Rea's home in North Bay burned to the ground. He was the town clerk at the time, and his office containing all the town records was in his home. Thus everything was destroyed, and many of the images and historical records of North Bay, Fish Creek, and the other small hamlets that make up the township were lost. However, it is believed North Bay had seven hotels, three stores, two sawmills, a planing mill, a shingle mill, two potteries, a blacksmith shop, a harness shop, a wagon and sleigh shop, three churches, a school, and a post office. Records reveal that as many as 35 canal boats were built in the "Bay."

In 1873, Walton Rogers, a master on the Erie Canal boat *Geo. W. Butterfield*, obtained two canal boats, the *Nettie Irene* and the *Emma Louisa*, named for two of his daughters. Built in North Bay, they were launched into Oneida Lake and then traveled south to Wood River. At

Jug Point, the junction of Fish Creek and Wood Creek that formed the Wood River, the boats traveled a short distance up Wood Creek to the "Higginsville side cut." Also known as the Oneida Lake Canal, the Higginsville side cut opened on September 12, 1835. It was located between Wood Creek and Higginsville and connected Oneida Lake to the Erie Canal. Built by the Oneida Lake Canal Company, formed in 1832, the canal was just six and a half miles long and cost $65,000.

North Bay dwindled in importance as Sylvan Beach began to grow and flourish. Located side by side, their borders were a fuzzy uncertainty. In 1886, the New York, Ontario and Western Railway built a loop into Sylvan Beach to accommodate large groups of vacationers. The completion of the Barge Canal in 1918 caused more great changes and improvements for Sylvan Beach. The midway of old had to be moved when Wood River was straightened to enter Oneida Lake, and new bridges had to be built.

Oneida Lake starts at Wood River on the east. Its sandy shores give way to the wide valley, nudging the Tug Hill Plateau on the north that spreads across the fertile land to Oneida River in the west. The shallow, blue lake is a paradise at 369 feet above sea level and 22 miles long. Its serenity is only occasionally disturbed by the sheer fury of a sudden storm. The lake was a convenient avenue to incorporate into the Barge Canal, which included parts of the old Erie Canal. It continues to operate to this day.

Many events, places, and people working together caused the creation of the only village in Vienna Township, Sylvan Beach.

One

The Beginning

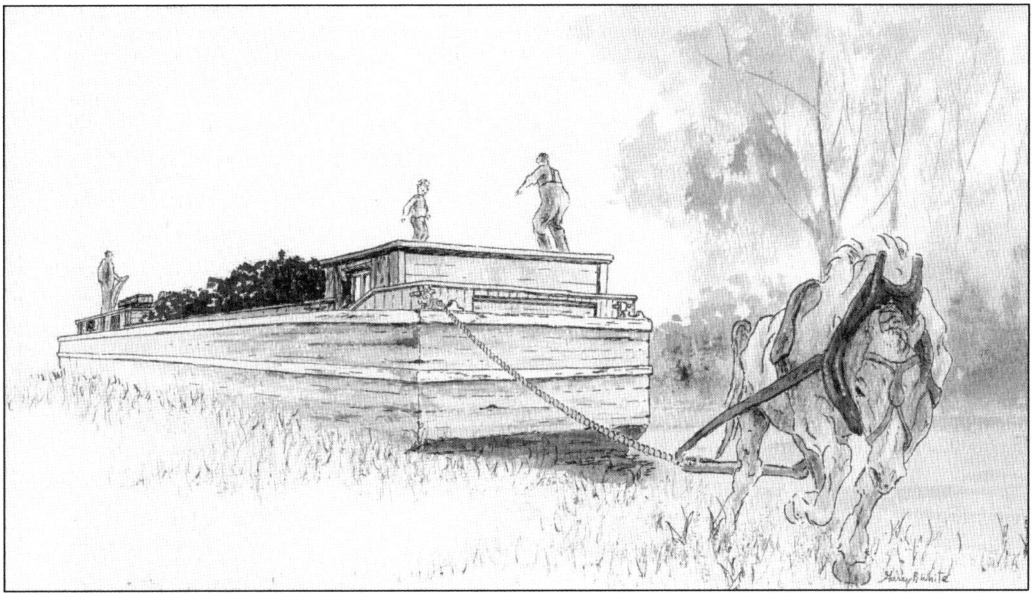

The idea of a canal system across New York State was first presented in 1792. It was not until 1804 that Gouverneur Morris created enthusiasm for a cross-country canal connecting the Hudson River to Lake Erie. Funds were sought from the federal government; however, they were unobtainable. The Erie Canal and all the canal systems in New York State were paid for by the people.

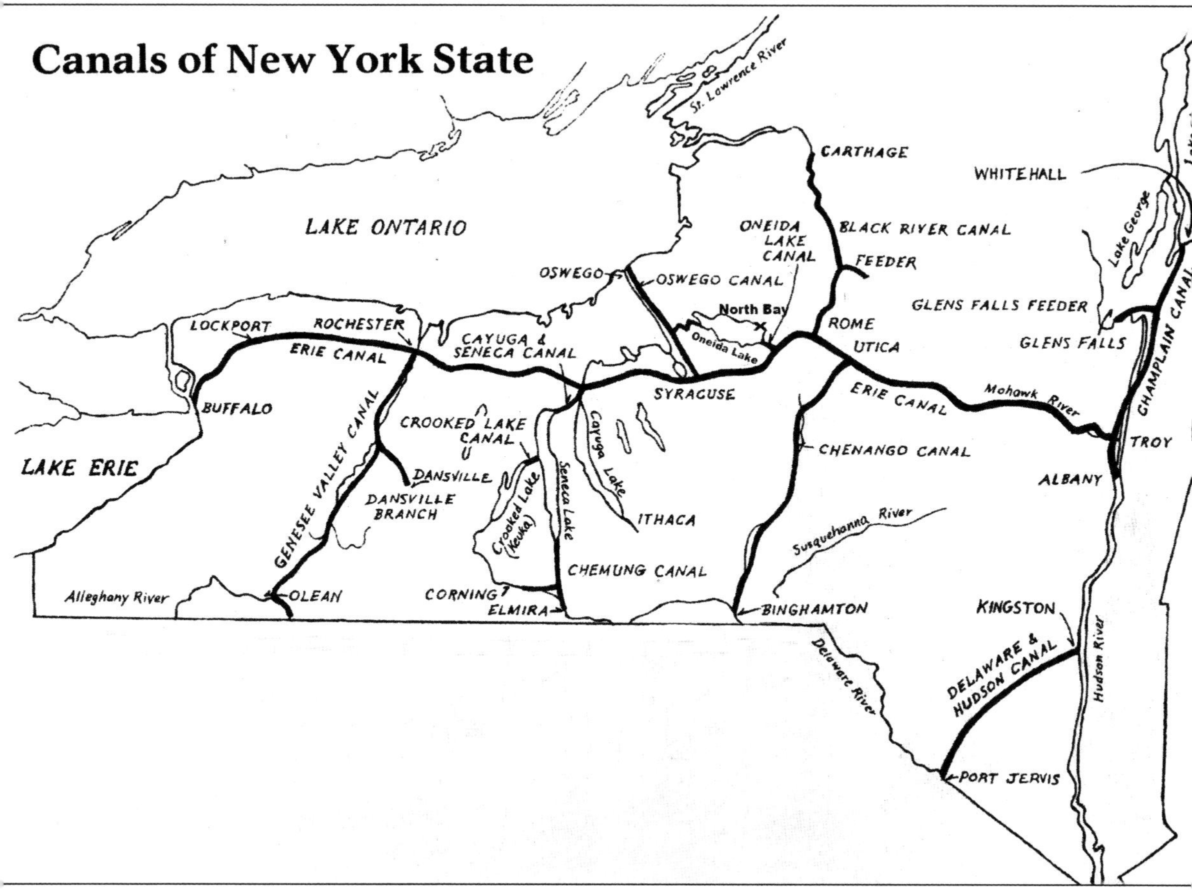

The history of the Erie Canal is not only fascinating but also a major stepping stone in the development of North Bay and Sylvan Beach as well as the state of New York. The completion of the canal instantly brought prosperity to all the small towns along its route. Syracuse grew from a small hamlet in 1820 to an immense city of 11,000 in 1840. An outcry from other small towns for a waterway connecting them to the Erie Canal resulted in a system with many small canals throughout the state. Some contribute the prosperity in North Bay to the Black River Canal that runs through Rome, but that is not likely because the Black River Canal did not connect to Oneida Lake. However, the "Higginsville side cut," also known as the Oneida Lake Canal, ran directly from Oneida Lake to the Erie Canal, and the Oswego Canal was connected to Oneida Lake on the west by the Oneida River.

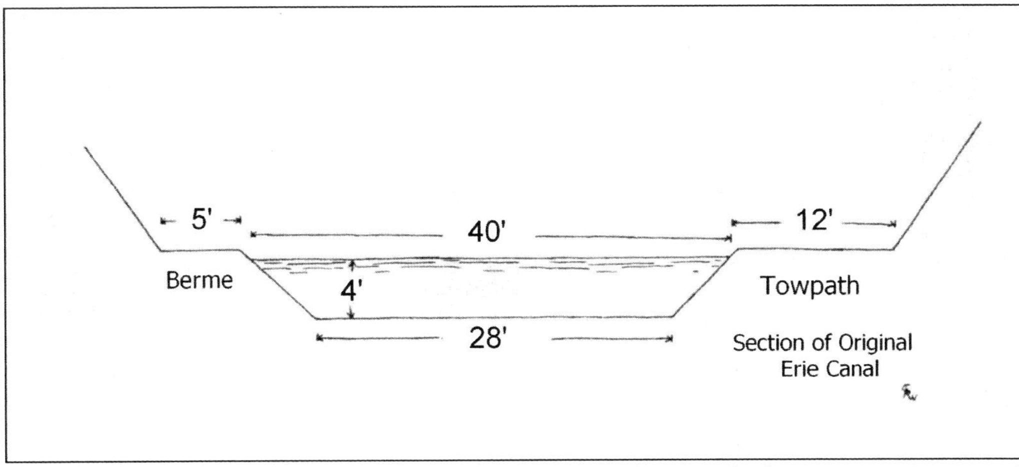

The original Erie Canal was four feet deep and stretched from Waterford near Troy to Tonawanda north of Buffalo. It included 77 stone locks that measured 15 feet by 90 feet. The total length of the canal from the Hudson River to Lake Erie was 363 miles. On October 26, 1825, the *Niagara*, a private vessel, was the first to travel the full length of the Erie Canal, reaching the Hudson River on November 1.

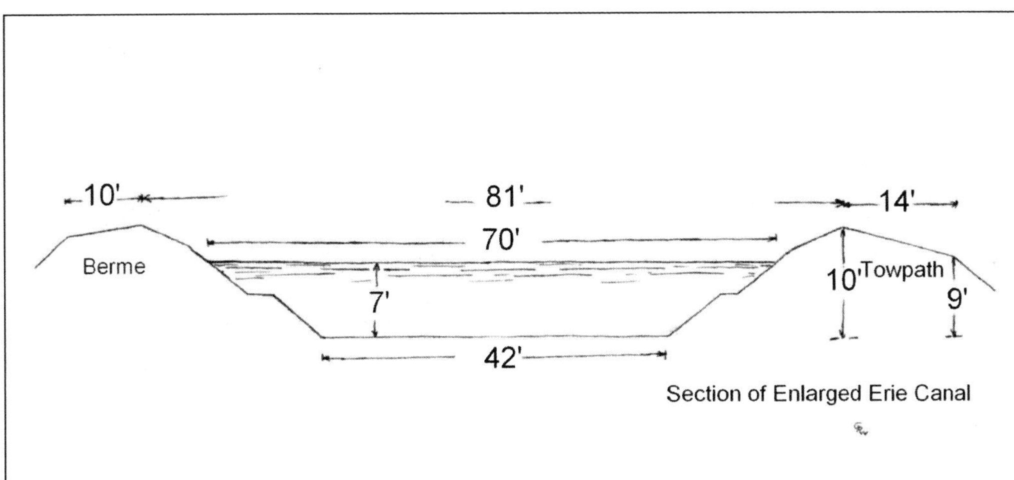

In 1836, the canal was straightened a bit, and the size was increased to 7 feet deep by 70 feet wide. The locks were enlarged to 18 feet by 110 feet. The smaller canals began to close, and the Black River Canal between Rome and Lions Falls was the last in 1917. The Barge Canal opened in 1918, and a new era began with steel boats and steam power, eliminating the need for the protected waterways of the "Old Erie."

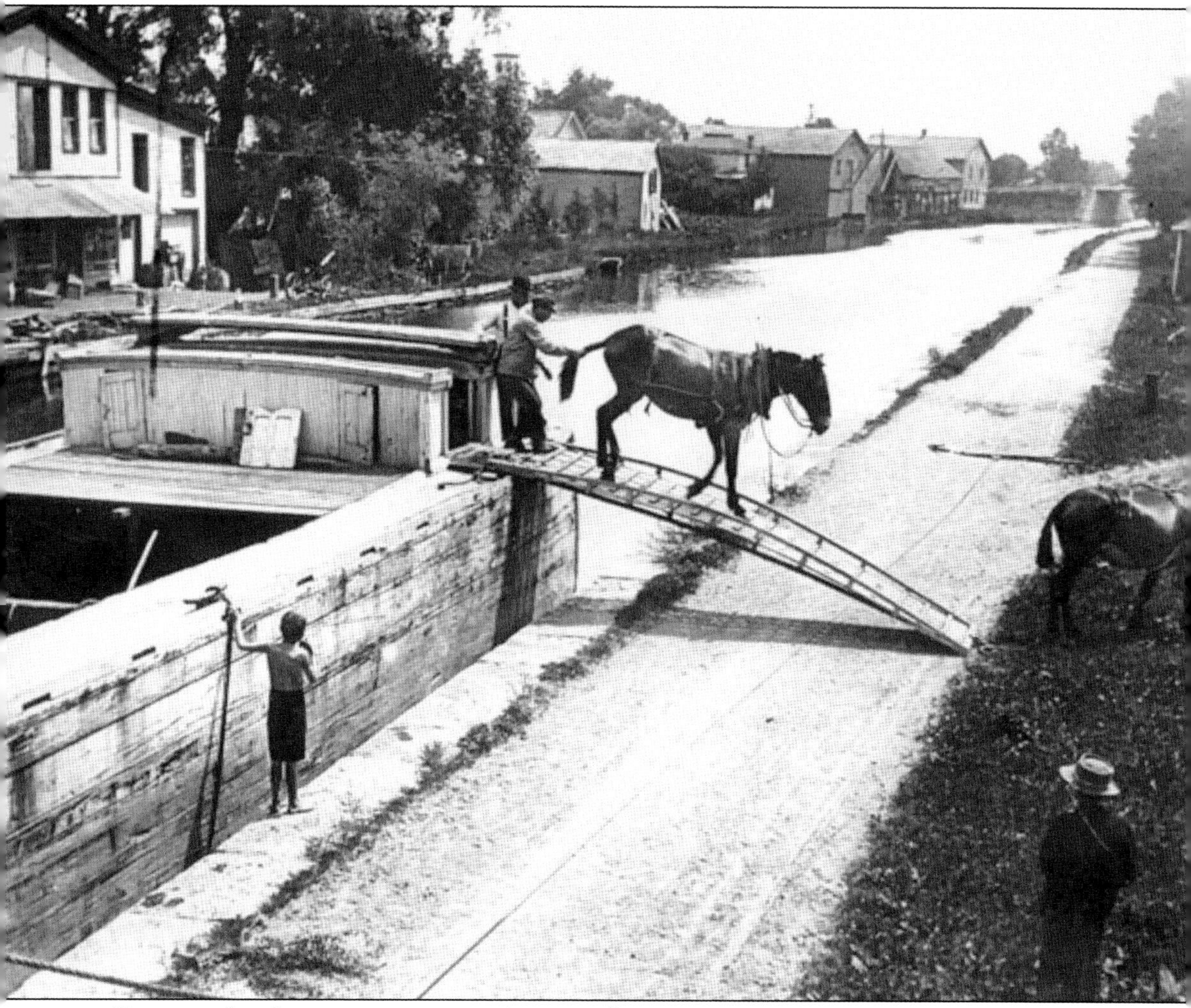

Horses and mules were a necessity when canalling was a way of life for pioneers of the old Erie Canal. Mules were most often used because their endurance was greater; on average, it took four hours to go 16 miles. Canal boats often worked night and day, seven days a week. The animals lived on the boats and easily became accustomed to walking the plank, which was referred to by the workers as "tailing off" or "tailing on;" however, it did take a bit of training. Eventually the animals learned that if their tails were twisted, it meant go ahead, and when their tails were pulled, it meant to stop. The unwilling were often towed aboard the first few times using brute force. A rope around the animal's girth ran to a pulley inside the boat with the other end of the rope connected to a team of mules that supplied the power necessary to lever their friend aboard. Free feed grew all along the canal in the form of grass; here one mule is enjoying a snack before starting his daily labor.

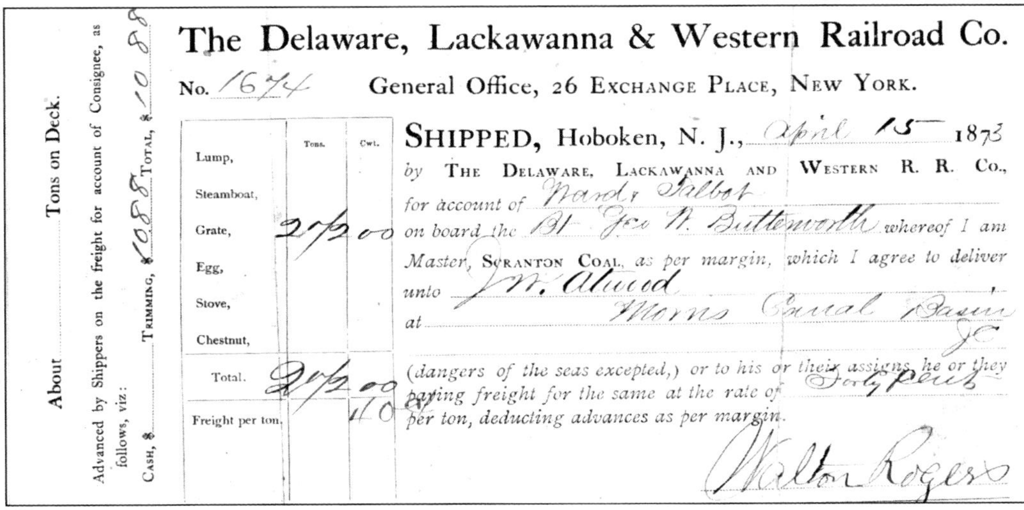

About .... Tons on Deck.

Advanced by Shippers on the freight for account of Consignee, as follows, viz:

Cash, $ .... Trimming, $10.88 Total, $10.88

The Delaware, Lackawanna & Western Railroad Co.

No. 1674 General Office, 26 Exchange Place, New York.

	Tons.	Cwt.
Lump,		
Steamboat,		
Grate,	272	00
Egg,		
Stove,		
Chestnut,		
Total.	272	00
Freight per ton,		40

SHIPPED, Hoboken, N. J., April 15 1873 by The Delaware, Lackawanna and Western R. R. Co., for account of Ward & Talbot on board the Bt Geo W. Butterworth whereof I am Master, Scranton Coal, as per margin, which I agree to deliver unto J. M. Alwood at Morris Canal Basin JC (dangers of the seas excepted,) or to his or their assigns, he or they paying freight for the same at the rate of Forty cents per ton, deducting advances as per margin.

Walton Rogers

The Erie Canal was closed and drained early in November each year. A number of boats chose to work during the winter months based in New York Harbor. During the years 1873 to 1879, Walton Rogers mentions being towed from Amboy, New Jersey, to Terrytown, and Hoboken to the Morris Canal Basin in Jersey City. He often carried loads of coal like this one at 40¢ per ton.

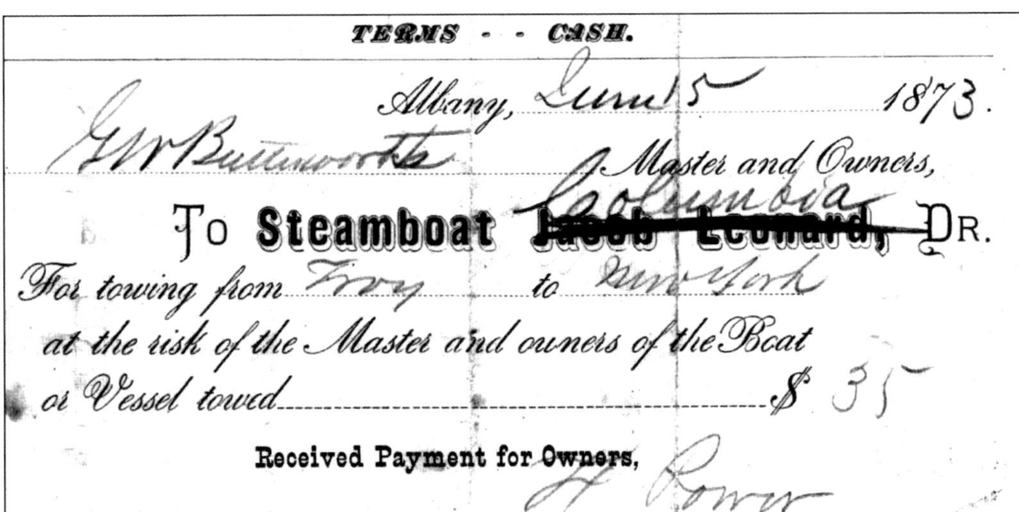

TERMS - - CASH.

Albany, June 15 1873.

G W Butterworth Master and Owners,

To Steamboat ~~Jacob Leonard,~~ Columbia Dr.

For towing from Troy to New York at the risk of the Master and owners of the Boat or Vessel towed $ 35

Received Payment for Owners,

H Power

On February 26, 1864, the *Columbia* transported Civil War troops from Norfolk, Virginia, to New York City. Casper Cook, a Fish Creek resident, was one of the solders on board. On June 15, 1873, Rogers engaged the *Columbia* to tow the *Geo. W. Butterfield* from Troy to New York City; he married Gertrude Bailey of Vienna. Rogers boarded his horses for the winter in Troy, quite often with Ed Wight.

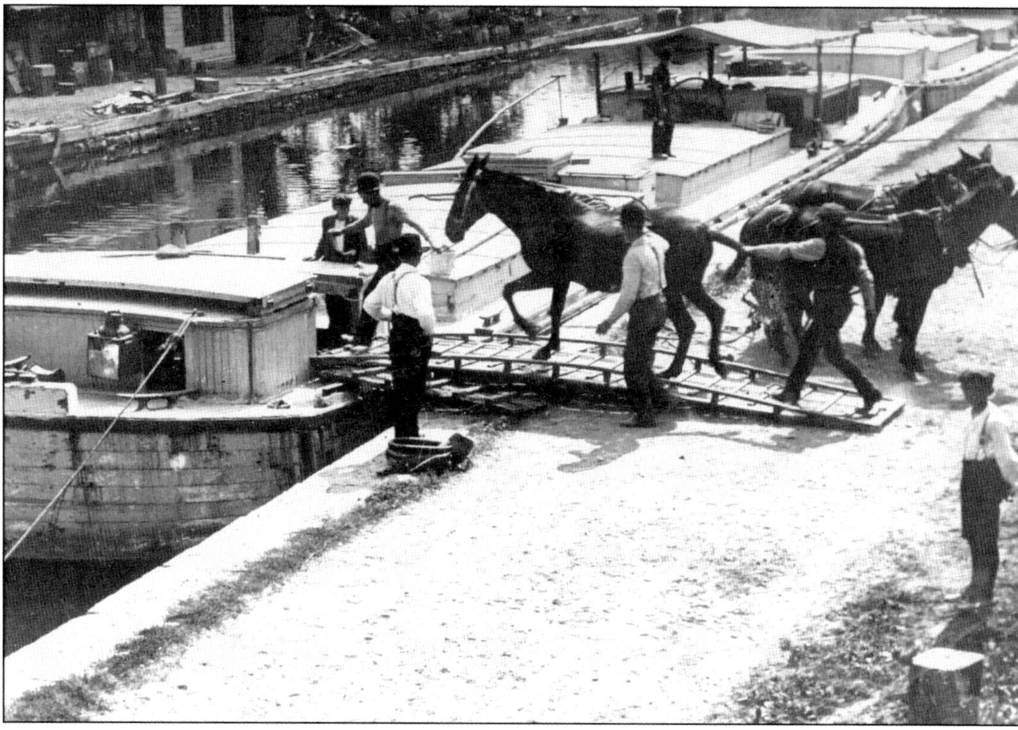

It appears to take three men to control this spirited young mule that was anxious to get to his stall on board. The boat is loaded and sets lower in the water, making it easier to load and unload the animals. In their endeavor to keep moving when they had a load to deliver, most boats had two teams, which allowed one team to rest on board while the other team worked.

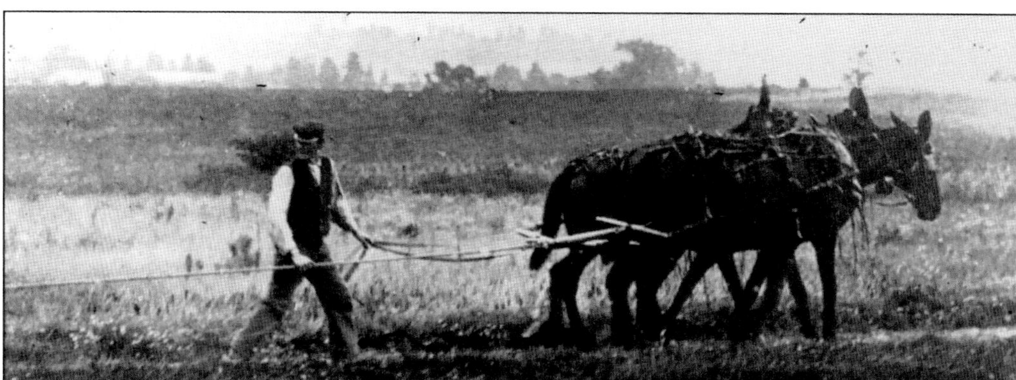

The designers of the original Erie Canal bypassed the lakes and rivers, including Oneida Lake, with a completely man-made channel. Animal power propelled the boats and barges on the canal, which required a continuous towpath for them to walk on. It was a wise decision, because mules did not break down like steamboats or produce the turbulence of a paddle wheel that would have seriously damaged the fragile banks.

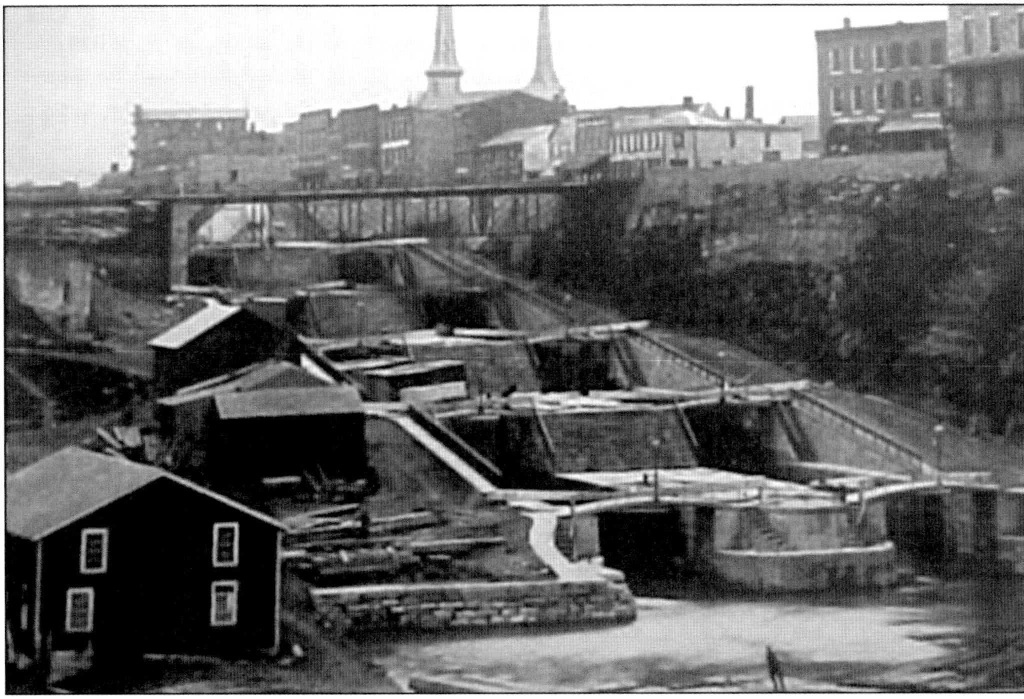

The most ingenious and indeed the most famous set of locks on the Erie Canal was in Lockport. Designed by Nathan Roberts, an assistant engineer, the locks raised a boat 70 feet to Lake Erie or lowered it into the canal. "Roberts Locks" were the great wonder of the Erie Canal, and photographs of his achievement were sought after throughout the United States and in other countries.

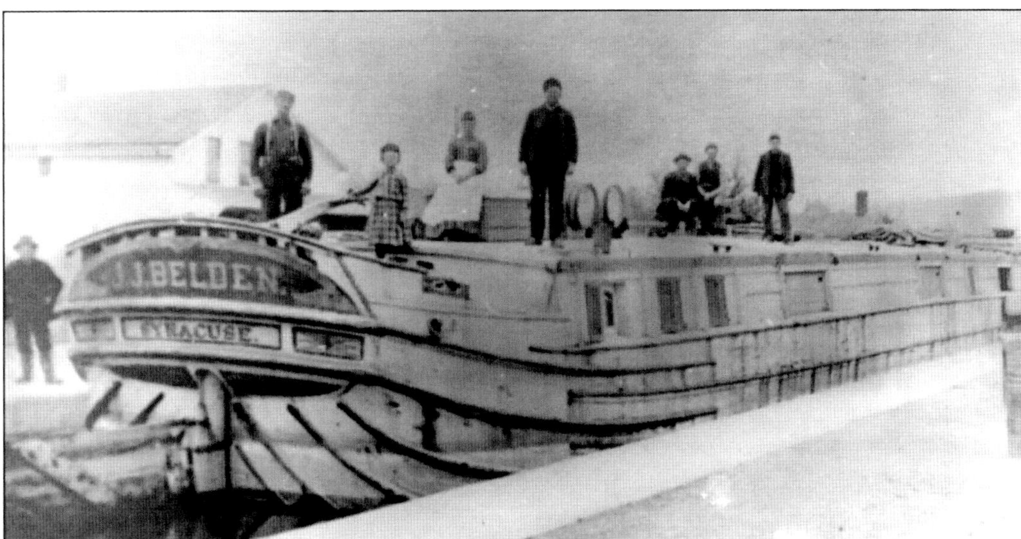

Designed to haul general freight as well as passengers, Line Boats like the *J. J. Belden*, shown here, were instrumental in transporting the mass migration westward caused by the development of the canal. Families from New England and Europe traveled the Erie Canal with their possessions and provisions to the vast, new frontiers that were opening for development. By 1833, half the boats on the Erie Canal were of this type.

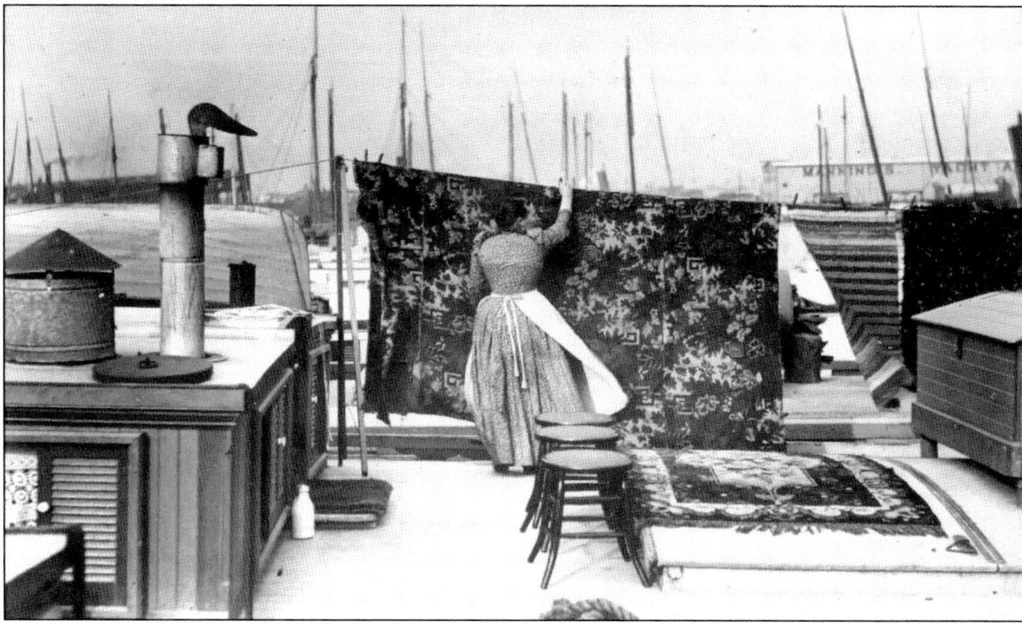

Making a home on a boat was not an easy task, but many accomplished the deed successfully. A woman's life involved cooking, cleaning, and washing, just as in any home. However, these ladies shopped in a variety of cities along the way and enjoyed a large number of friends living on similar boats. Diaries from the late 1800s reveal a constant stream of friends visiting from boat to boat.

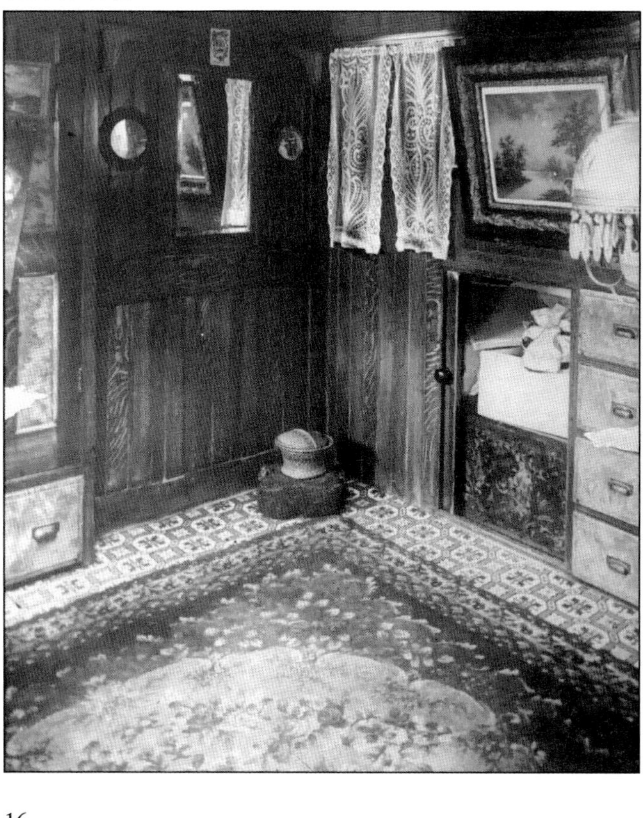

Freight boats owned and operated by families required a more complete living facility. A "woman's touch" is easily seen in this main cabin with almost all the comforts of a shoreside home. Mules for hauling the boat were kept in the forepeak along with quarters for drivers. The Rome-to-Utica section opened in 1819, and by 1845, 4,000 boats and barges were in operation on the Erie Canal.

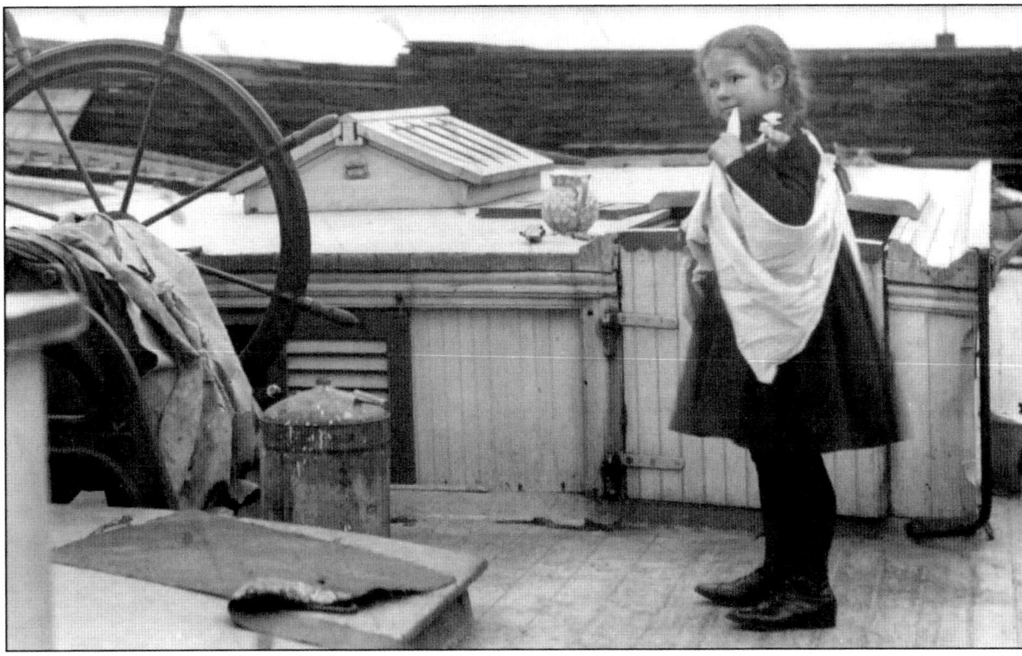

In 1921, a government study showed that children on canal boats were at a distinct disadvantage. Poor school attendance, working excessively long hours, a lack of access to doctors, and little recreation were a few of the problems mentioned. The study did not mention that the problems were shared with a great number of farm children across the country.

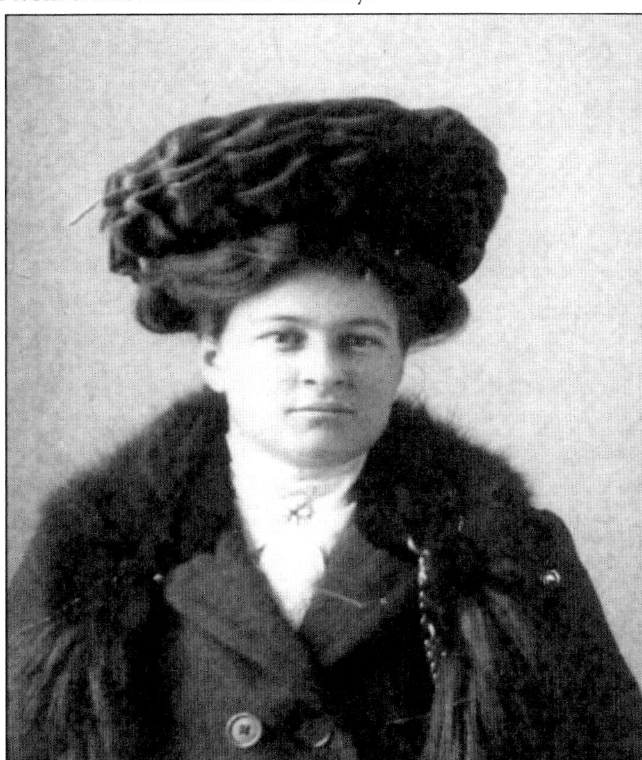

Emma Louisa Rogers was born on April 23, 1879, at 12:40 a.m. aboard the *Nettie Irene*, a boat on the Erie Canal. Dr. Stevens of 12 Granwich Street in New York City and a lady from a boat nearby attended. Rogers grew up on a canal boat, married Walter Collins, and spent the remainder of her life in North Bay.

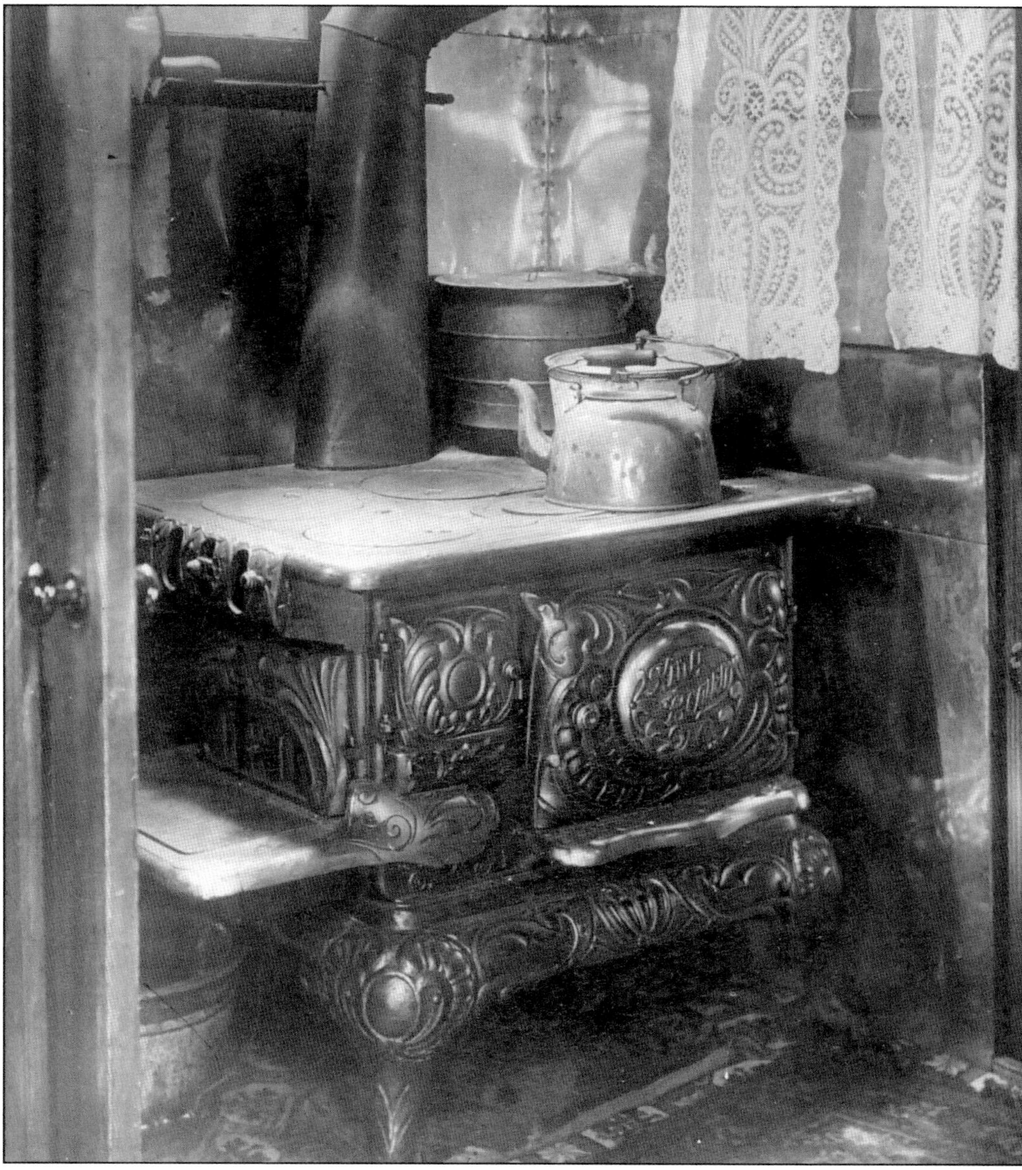

In early April 1877, a lady visiting the *Geo. W. Butterfield*, a boat working on the Erie Canal, gave little Nettie Irene Rogers a doll, and on April 16, her dad bought her a set of miniature dishes for a $1. During the early years before the age of technology, 90 percent of the children in this country attained some schooling and could at least write their names; however, in most cases, they learned how to make a living from their parents. Little girls became wives and mothers, and little boys took up their fathers' trade or apprenticed for years to attain a position. Higher education was for the rich and not for the common people who had to work long hours every day to achieve the American dream. Stoves like the one shown here were in homes across America at the dawn of the 20th century, but this one was on a canal boat. Double doors separated it from the rest of the living space, but they could be left open during the cold winter months to provide heat.

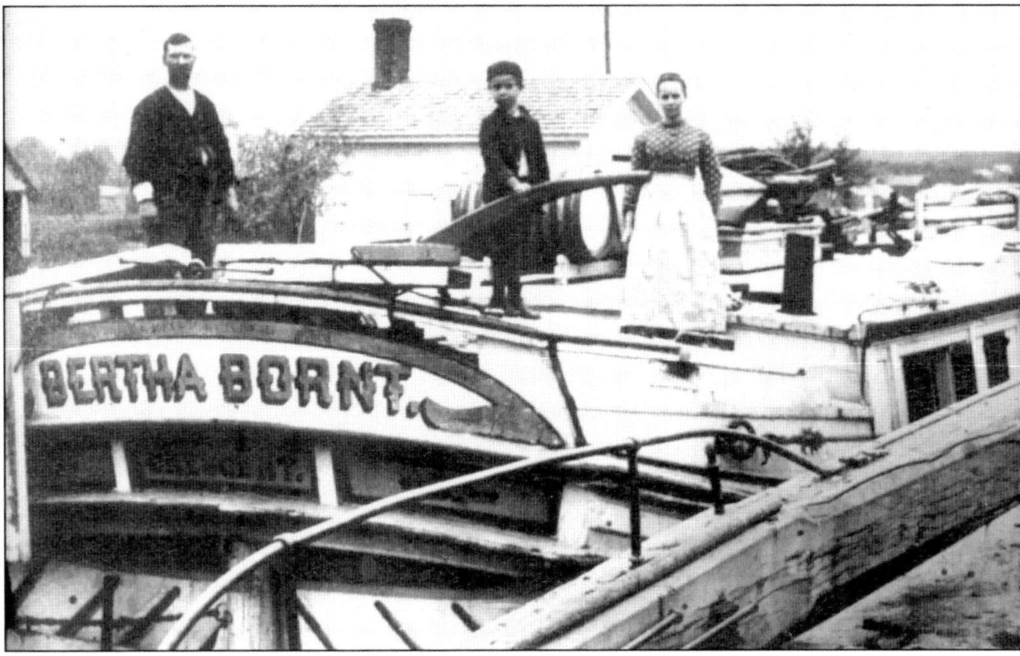

On November 26, 1825, Gov. Dewitt Clinton traveled the full length of the canal aboard the *Seneca Chief* and then went on to New York Harbor. He poured water from Lake Erie into the Atlantic Ocean, thus performing the "Wedding of the Waters." Children worked alongside their parents with little time for play. This young man seems to be accustomed to manning the tiller.

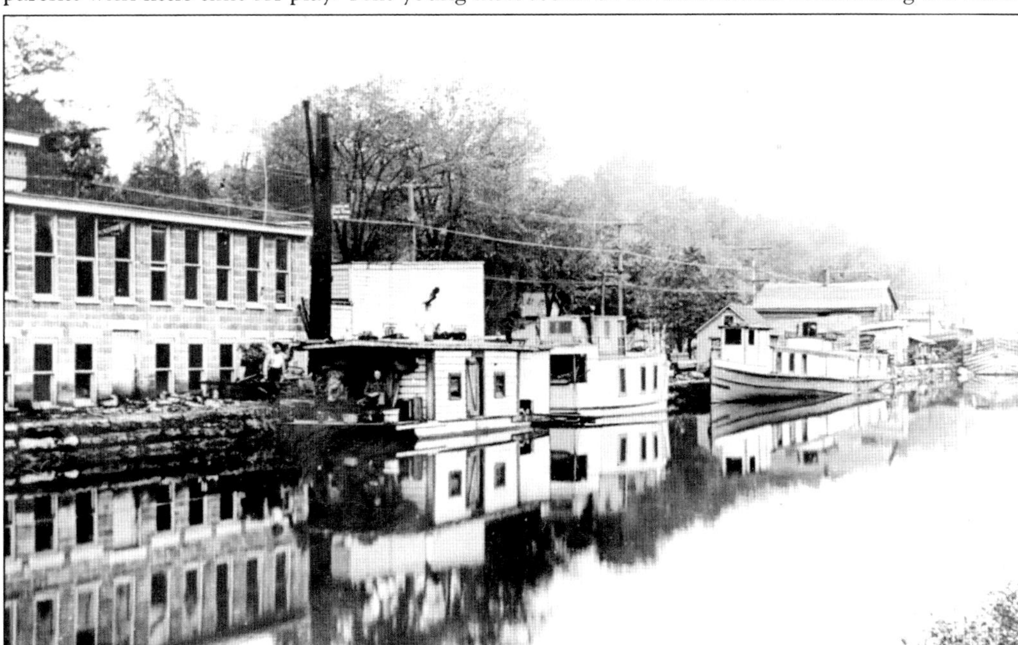

As illustrated in this late-1890s photograph, the old meets the new. Steam-powered vessels are docked next to Laker boats and state repair barges. A new era of canal improvement began in 1884, leading inevitably to the Barge Canal. The need for a protected waterway no longer existed, and larger vessels with greater power increased the interest in longer, concrete locks.

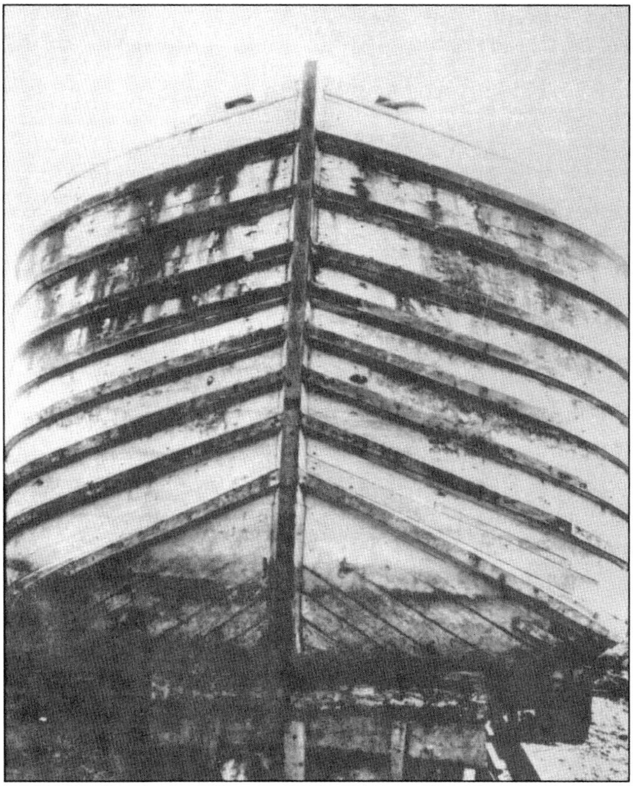

Early boats on the Erie Canal were more gracefully designed with an upsweep to the bow and stern based on hull shapes of boats commonly used on the lakes and rivers. The box shape was eventually incorporated because it was less expensive to produce and capable of larger tonnage within the same dimensions. It is easy to mistake the early Line Boat for the larger, heavier Laker boat common to the canal in later years.

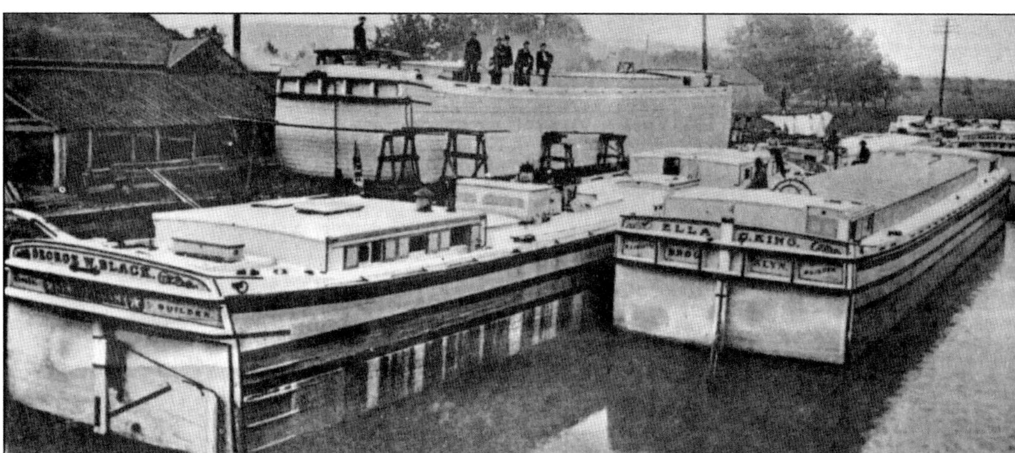

Bullheads and Lakers were close in appearance. Both were expensive to build, and both had a cabinlike cover running the full length. Most often, they were used to transport cargoes of flour or grain and other produce requiring a dry hold. The enlargement of the Erie Canal system allowed the construction of boats with a larger capacity. The Lakers and the Bullheads survived this change.

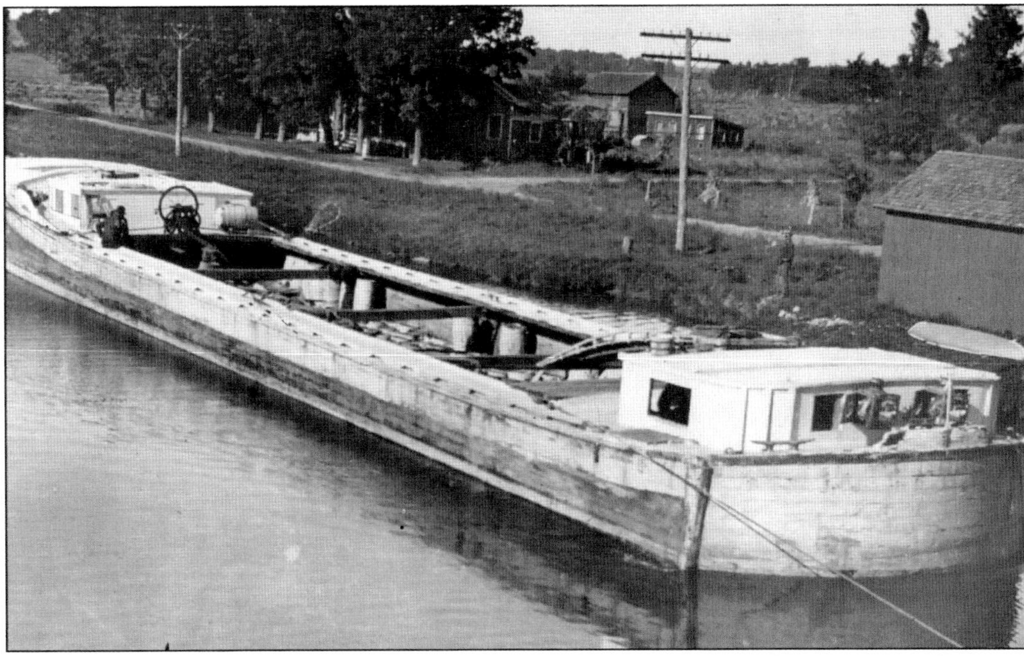

An open scow was used for hauling sand, gravel, construction stone, and coal. On March 9, 1877, Walton Rogers, master of the *Geo. W. Butterfield*, proceeded to Amboy after breaking the ice around the rudder. In Amboy, the boat was loaded with 219 tons of chestnut coal for delivery to Terrytown. He was paid 21¢ per ton (delivered), plus the cost of towing.

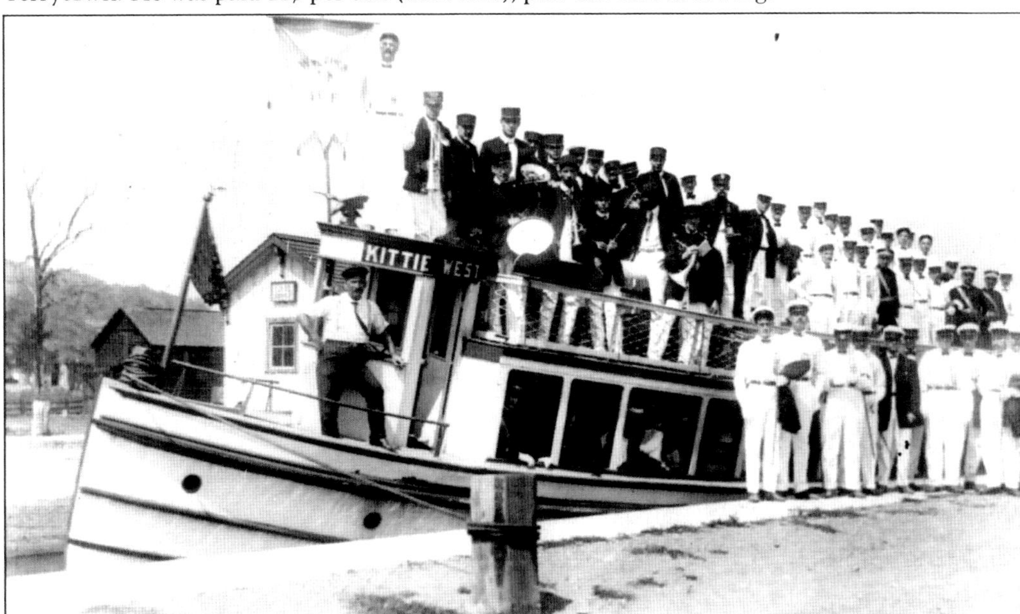

These long, narrow passenger boats could transport people a longer distance in greater comfort than a Line Boat. They were primarily used on the level stretches between Utica and Syracuse or Rochester and Lockport. Boats, such as the packet *Kitty West* at lock 25 in Rotterdam, were a vast improvement over the horse and wagon of earlier years, but they became virtually extinct with the development of rail passenger service.

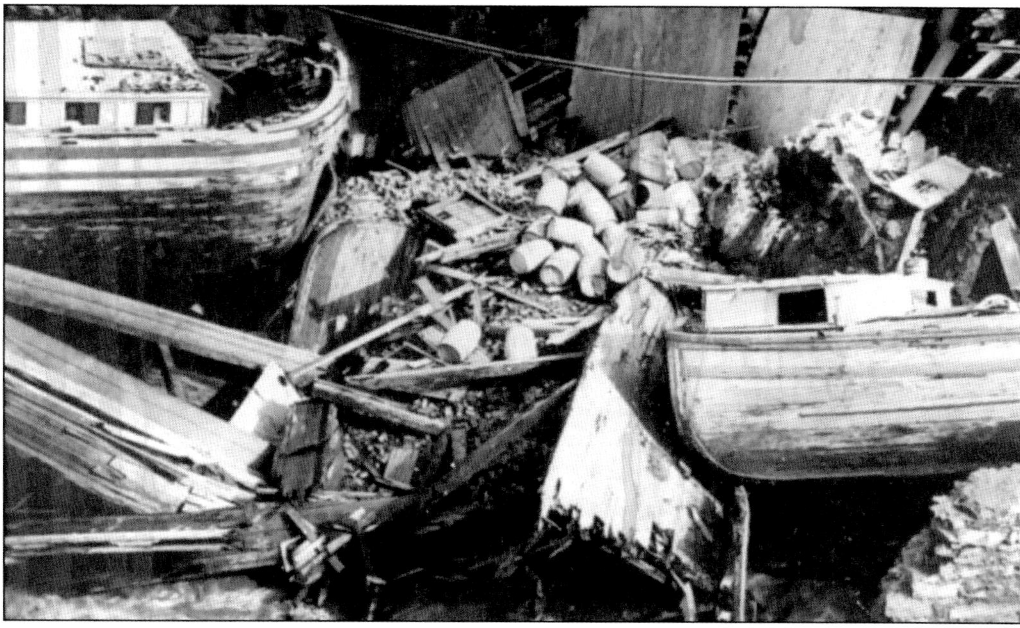

With the advent of steel construction and self-propelled boats, the Erie Canal was quickly becoming obsolete. Boatmen complained they could not compete against rival canals and the railroad. In an effort to aid the commercial haulers, all tolls were eliminated in 1882, but this accomplished little. Accidents were increasing; the one shown in these 1907 photographs was dubbed the "worst wreck in the late years of the Erie Canal."

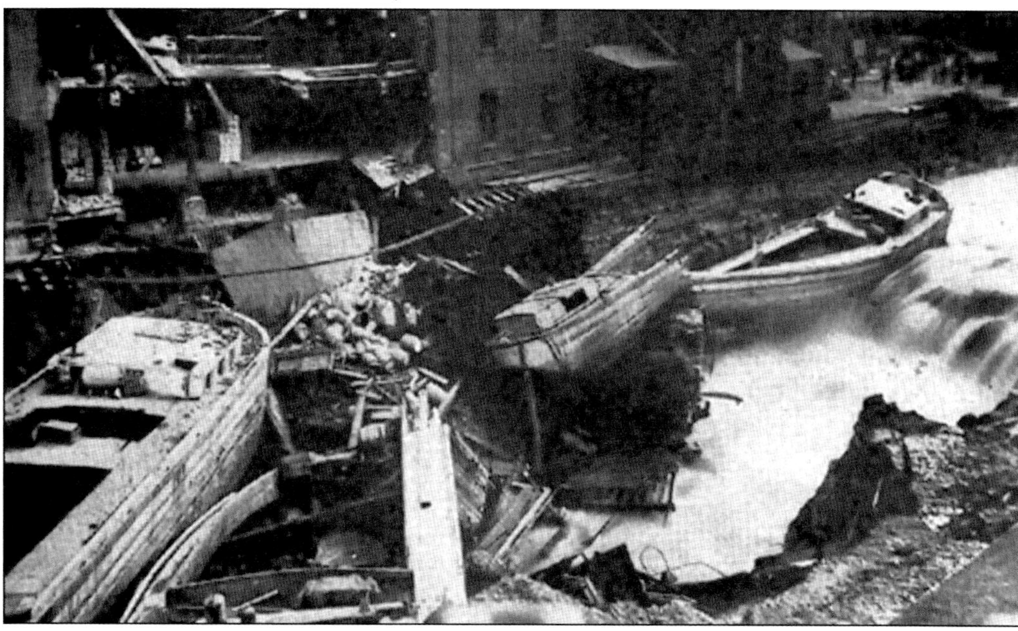

The accident occurred late in July when masonry arches broke and dropped the bed of the canal into the Onondaga Creek in Syracuse. Ultimately traffic was held up for a total of seven weeks and two days. The answer was clear: a larger canal with a greater capacity was needed. The New York State Barge Canal opened in 1918, using part of the old Erie Canal and the advantages of Oneida Lake.

Two

The Growing Years

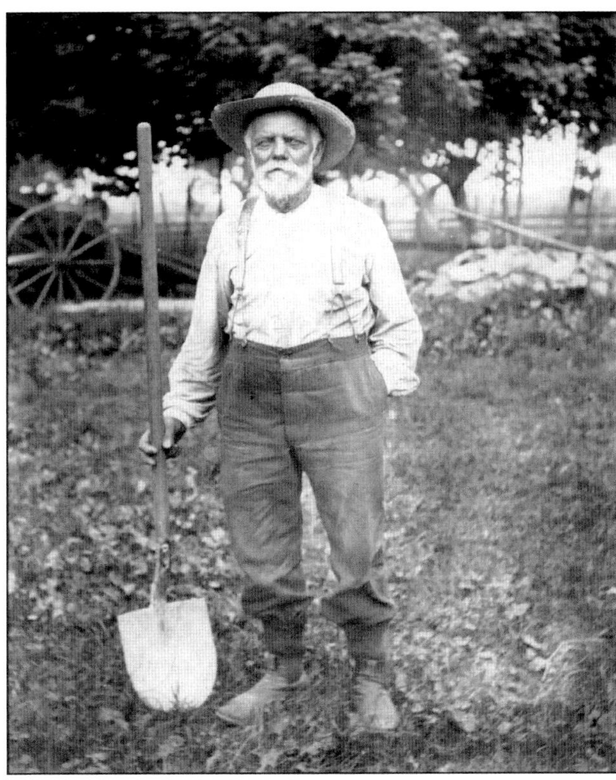

The first permanent settlers on the northeastern shores of Oneida Lake were farmers. As North Bay began to grow, some farmers diversified, and they were joined by merchants and professionals eager to invest in the area. By the early 1800s, there were as many as 37 sawmills in the general area. The lumber built homes, canal boats, and businesses, but still the farmers were the mainstay of the economy.

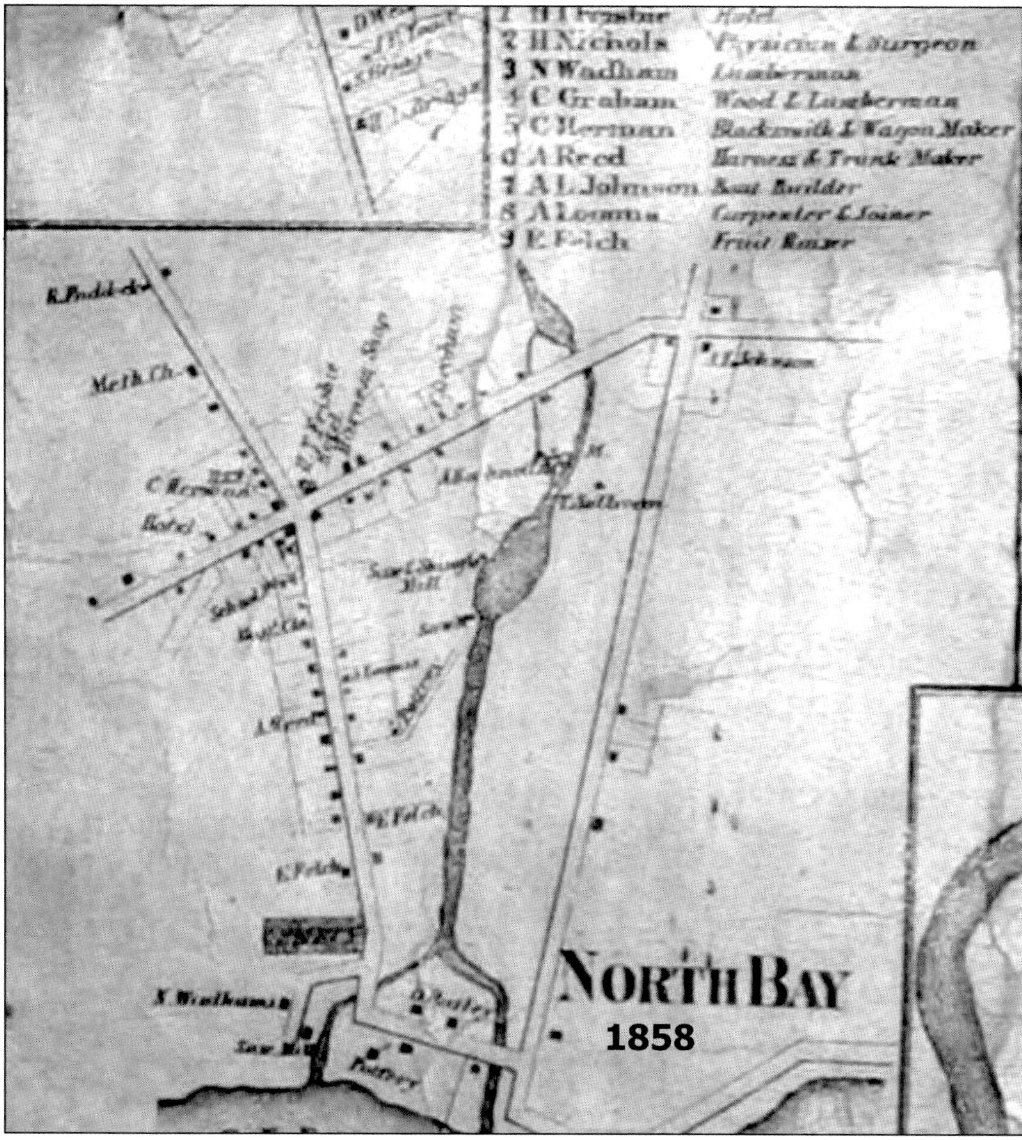

The face of Oneida Lake in 1858 was much different from the shoreline of today, and the cove in North Bay was deeper and more defined. The creek that ran through the center of the town, Mill Stream, known today as Murray Brook, forked at the lower end before entering the lake. Residents at the time included A. J. Johnson, a ship builder; A. Loomis, a carpenter/joiner; N. Wadham, a lumberman; C. Graham, a wood and lumberman; and C. Herman, a blacksmith and wagon maker. Old-timers say the changes in the lake came about because of the heavy forestry carried on during that era, allowing a faster runoff that carried more sand and dirt into the lake, filling it in. A rich deposit of clay near Mill Stream in North Bay was the reason five potters decided to build their businesses there. This 1858 map clearly shows the creek running through North Bay forked at the lower end, and it shows the location of at least two potters.

Around 1847, Dwight Graves sold Peel (or Perlee) H. Webster a piece of property located in North Bay. Webster owned a small pottery that produced stoneware from 1848 through 1850. This jar is an example of the early stoneware he made in North Bay and is very rare. His potter's mark was "P. H. Webster/North Bay."

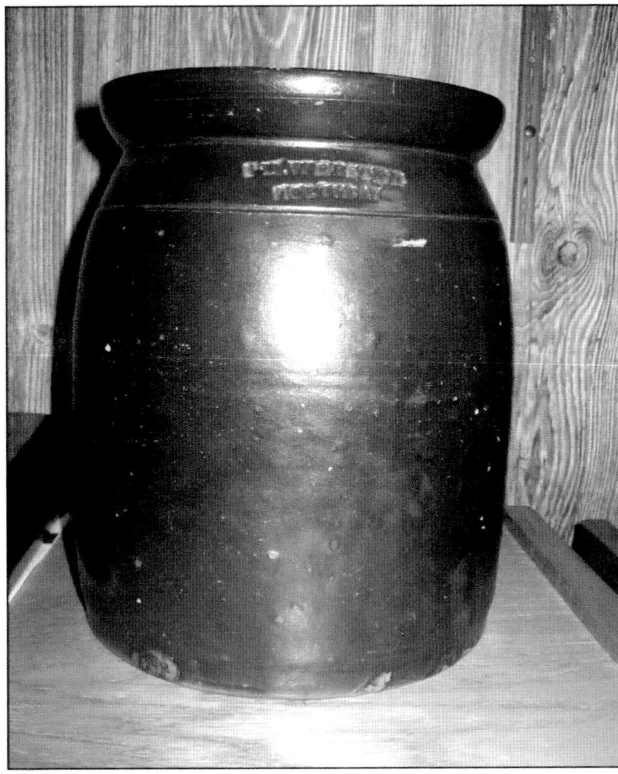

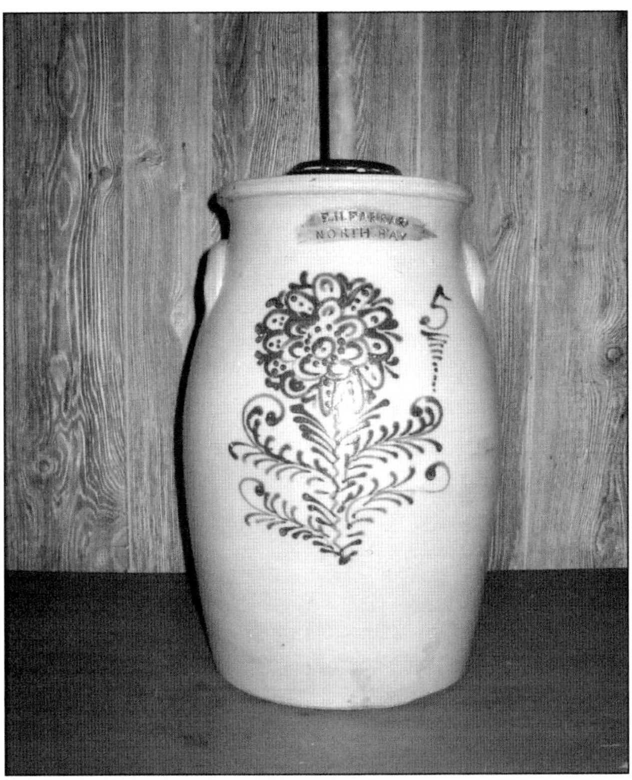

E. H. Farrar, a potter from Geddes in Onondaga County, arrived in North Bay in 1850 or early 1851. He stayed in North Bay for a very short time and only produced a small number of stoneware pieces. This five-gallon milk churn, marked "E. H. Farrar/North Bay," is an example of his work.

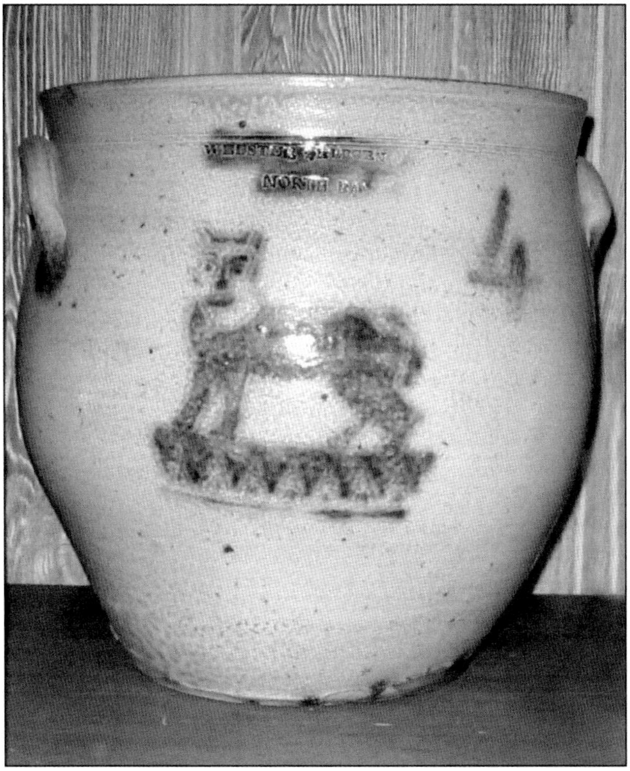

Around 1850, Peel H. Webster was joined by Symmis Bergen, a local physician, and the business grew. It is presumed that Bergen financed the operation, which allowed for the growth. This very rare piece of stoneware bears the mark "Webster & Bergen/North Bay." This example is one of two known to exist; the other one sold in October 2007 for $12,500.

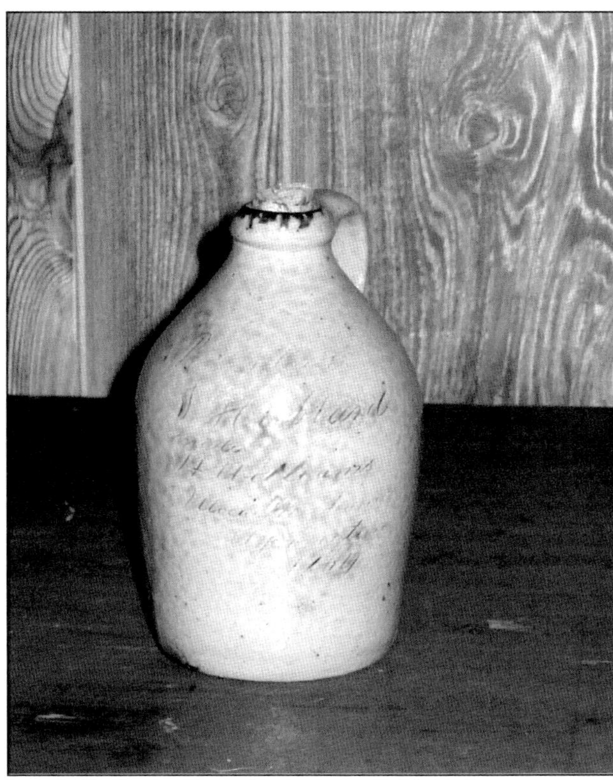

Henry Williams, a Welsh potter, worked in Utica's White Pottery, where this small stoneware jug bearing his name and the date 1846 was produced. In 1850, he arrived in North Bay with his family. Two more children were born; one, a son named Charles, became a potter and worked with his father in the 1860s. Williams Kiln in North Bay only produced earthenware and, in later years, only flowerpots.

John C. Waelde, a German craftsman from Wittenberg, settled in North Bay by 1851. Unlike potters before him, he stayed and produced stoneware through 1875. His kiln turned out a large variety of quality stoneware before his death around 1880, making his stoneware more available to collectors. Waelde produced both hand-painted (or slip cup) and stencil patterns. This two-gallon jug is an example of his hand-decorated stoneware.

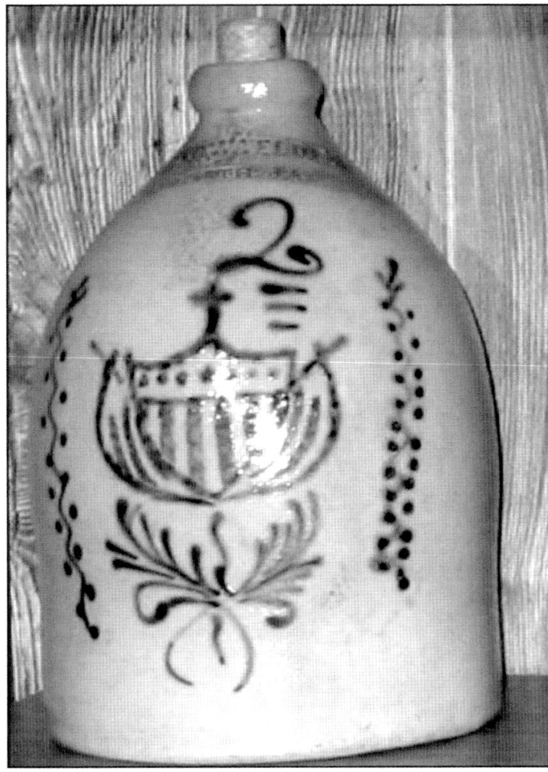

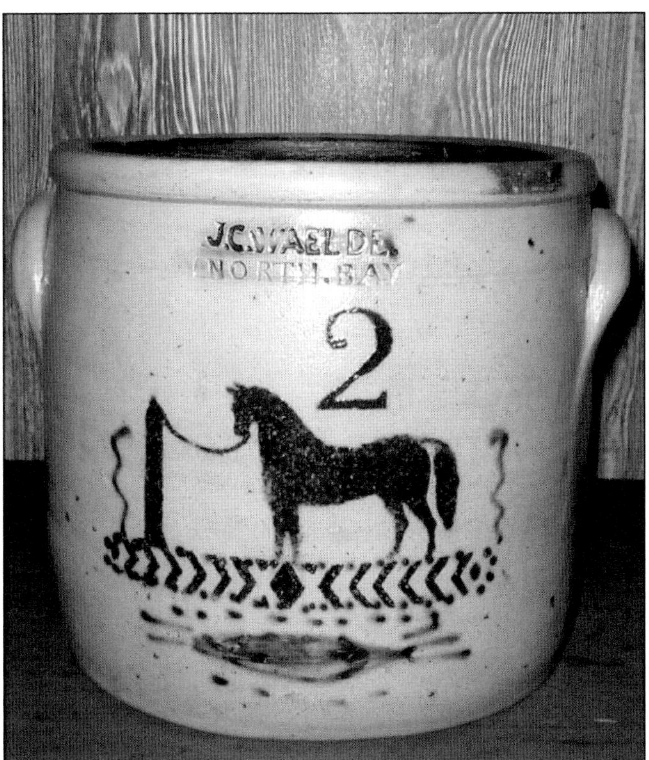

Waelde stoneware was more popular because of the appealing decorations he applied by hand or by the use of stencils. This two-gallon pot shows an example of his stencil work. Other examples of stoneware found bearing his mark include a variety of bird, deer, cow, eagle, and leaf stencils.

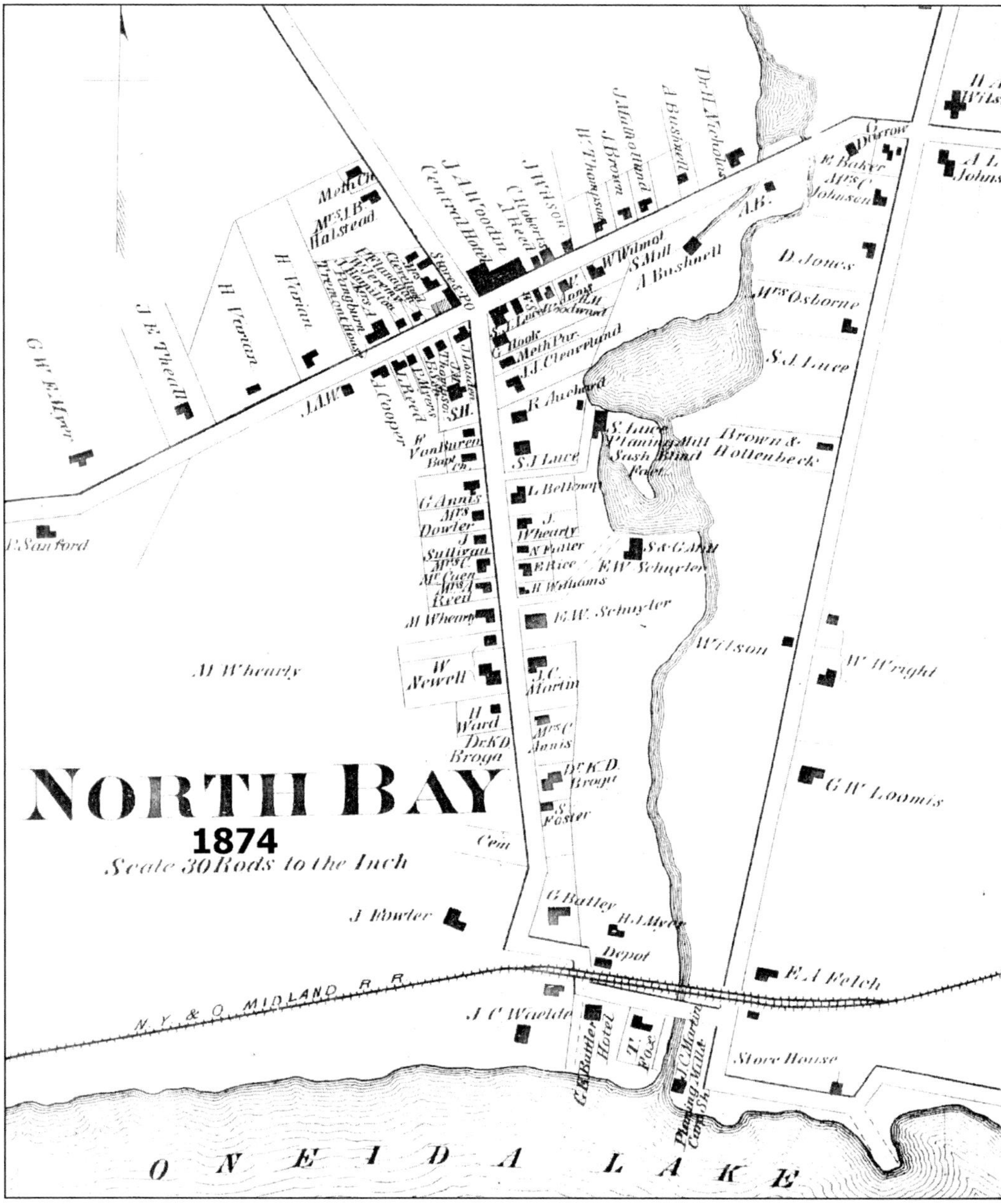

North Bay is a quaint village with gentle, rolling hills formed around a valley that faces Oneida Lake. The development of the Erie Canal in 1825, the Higginsville Canal in 1835, and the Black River Canal in 1851 contributed to the growth of North Bay in the mid-1800s. At one time, it was an important location for shipping lumber and boatbuilding. Fishing was a great source for sport, income, and food for the pioneers. Oneida Lake rivaled Lake Ontario for its production of Atlantic salmon as well as game fish. The pioneers selected North Bay because of its natural bay and a small stream that afforded a convenient means of power. Nathan and Amanda Auchard moved to North Bay and bought the eastern half of lot 95 of the Scriba Patent early in the 1800s. They had three daughters, Jane, born in 1850, and twins, Mertie and Amanda, born in 1857. Jane married James Louden. He opened the first store. Mertie married Albert S. Annis, the proprietor of a shipyard and the town supervisor in 1896 and in 1921.

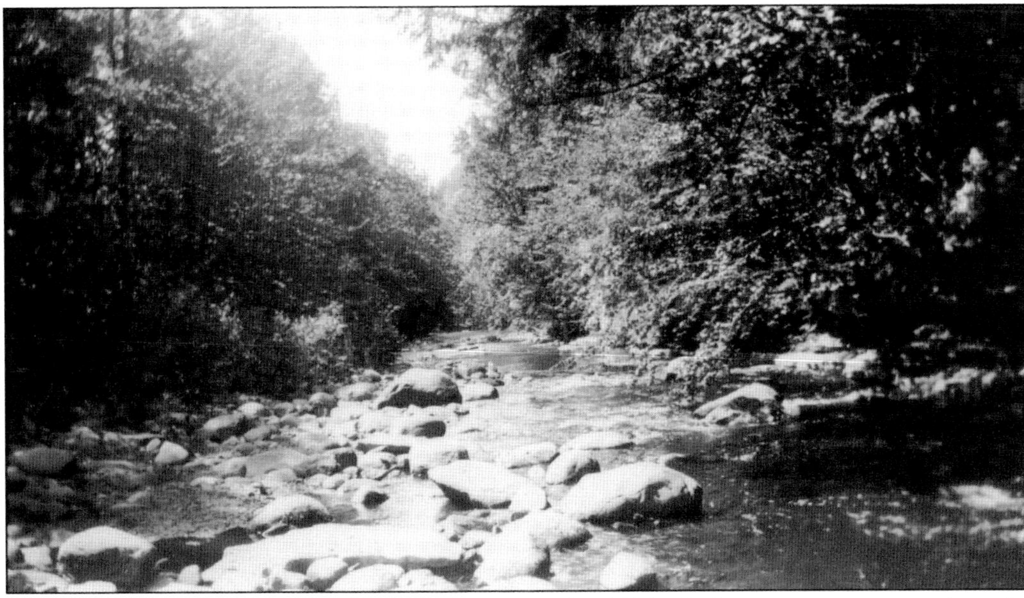

The Murray Brook, known as the Mill Stream in the 1800s, finds its origin in a pond on the Tug Hill Plateau. Not large enough to provide navigation, it wanders past Murray Cemetery on its way south. An inconsequential little stream fed by various springs along its path, it crosses Bushnell Pond by Route 49 in North Bay, then runs through the valley and into Oneida Lake.

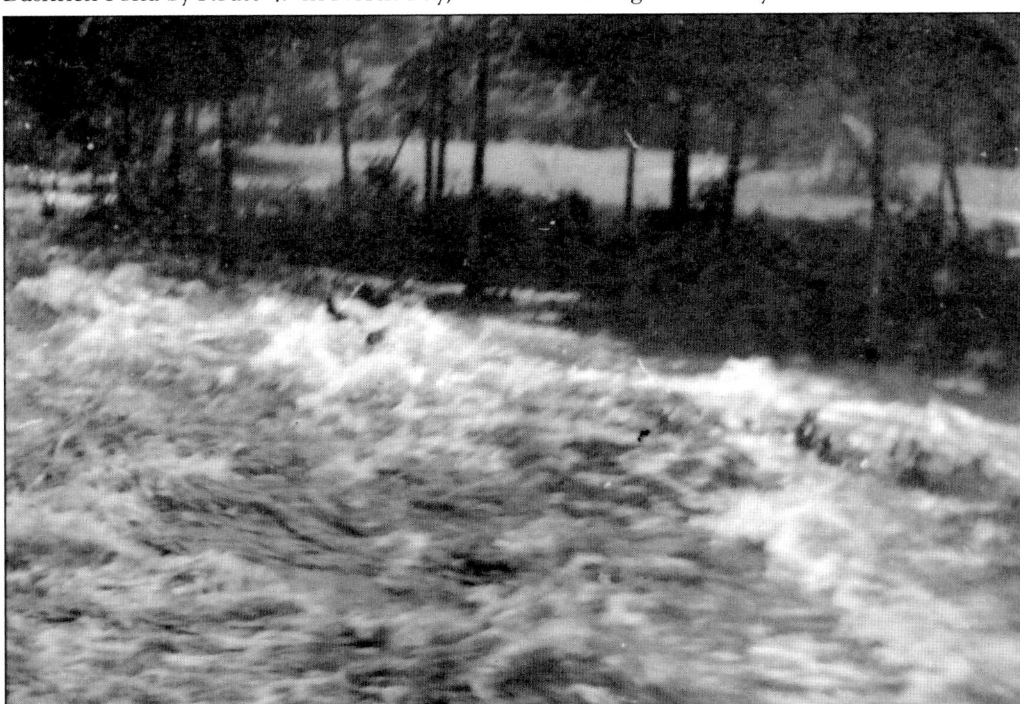

Water cannot be compressed, and when obstructed, it will find a way to continue on its course. Through the decades, the course of Murray Brook has often changed, sometimes by the hand of man and other times by the forces of nature. The fork at the lower end of the brook disappeared by 1874.

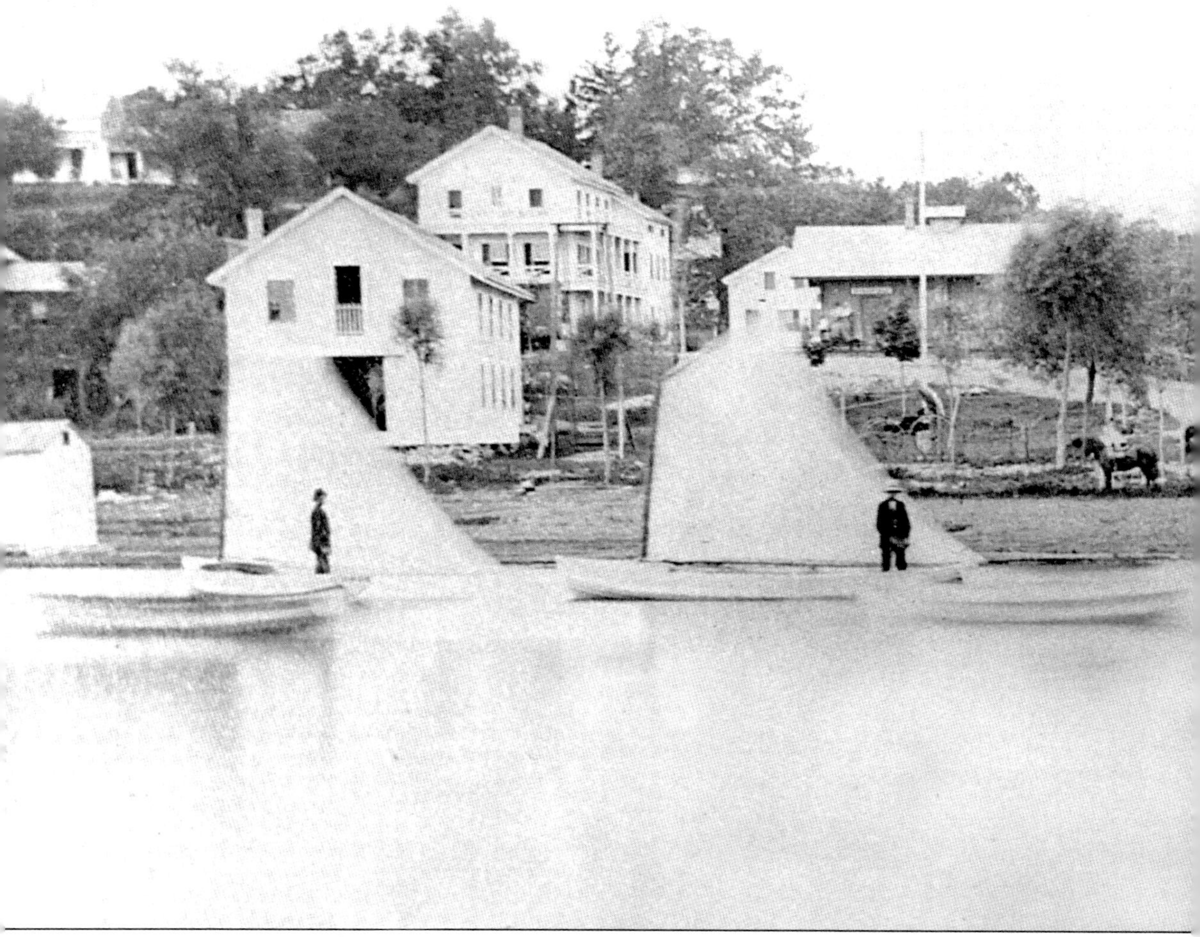

Henry J. Myer arrived in 1832 and built the first hotel east of the four corners in North Bay, but it burned. He then built the Tremont House west of the four corners, but it too burned. Records reveal Myer built at least 10 houses and 20 Durham boats. The New York and Oswego Midland Railroad built its first station in September 1869, and the new Myer Hotel was ready to greet passengers. The railroad station was struck by lightning and burned in May 1878. The Myer

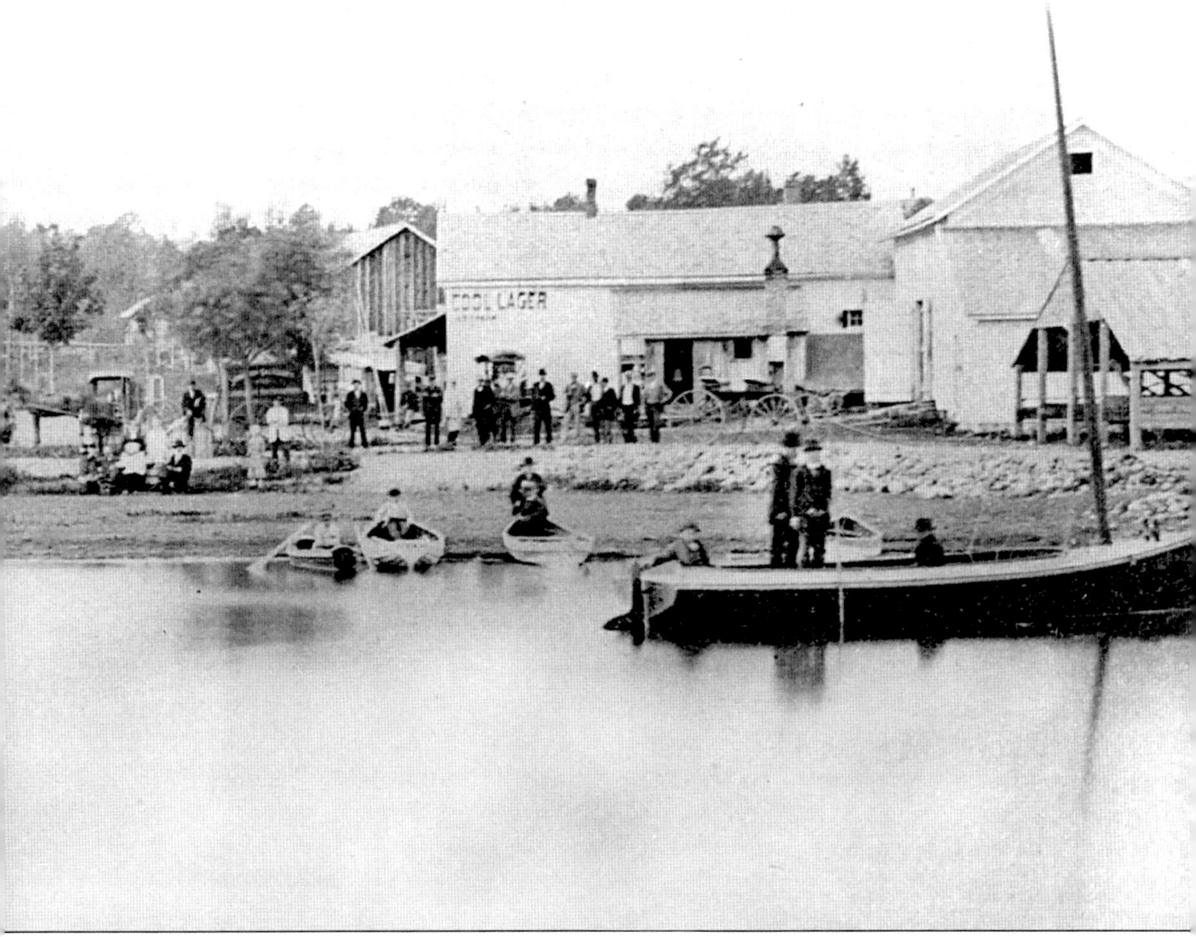

Hotel, directly across from the station, was utilized as a ticket office and waiting room until the new station was completed in October 1878. The large hotel on the left with the verandas is identified as the Butler Hotel on the 1874 map. The Myer Hotel is the white building behind the railroad station.

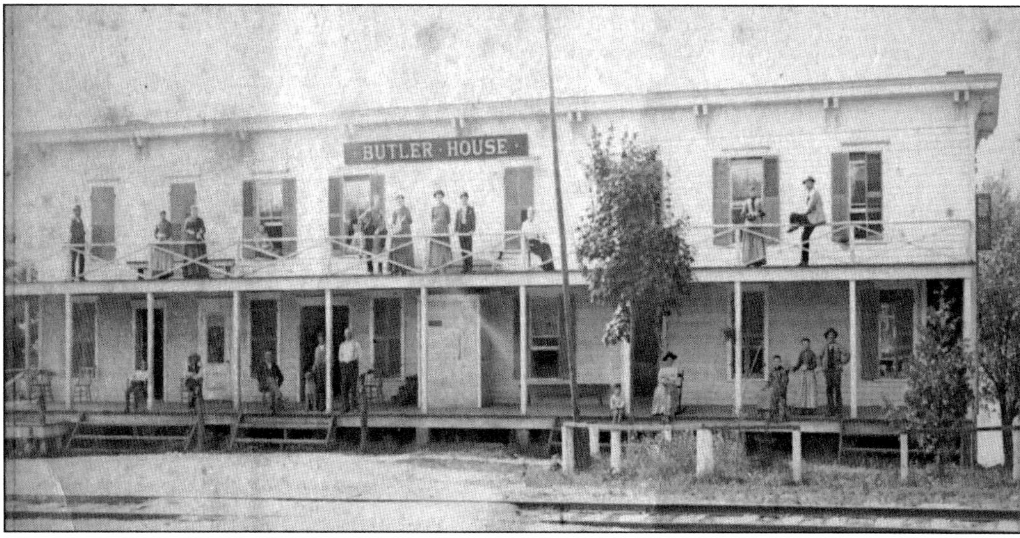

The original Butler House was built and operated by George Butler. As made apparent by the railroad tracks visible in front of the hotel, it was located across from the station on the lakeside in the late 1870s. The New York and Oswego Midland Railroad ran closer to Oneida Lake in North Bay than any other place along the line. The hotel was modified at some time and sold to Elmer Horton.

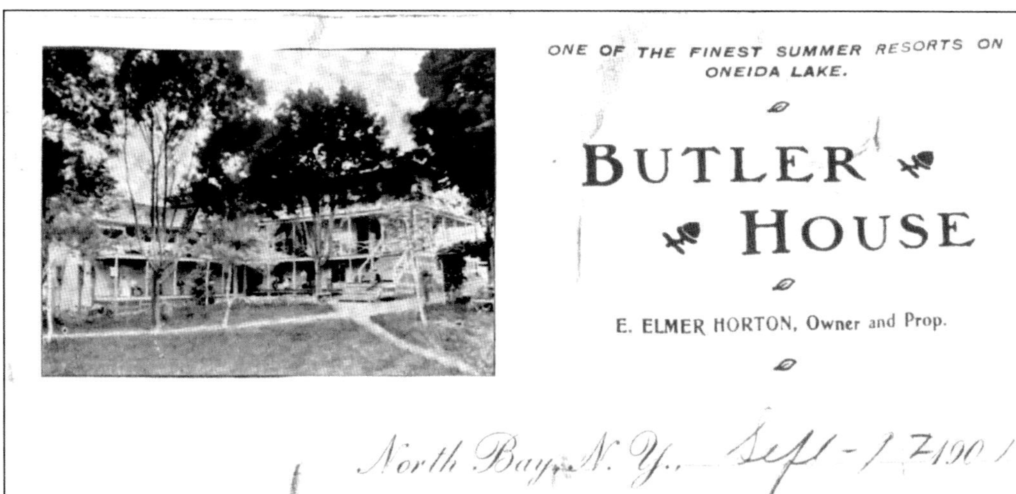
ONE OF THE FINEST SUMMER RESORTS ON ONEIDA LAKE.

BUTLER HOUSE

E. ELMER HORTON, Owner and Prop.

North Bay, N. Y., Sept-17 1901

When owned and operated by Horton, the Butler House continued to be one of the finest lakeside resorts conveniently located near the rail station. Verandas on every floor allowed vacationers to enjoy breezes off Oneida Lake. This letterhead shows the back of the hotel as seen from the lake only a few yards away. The Butler House burned in the early 1900s and was not rebuilt.

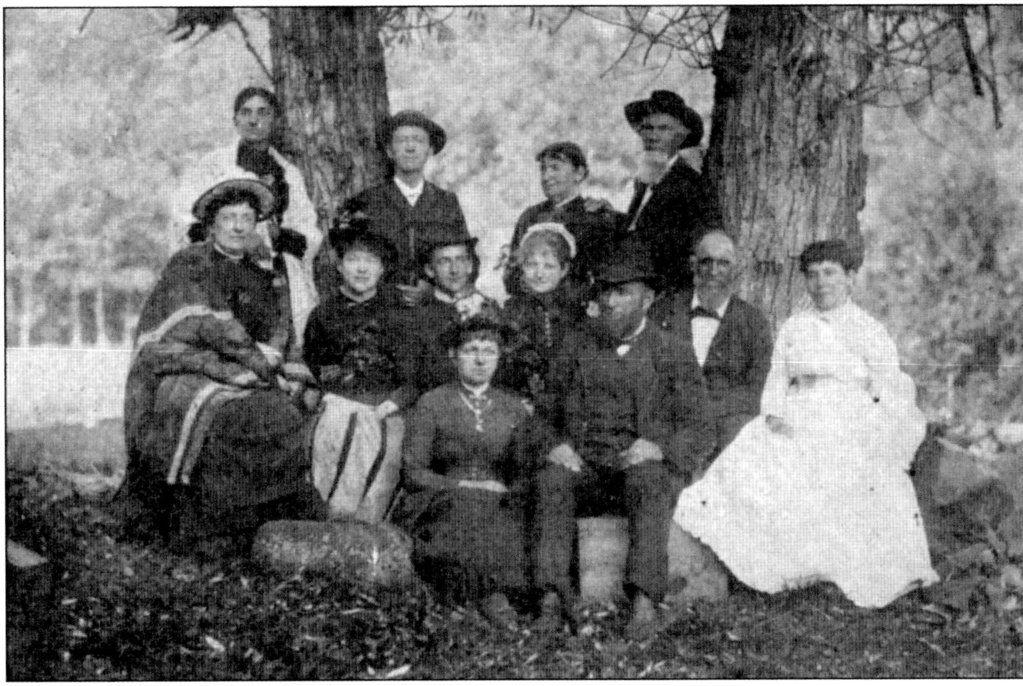

In the late 1800s, the valley in North Bay was known by many names, such as Butlerville and Myer's Grove. Charles W. Lanpher of the New York and Oswego Midland Railroad created a picnic and camping area in the valley. This tintype from about 1878 shows vacationers who arrived on the train or by an excursion boat docked at the North Bay pier behind the Butler House. The pier remained until 1915.

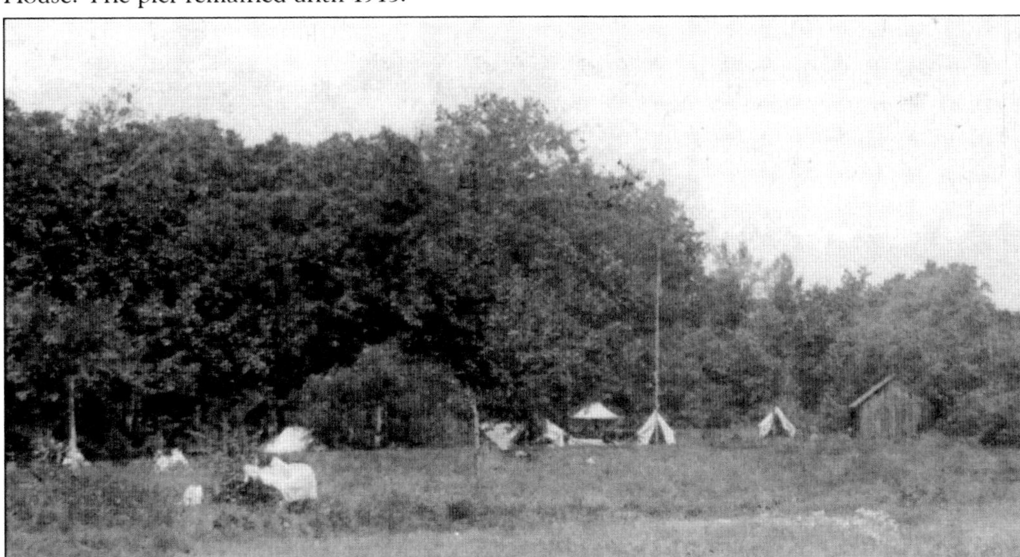

Lanpher chose Myer's Grove, in the valley behind Myer's Hotel, because of its close proximity to Oneida Lake and the railroad station. The first picnic was held on June 27, 1877. During 1877 and 1878, people came by railroad and lake steamers from as far away as Oswego, Norwich, and Cortland. The Central Hotel operated a free "bus line." In July 1877, one train was 20 cars long.

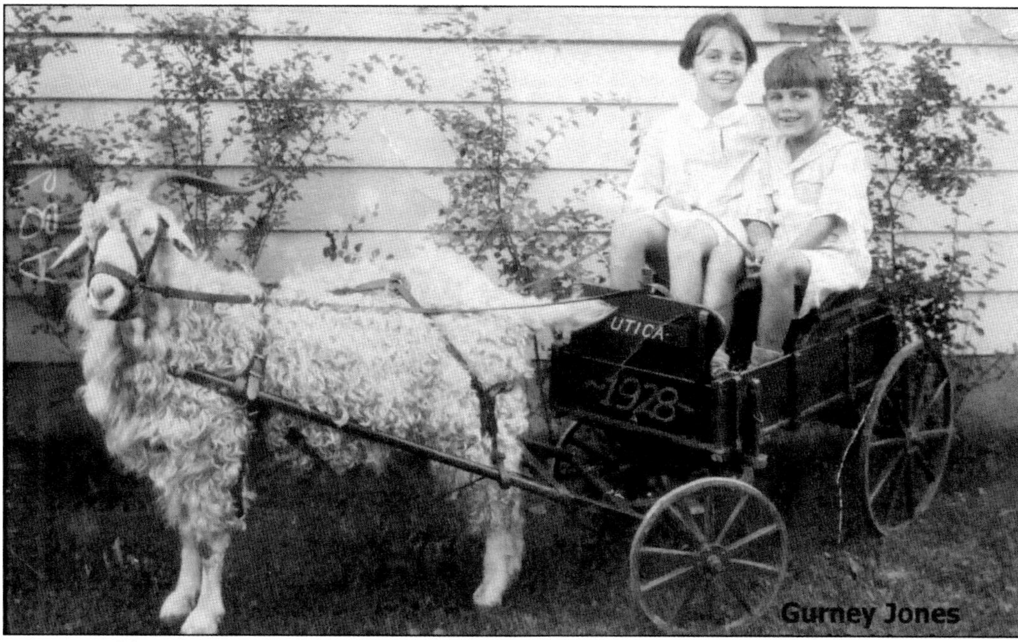

Five-year-old Gurney Jones and his sister Doree pose on their goat mobile in the early 1920s. They spent their summers at their grandparents' home on Oneida Lake. Charlie and Caroline Schafer lived on Lakeshore Drive just west of the valley. It is still home for Gurney and his wife, Jer. Over the table in their little breakfast nook hangs the light from the old New York, Ontario and Western Railway depot.

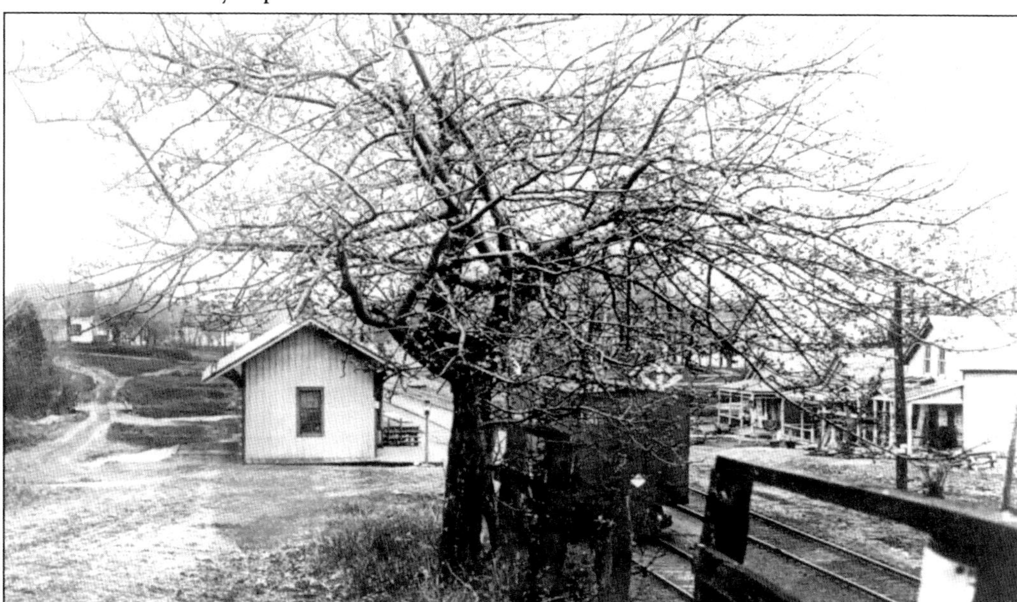

This photograph looking down Lake Hill was taken around 1920. In it, the hotels that were so popular during North Bay's grander days are gone. All the early hotels burned except the Central Hotel, now known as the North Bay Hotel. Opposite the train station is the new Horton's and a man working on his roof. The stone that reinforced the embankment below Brayton's is still there.

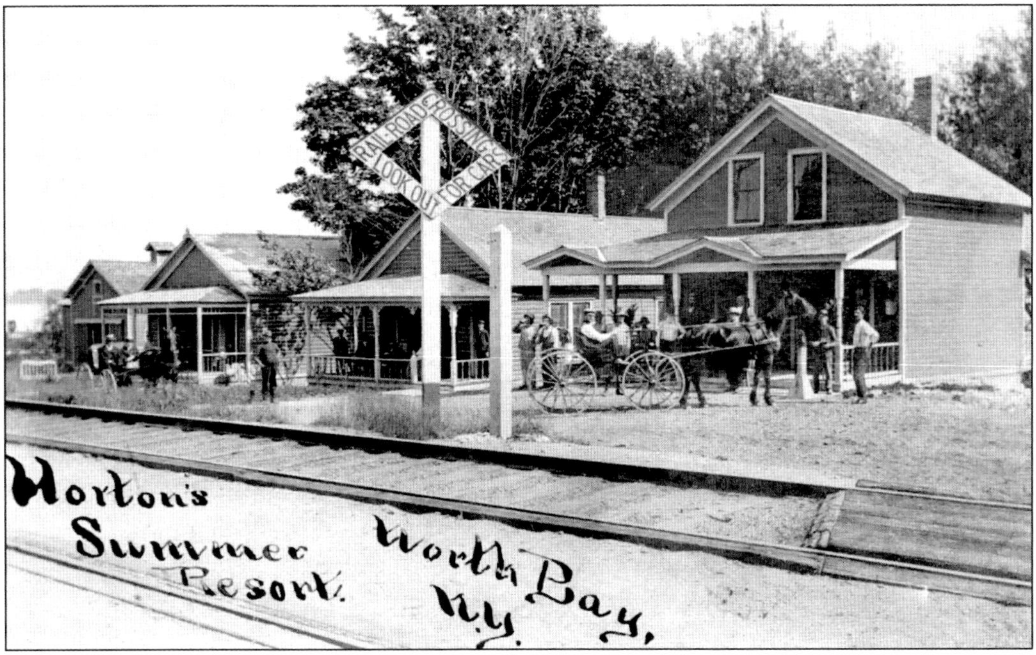

After the Butler House burned, Elmer Horton built the hotel shown on the right in this picture taken in 1919. He also owned the two buildings adjacent to his hotel and eventually incorporated the one next door into the original hotel. This allowed for a larger living space as well as the hotel and a tavern.

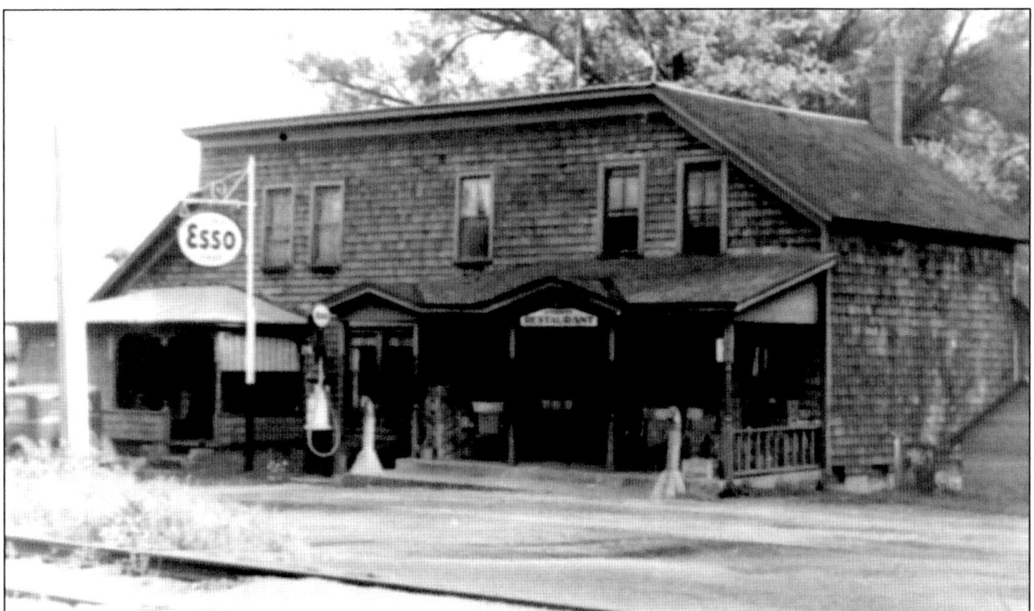

Charlie Strader was an upholsterer who lived in New York City. While visiting North Bay, he met Emma Heller, and they were married. He bought the Horton property and used it as a restaurant and tavern. Behind the building was a favorite swimming beach for visitors and townsfolk alike. At one time, it was a gas station known as Strader's Crossing because of the railroad crossing in front.

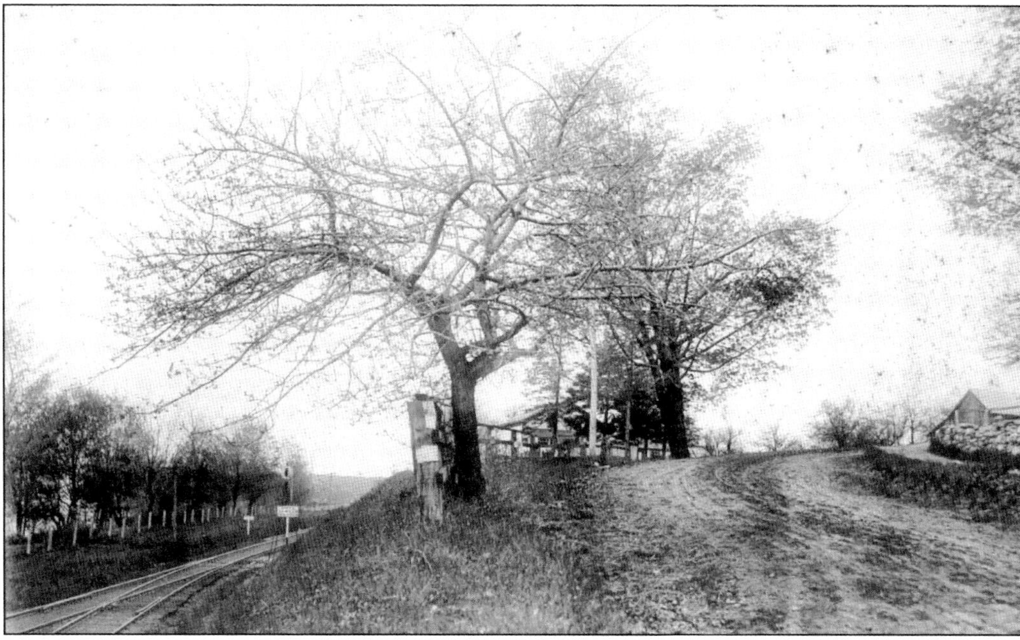

In 1874, a property on West Lake Street at left next to the cemetery on top of Lake Hill belonged to J. Fowler. A structure was built on this site to be used as a paint shop. The New York and Oswego Midland Railroad was new, and the land was largely undeveloped along the water's edge on Oneida Lake at the west end of Lakeshore Drive.

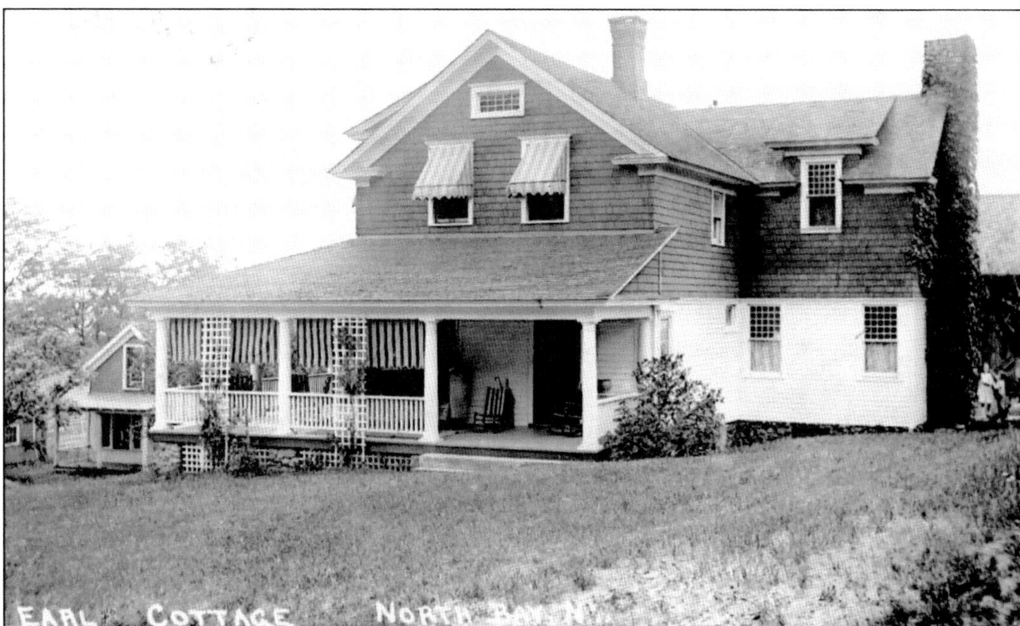

Howard J. Earl obtained the property from Harrison W. Coley in 1908. He remodeled the paint shop into a comfortable cottage with cabins to rent to summer tourists. In 1922, after Earl's death, William Alsever, C. E., created a map of the holdings belonging to his wife, Mary J. Earl. The area was called the North Bay Park and encompassed nearly all the property on the lake at the west end of Lakeshore Drive.

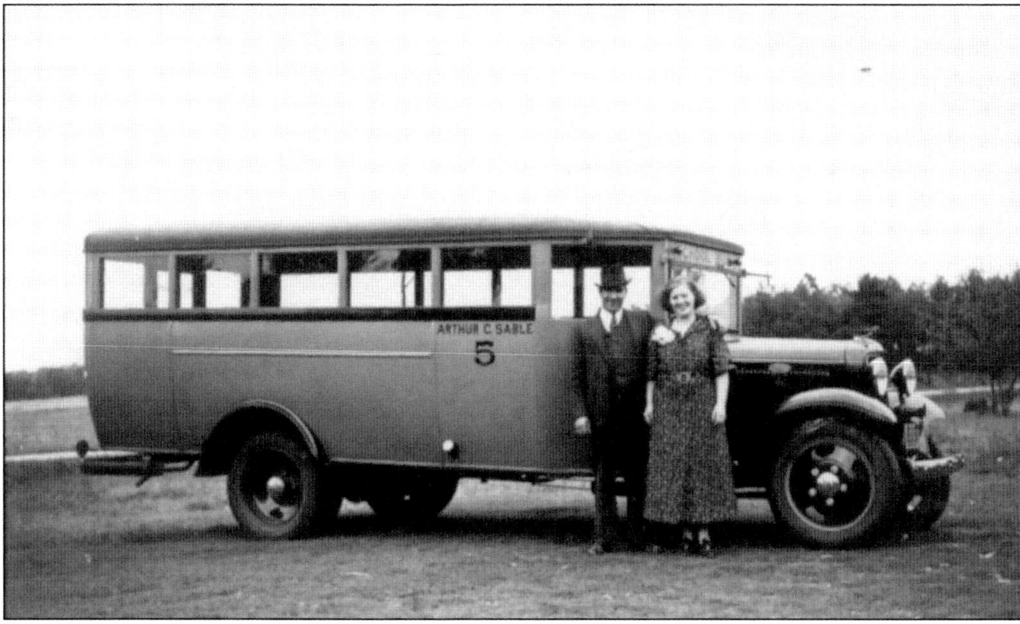

In 1936, Arthur Sable and his wife, Esther, started a bus company. Their first vehicle, No. 5, was contracted to the Camden Central School system in Camden. Esther was the granddaughter of Walton Rogers. Her mother, Emma Rogers Collins, was born aboard the *Nettie Irene* on the old Erie Canal.

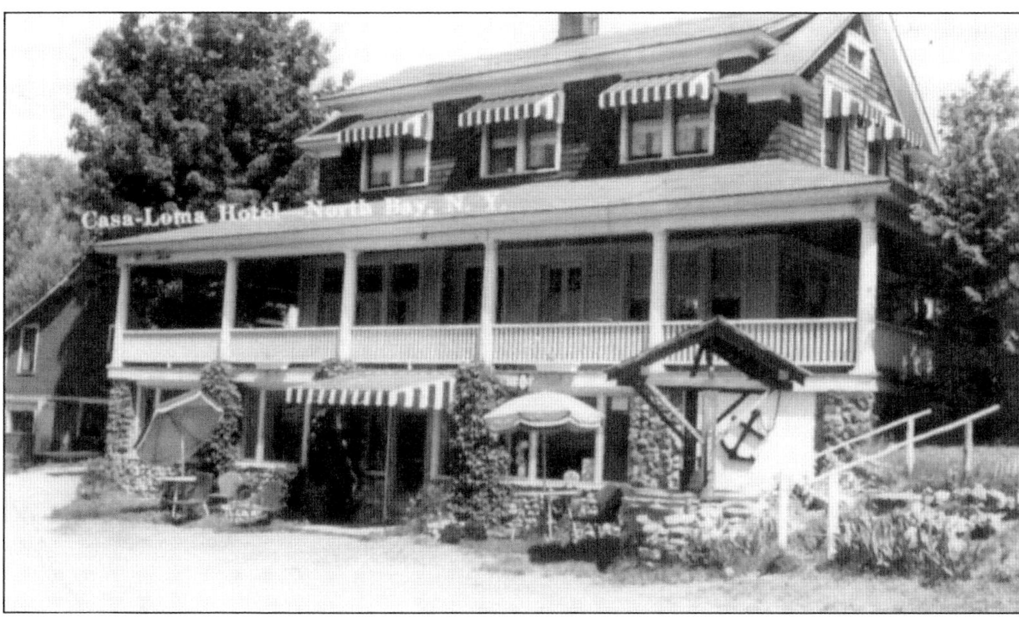

In the mid- to late 1940s, the Sables bought the Earl cottage for $5,000. It was very nicely furnished, and there was even a car in the garage. The Sables remodeled and opened a restaurant offering fine dining and a comfortable hotel overlooking Oneida Lake.

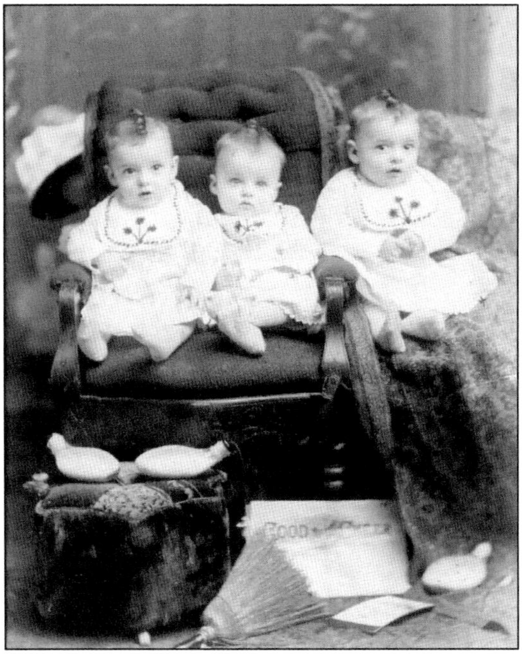

The first post office was established in 1840, and the first postmaster was Hiram Higby. Hiram owned a store where James Louden had his establishment on West Lake Street. On October 23, 1885, the Loomis triplets, Oliver, Eugene, and Crawford, were born on East Lake Street in the second house on the right facing north. Charles Loomis, their father, was a farmer.

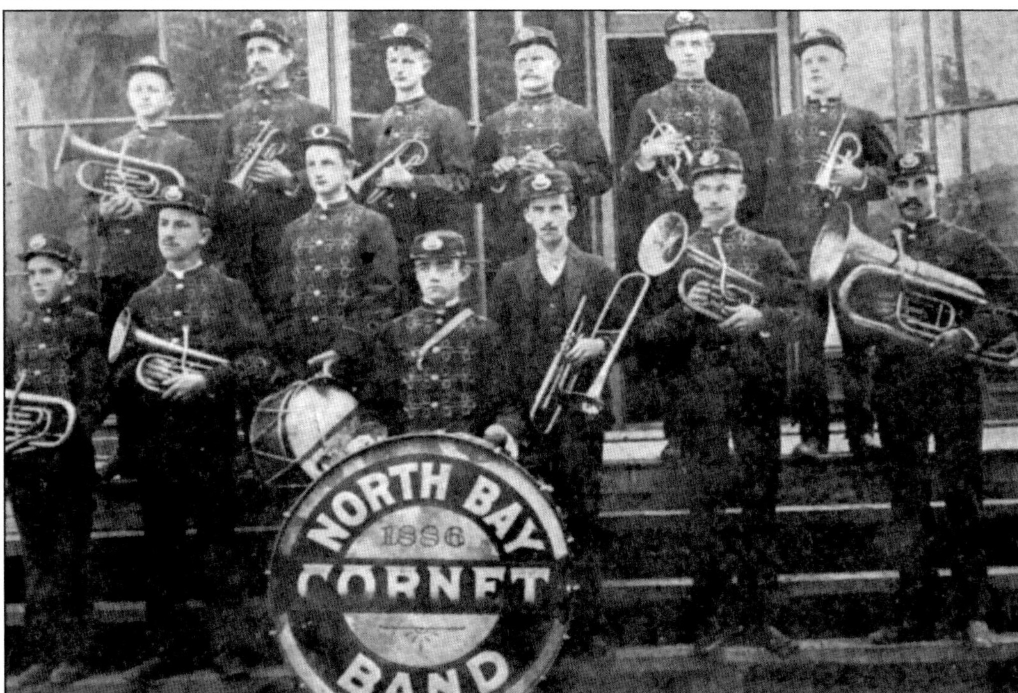

This is the North Bay military band in 1886. William Bowman, editor of the *Vienna News* from 1877 to 1881, was the leader. From left to right are (first row) George Janes, Lawrence "Ed" Allen, Bert Montross, Fernando Joslyn, Joseph Laffinwell, Charles Allen, and Elmer Matthews; (second row) Harry Montross, Charles Mulholland, Edwin Montross, John Scullen, Bowman, and Howard Janes. Edwin was the grandfather of Bob Montross, a past historian of North Bay. Harry and Bert were Edwin's brothers.

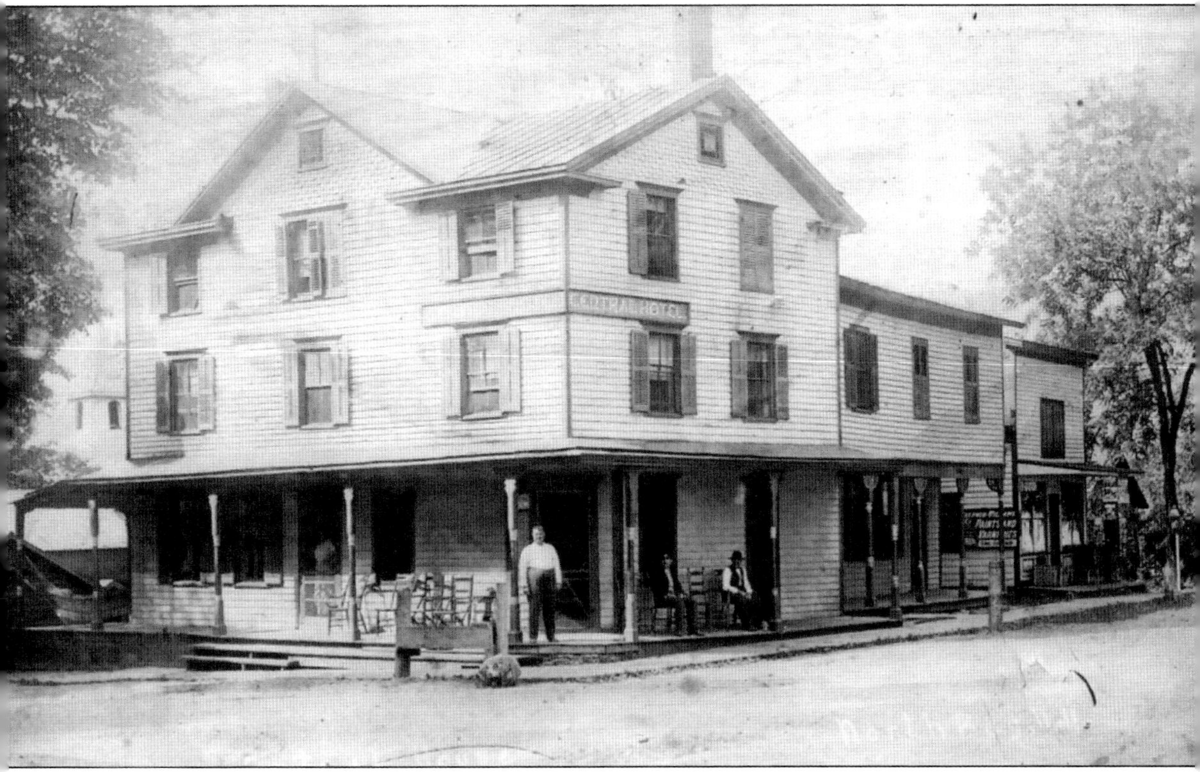

The first Central Hotel was located on the eastern part of the four corners. In July 1877, Mr. Tallman was reputed to be an excellent landlord. After the hotel burned, Josiah Cleveland built the second Central Hotel on the west side of the four corners on a West Lake Street lot formerly occupied by James Louden. The oldest hotel in North Bay, it is now known as the North Bay Hotel. The third floor, removed after a fire in 1961, was a popular dance hall. The Dixon brothers played there in the 1930s, with John Dixon on the drums, Joe Dixon on the saxophone, and Stan Dixon on the piano. Around that time, Marge Montross had a tea shop in a section separate from the hotel proper. She fascinated children by reading their fortunes in tea leaves. In 1932, a group of men met with Fire Chief Frank Ernwein from Oneida and Cappy Mayer of Durhamville in the ballroom of the hotel, and the North Bay Volunteer Fire Department was formed.

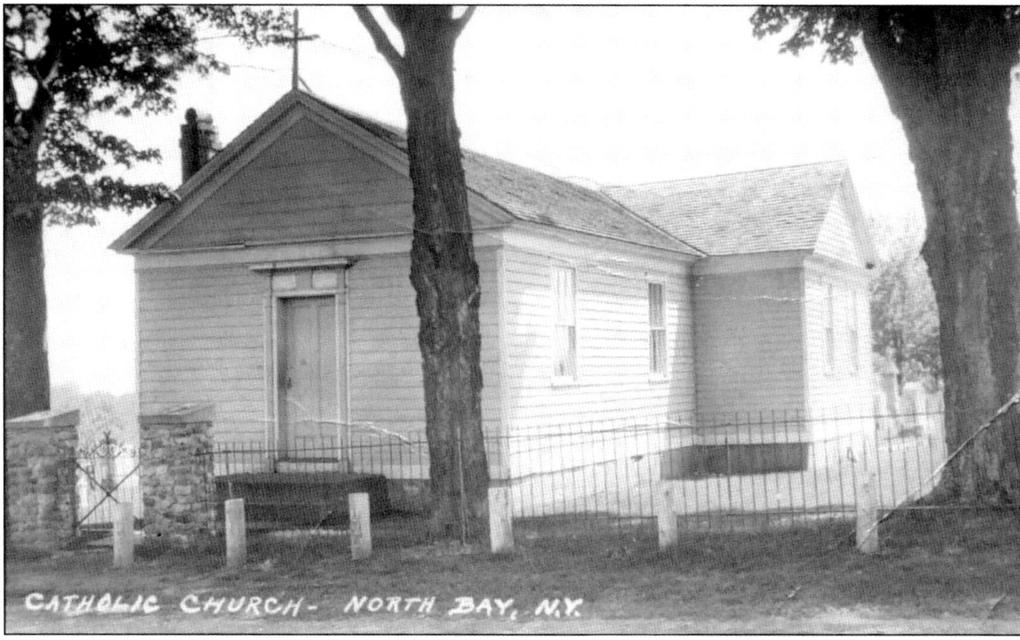

The first Roman Catholic mass in North Bay was held by Father Quarter in the home of Maj. Daniel Mulholland in 1835. In 1843, Mulholland donated land about a mile north on Mulholland Drive near the entrance to the cemetery, and the St. Peter and Paul Catholic Church was built. Father Beechman said mass from 1843 until 1873.

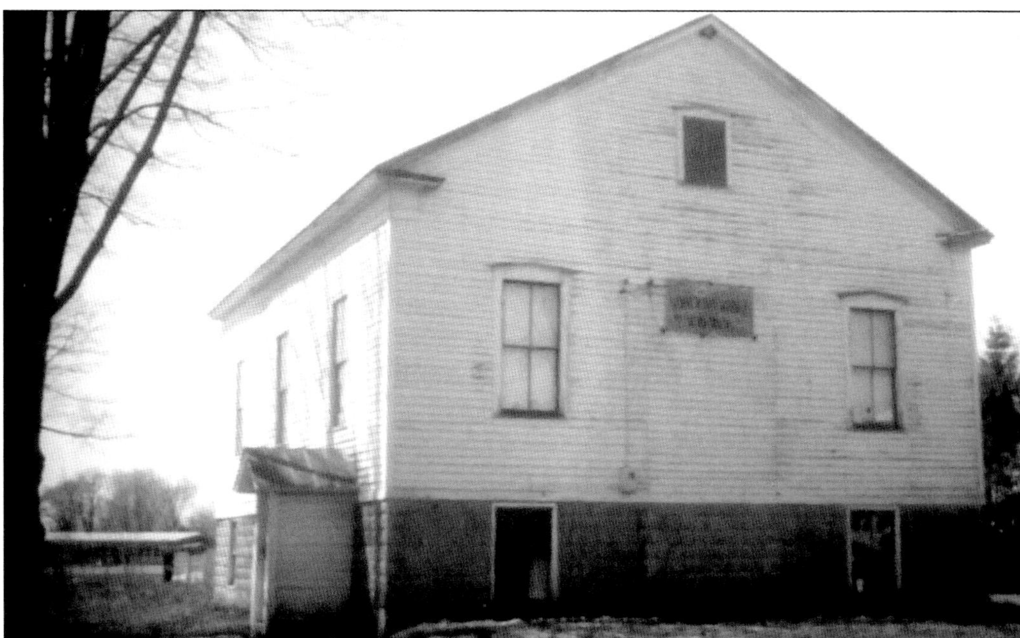

Henry J. Myer built the Baptist church in North Bay in 1862, and it was a busy church. Just one of many fund-raising events to benefit the church was an excursion and basket picnic aboard a steamboat to Frenchman's Island in August 1877. Tickets sold for 40¢. At that time, the steamboats *Manhattan* and *Sue* were active in North Bay.

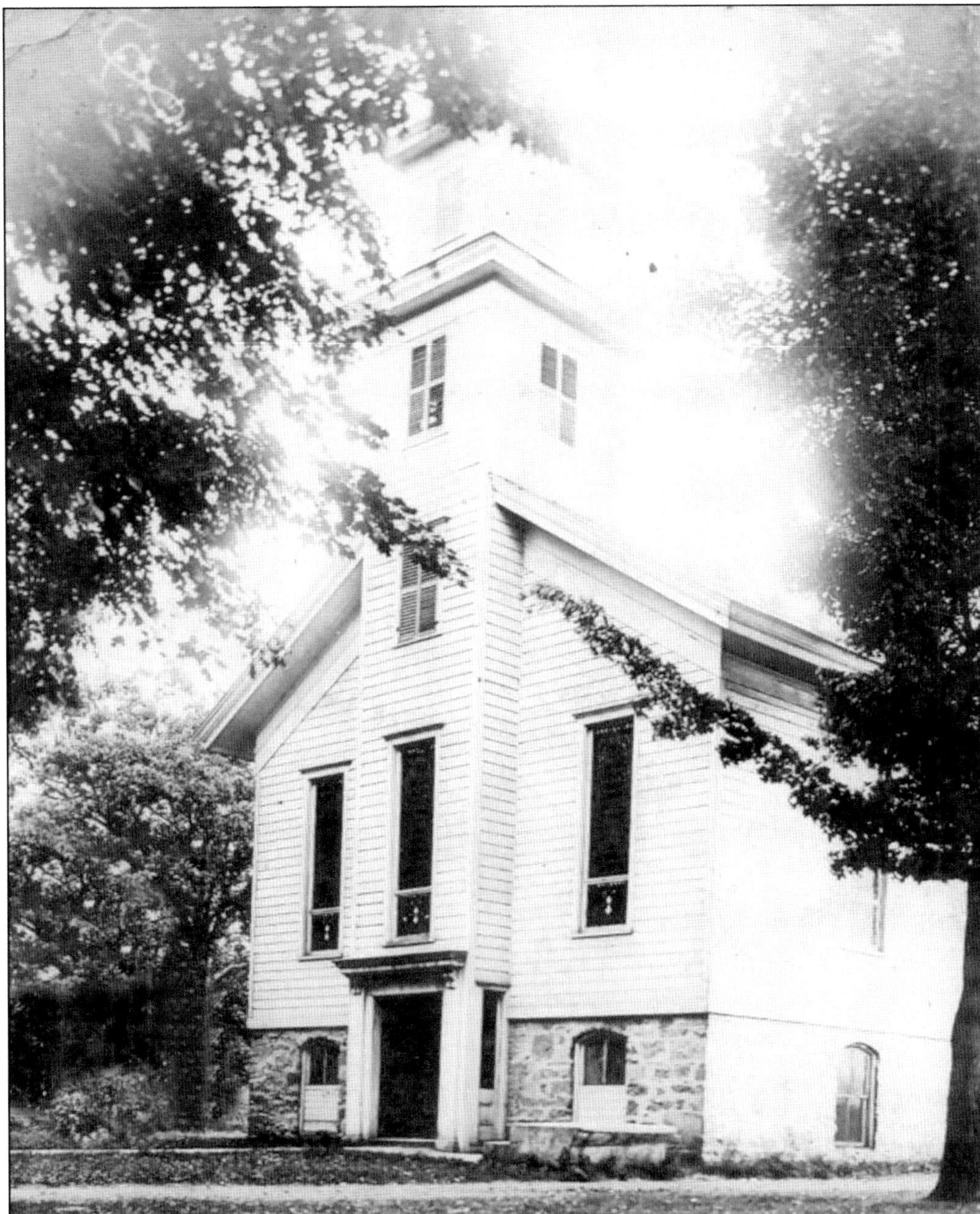

As early as 1874, the congregation of the North Bay Episcopal Methodist Church on Mulholland Drive discussed building a new church. However, no steps were taken until December 4, 1878, after a sermon by Elder Skeel. Using a blackboard to assist him, Skeel illustrated the church's need and the possibilities. Committees were formed, and the building of the new church was begun on West Lake Street beside N. McCormick's grocery store. Completed in December 1879, it was dedicated in January 1880. It closed on December 31, 1967, and was sold. In 2006, the old church received a shiny, red metal roof, and remodeling the grand, old building into two apartments began. Much of the fine, old woodwork is being preserved by new owner George Baker. Baker is the husband of the first elected woman supervisor in North Bay.

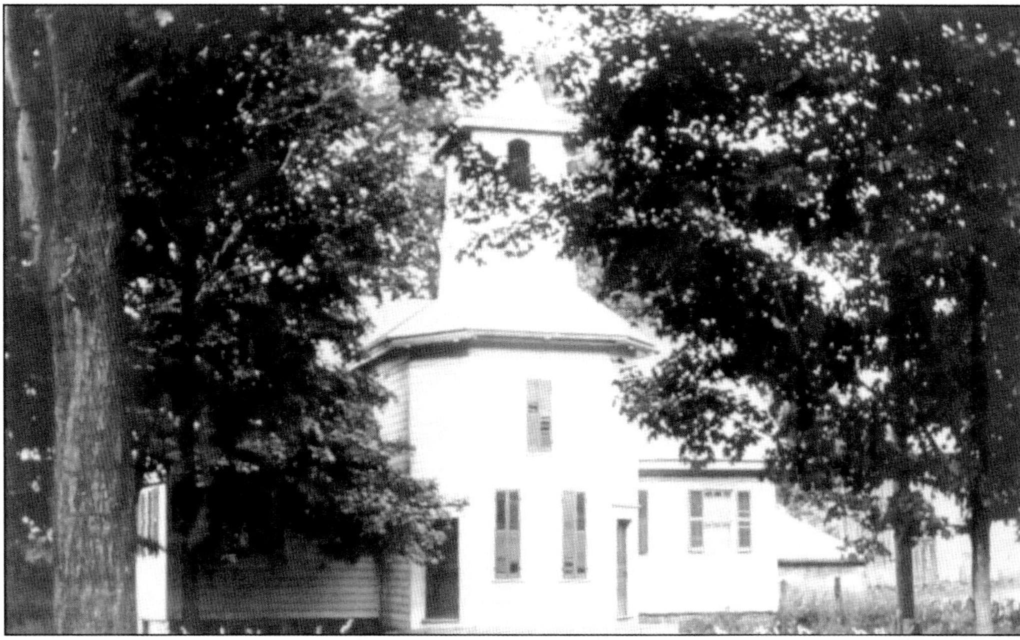

The North Bay Elementary School was located on West Lake Street one door down from the Central Hotel. It was built in the mid-1800s and was used to educate young minds until the North Bay Area School replaced it in 1956. It was sold and remodeled and is still in use as duplex apartments.

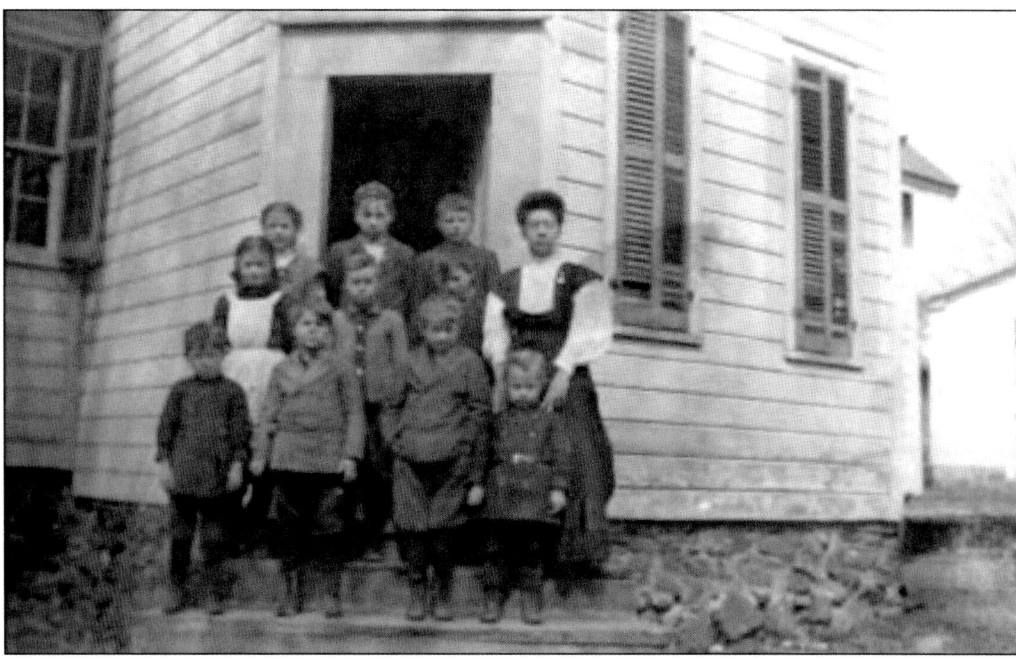

Masie A. Tuttle was a teacher at the North Bay Elementary School and is shown here with her class in 1909. In the two-room schoolhouse, the children were educated through the eighth grade. Those wishing to further their education usually took the train to Oneida or Camden where there were high schools.

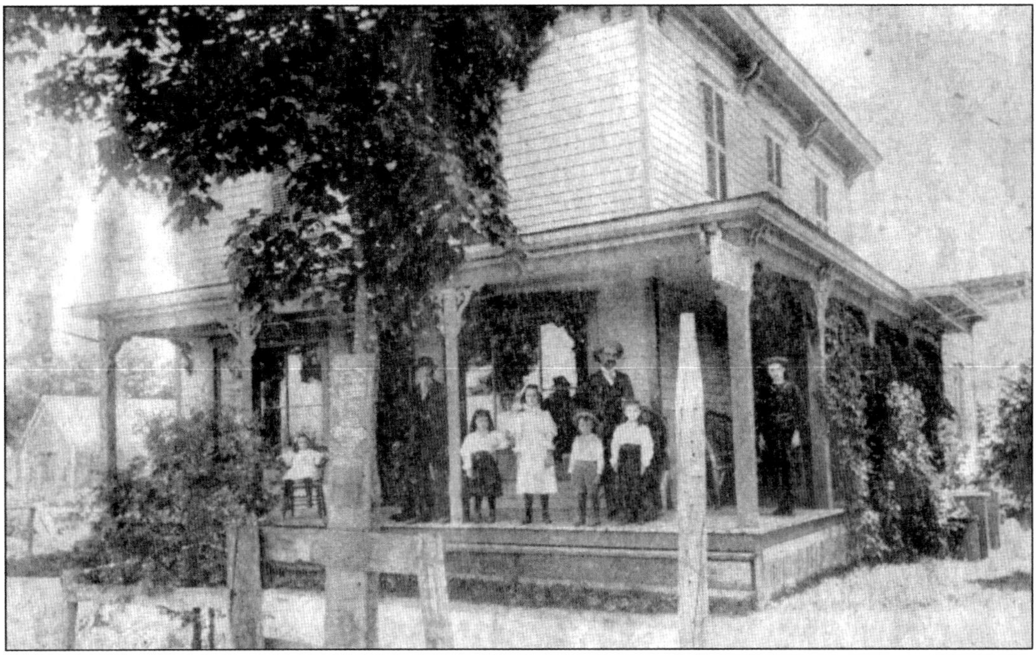

Prior to 1870, James Louden built the first grocery store in North Bay on the corner of West Lake Street south of Main Street. Known as Jimmy Low's, it may have offered a few yards of calico as well. Photographed around 1893, from left to right are Emma Theall Bates, James Louden, Ola Annis Campbell, Gertrude Theall Kilts, Edith Theall, Lola Annis Penoyer, Edith A. Wells, and Frank Broga.

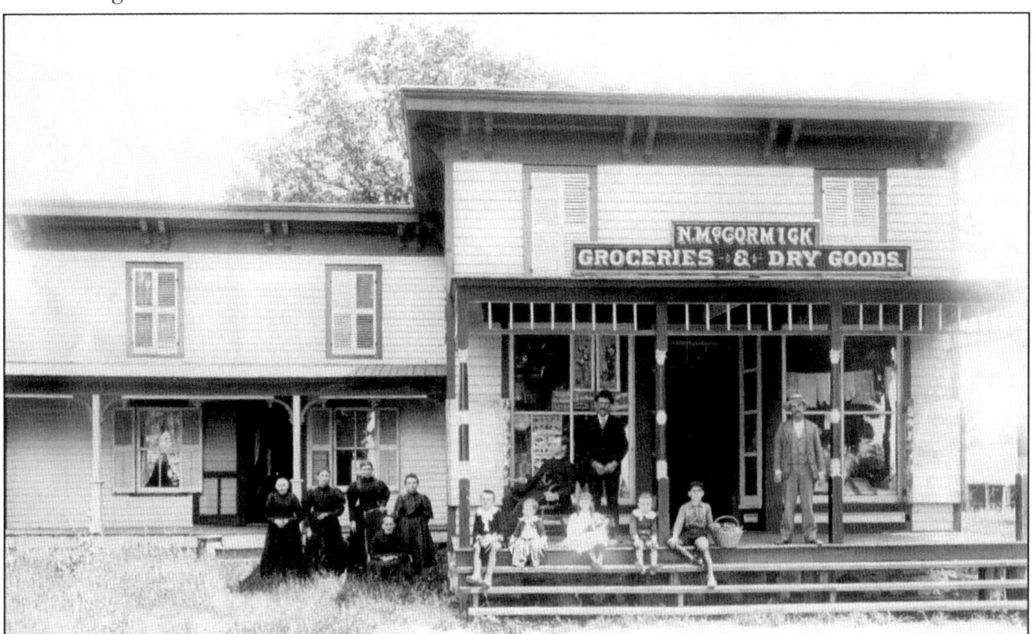

The McCormick Grocery and Dry Goods Store was built in the late 1800s. It was one of the first general stores in North Bay. Serving as a residence and a store, it was located on West Lake Street next to the Methodist church. Today it is a private residence.

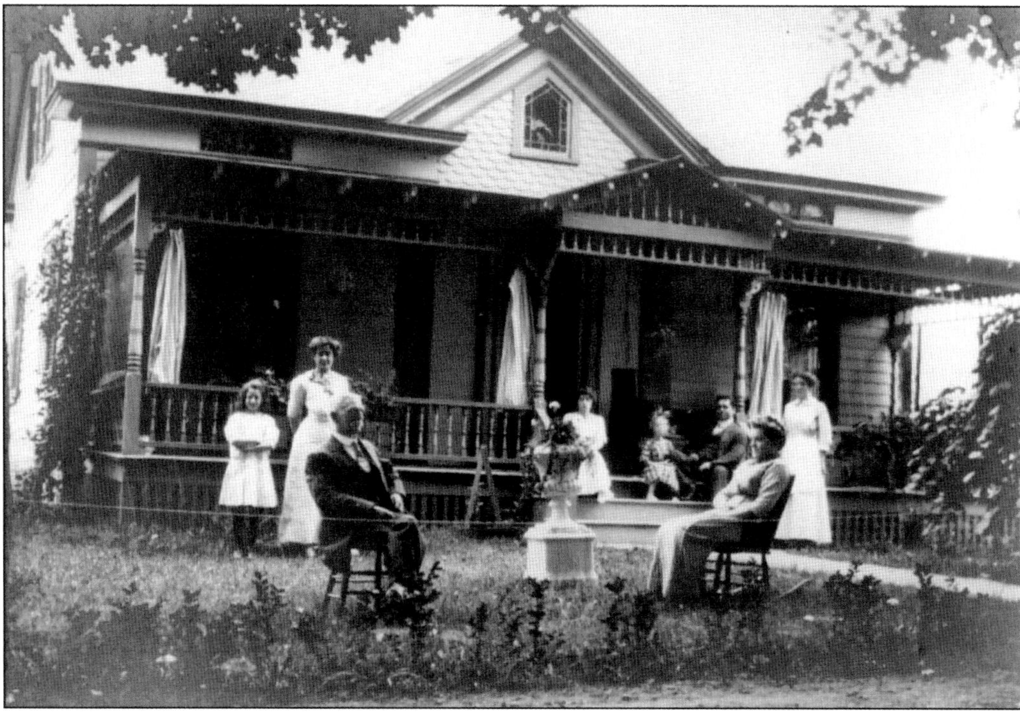

Facing north, Dexter Nichols Groceries and Dry Goods was the third building on the left on Mulholland Road. The structure served as a residence and a general store. Pictured in the early 1900s, Nichols is seated and the young girl to his left is his daughter Sara Nichols Warren. Her children, not shown, are Sid, Jean, and Virginia Warren. The names of the rest of the people are not known.

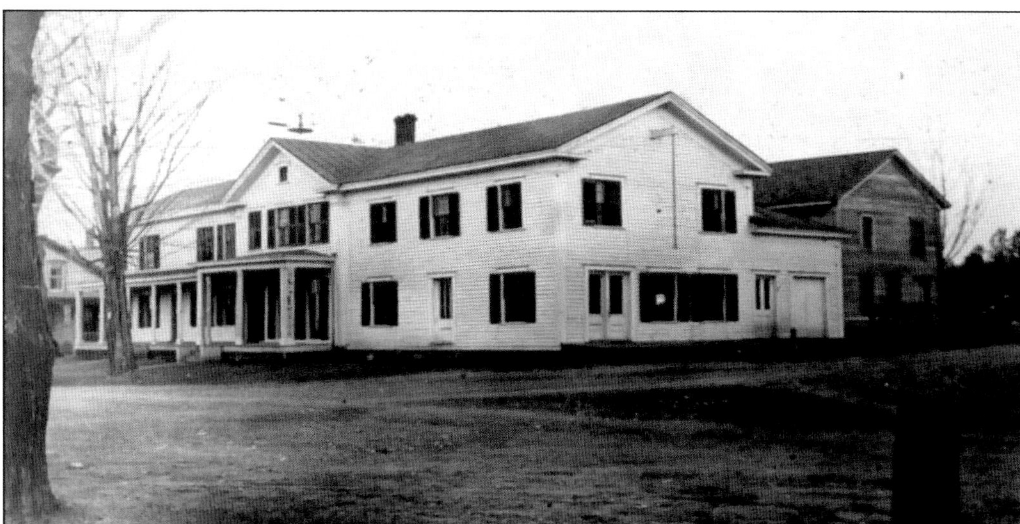

Facing north, the Paddock House was located on the corner of Mulholland Drive and Main Street at the four corners. It served as an apartment building and housed businesses. After his bakery burned in 1887, Henry Woodard moved his business to the east end of the building. During the 1920s, Mattie Woodard sang a little song as she carried a basket about town, selling her father's baked goods.

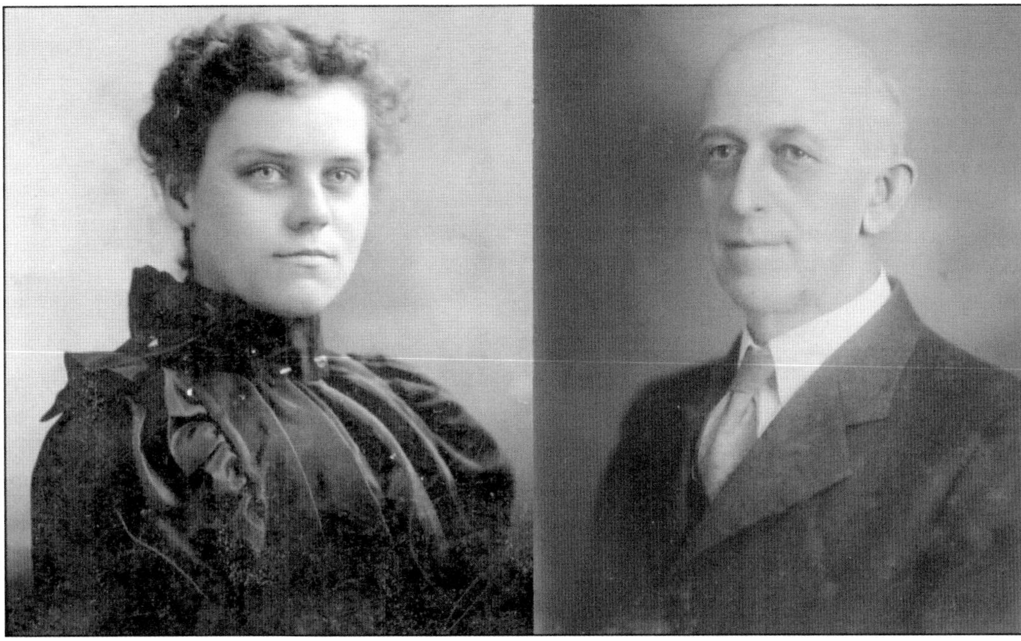

In 1901, Jessie Cook, a schoolteacher, married Harley R. Phelps, a dairy farmer. Phelps bought the valley in North Bay, and they worked together to build a life. Their first home was a small shack by Murray Brook, and he built a barn on the east side of the valley.

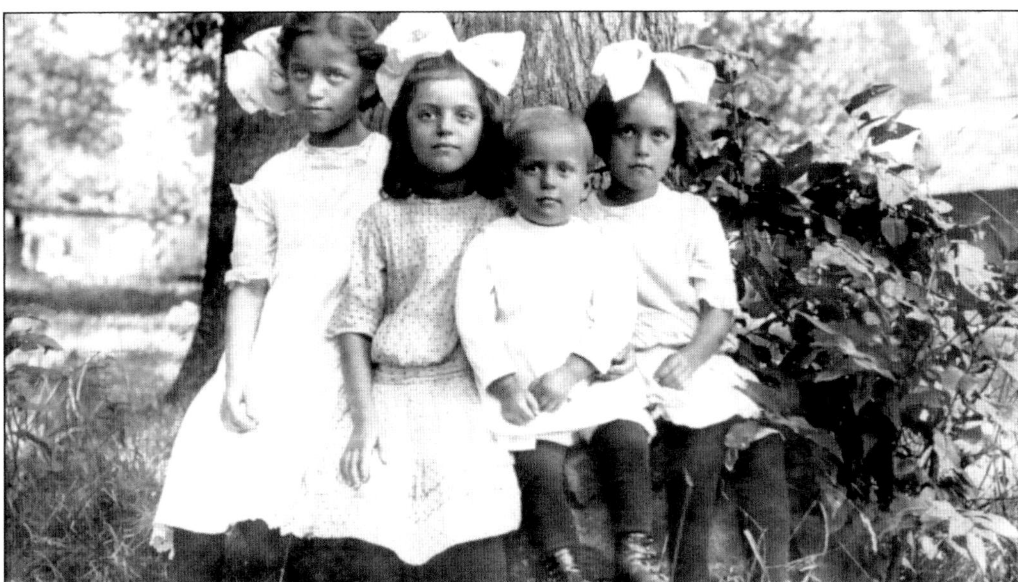

The Phelpses had four children. Pictured from left to right are LaVanch, who became a home economics teacher; Ruth, who became an elementary teacher; Russell, who ran the farm, the town water system, and the canning factory and was a founding member of the volunteer fire department; and Elizabeth, who became an accountant and a seamstress.

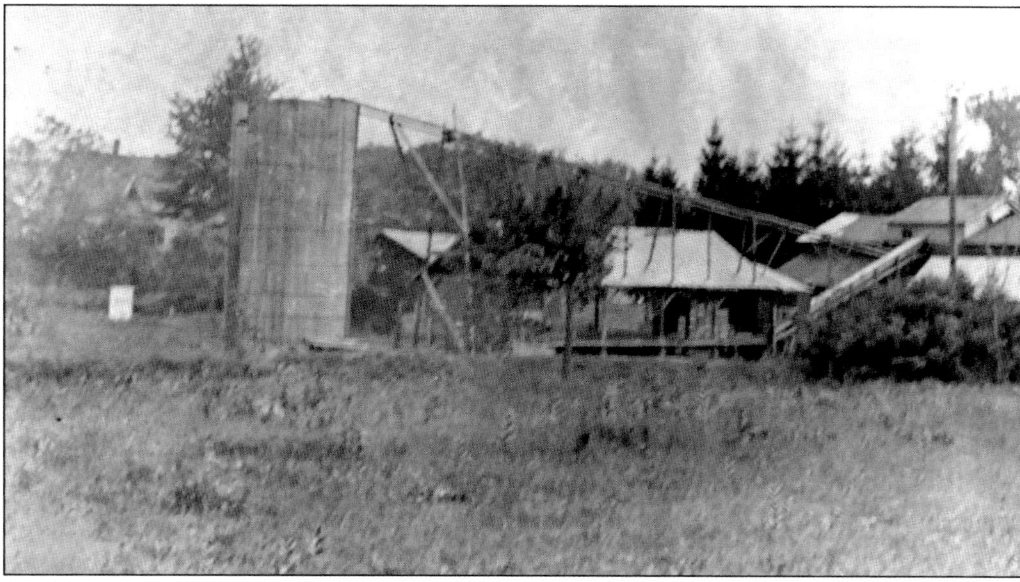

In 1906, when Harley R. Phelps opened the Har-Phel Canning Company, North Bay had dwindled in size. The loss of tourism to Sylvan Beach had a heavy impact on the little hamlet. Rebuilt in 1924, the factory was the only industry of that type left when it closed in 1951. During World War II, they packed and shipped 16,000 cases of beans and corn per year to the front lines.

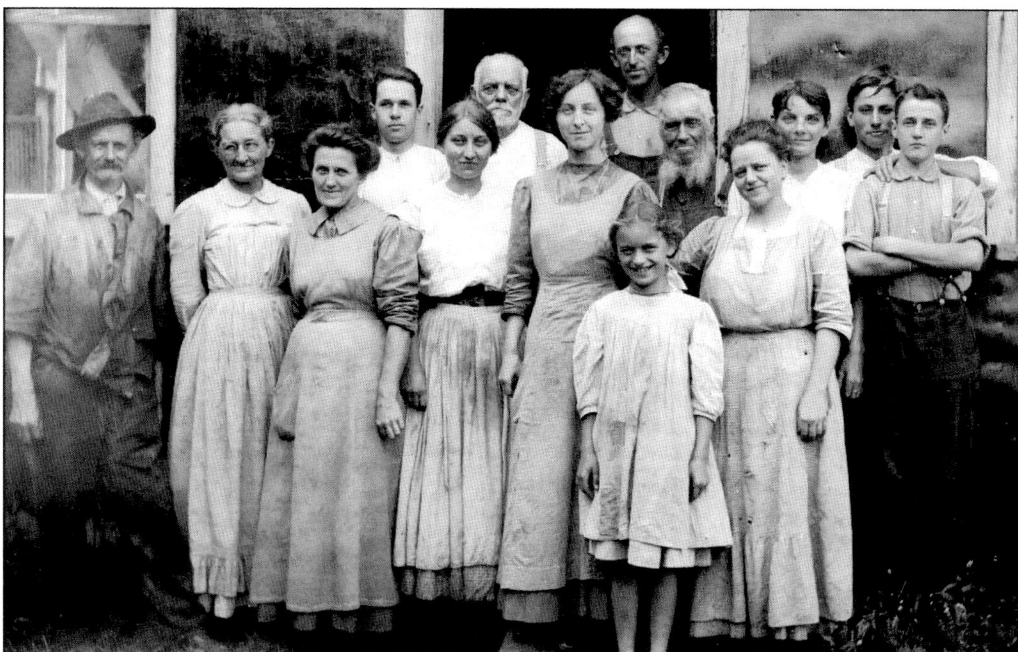

Nearly everyone in North Bay worked in the factory at one time or another. From left to right, this group from 1912 includes (first row) William Janes, Mrs. William Janes, Mary Allen, "Totsie" Barnes, Esther Allen Evans, LaVanch Phelps, and Mrs. John Fox; (second row) Frank Van Buren, Civil War veteran Casper Cook, Harley, Henry Nash, Howard Fulton, Thomas Griffing, and Ward Van Buren.

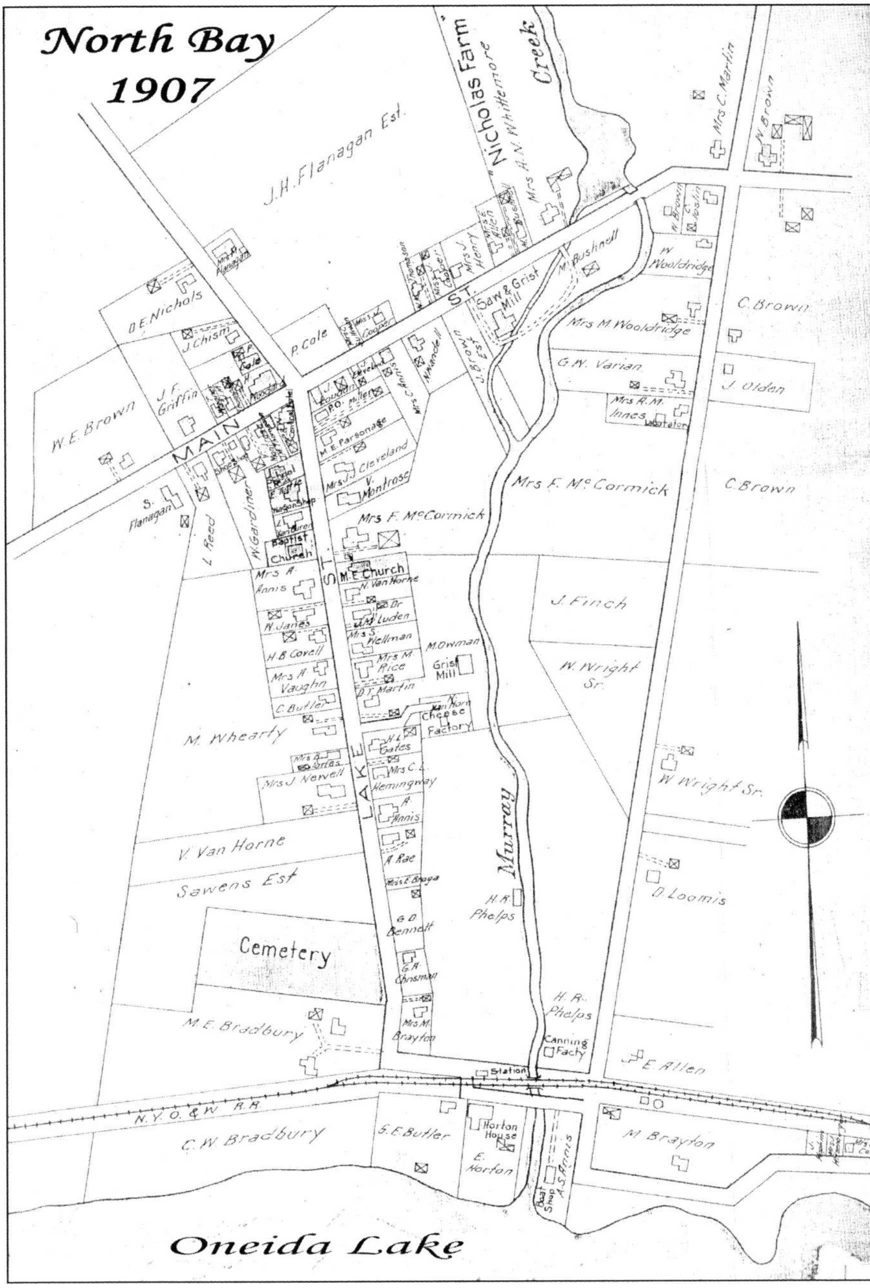

Of the seven hotels active in the 1800s, only two remained by 1907, the Central Hotel at the four corners on West Lake Street and the Horton House on the shores of Oneida Lake. Passenger trains full of vacationers eager to experience the peace and joy of Oneida Lake no longer patronized the North Bay station, and all the potteries had long since closed. However, some commerce continued. There were still two gristmills and a sawmill, N. Van Horne still ran his cheese factory, Velsor Montross had his blacksmith shop, and E. Tuttle had his wagon shop. In addition, there was a laboratory on East Lake Street, a canning factory, a shoe shop, and Albert Annis continued to build and repair a few boats. Farmers, the backbone of any community, produced milk and food that was transported to the cities by the New York, Ontario and Western Railway.

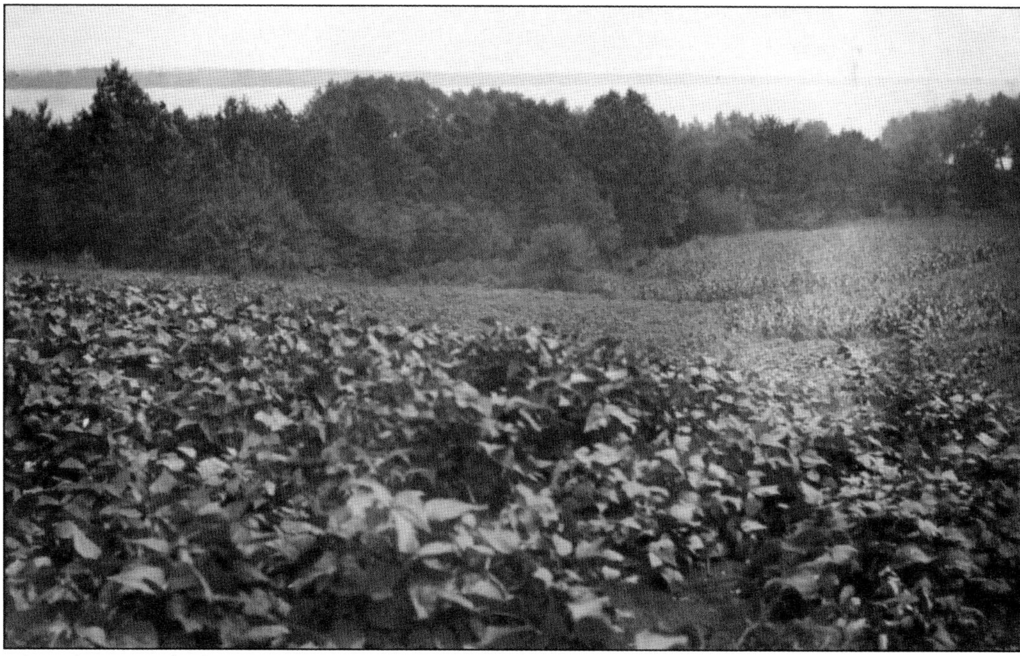

This photograph shows a field of beans and corn overlooking Oneida Lake on East Lake Street around 1915. The plantation was one of many fields the H. R. Phelps canning company used to grow the produce it canned. This field contained the ingredients for the company's famous succotash made with sweet corn and lima beans.

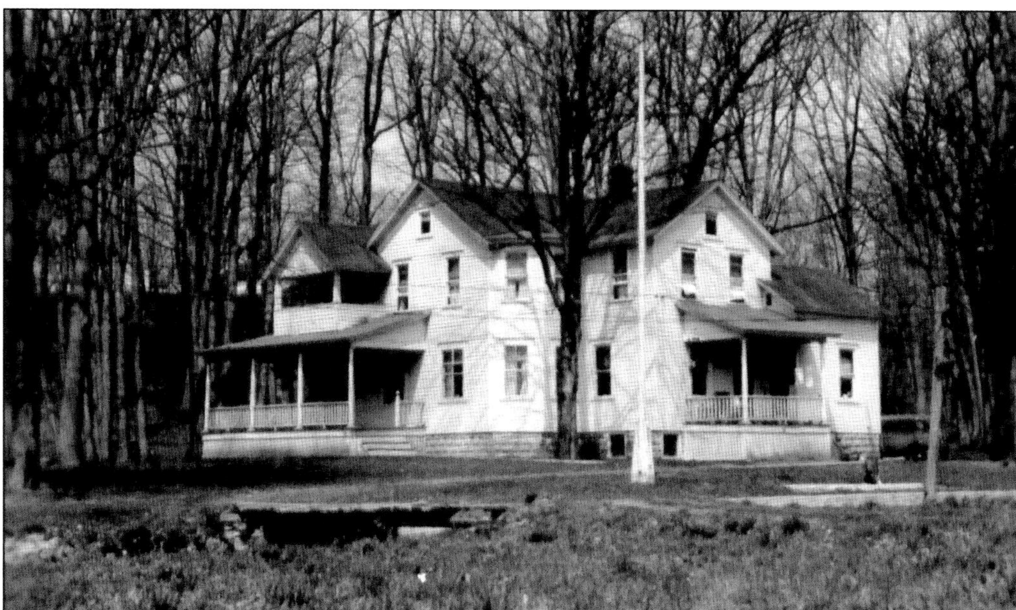

Although seven years old at the time, Harley R. Phelps's son Russell said he helped to build the house in the valley in 1917. The "house of seven gables" only cost $4,000 to build, but it had five bedrooms and a large, warm kitchen that received many visitors from all walks of life. Located near the railroad station, many people found shelter behind its doors during the cold winter months while waiting for a train.

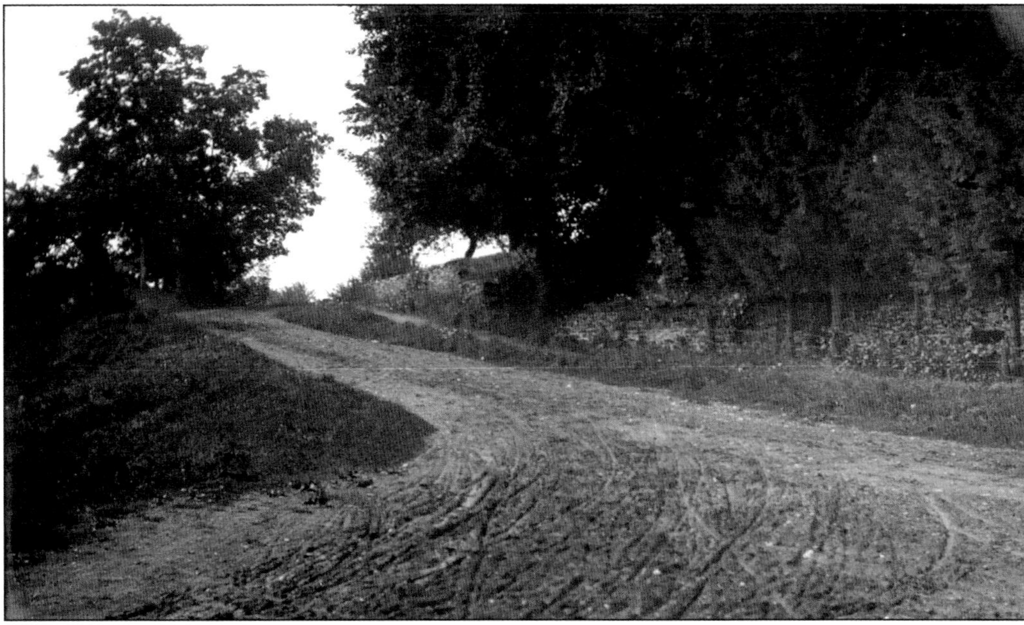

This is Lake Hill leading to the North Bay depot in the early 1920s. In 1925, Sykes rail bus No. 801 was put into service on the northern division of the New York, Ontario and Western Railway. It carried passengers between Oneida and Oswego. Locals referred to the self-propelled railroad car as the "Tooneville Trolley." It continued in service until 1926. Regular trains at that time were usually comprised of boxcars and coal cars.

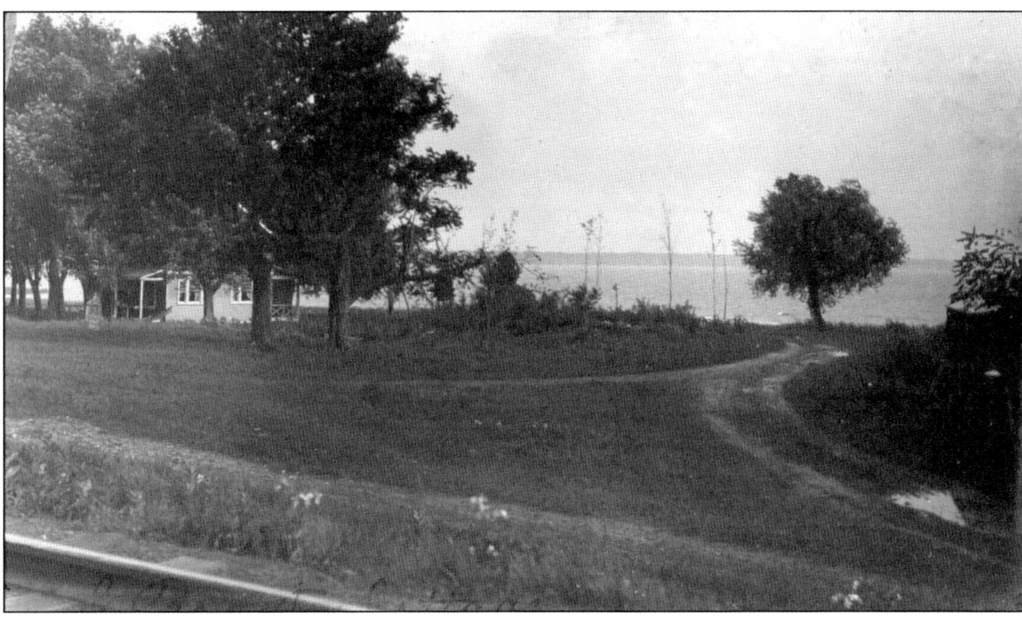

Lakeshore Drive in early 1900 was largely undeveloped, having only a few cottages. The Brayton family home was built after their hotel and is shown in this picture. Lloyd Hepburn built a cottage in the 1920s after he married a Brayton girl. Lloyd was actress Katherine Hepburn's uncle. It is said that Katherine visited her uncle one summer. A signed picture of the star hung on the wall near his front door.

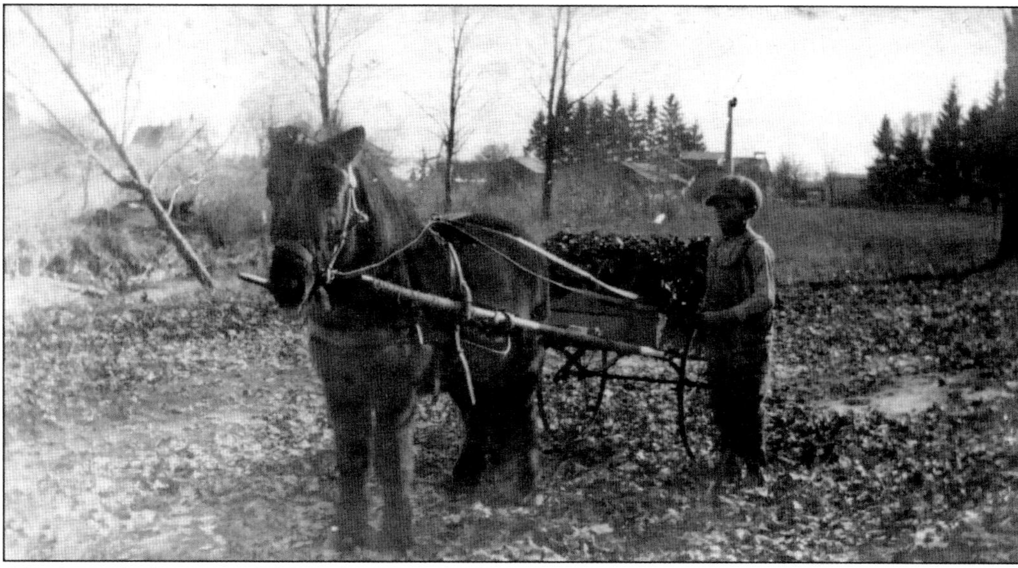

All through history, children have worked alongside their parents to survive and achieve. This photograph, appropriately dubbed "the farmer," was taken during the fall of 1919 and is a prime example of child labor. This young boy is using his pony and cart to do chores around the farm.

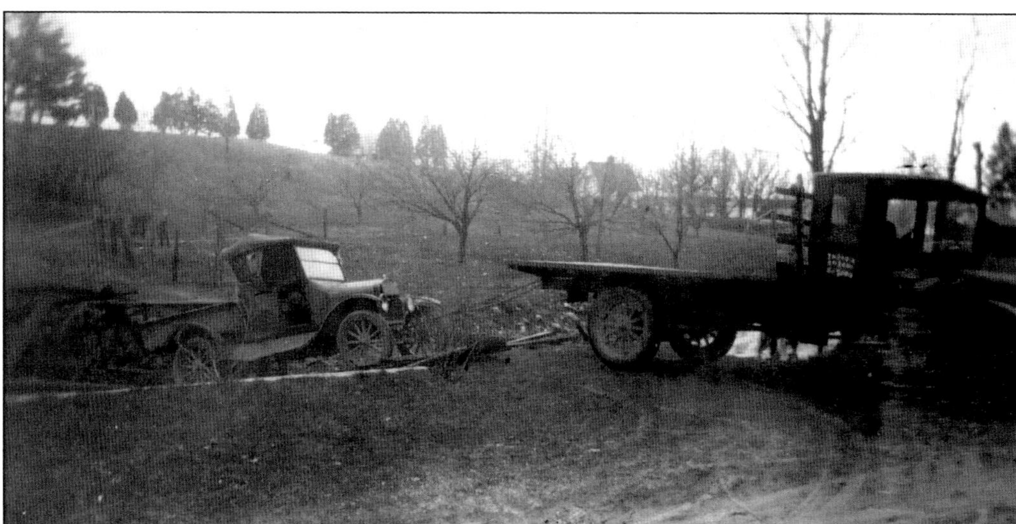

Trucks were a vast improvement over the horse in most cases, but, as seen here, they sometimes got stuck, and early models often broke down. Horses, on the other hand, did not run out of gas and did not get stuck very often. These two old work horses that were used on the farm and at the canning factory are at work in the valley in North Bay in the mid-1920s.

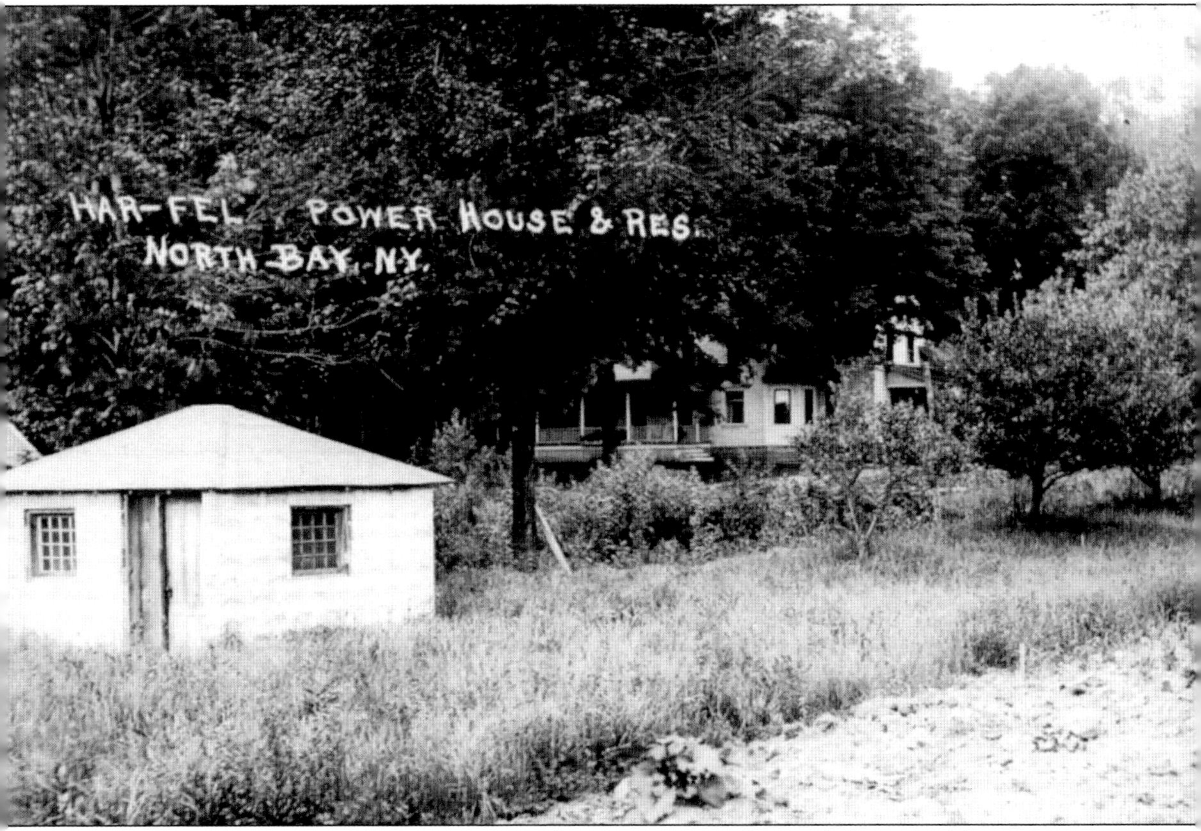

In 1922, the public service commission granted authority to Harley R. Phelps to build, maintain, and operate an electric lighting system in North Bay. He built a hydroelectric dam for the purpose, and on February 10, 1924, a radio broadcast from Buffalo credited Phelps with this accomplishment. Between 1923 and 1927, Harley, his son Russell, and Ur Dutcher wired all the homes and businesses in the community for electricity. Around the same time, Phelps built an award-winning spring water system that provided the town with clean, clear drinking water. When Russell sold the water system to the town in 1972, a water district was formed. He continued to take care of the maintenance for several years; however, they made him remove the rainbow trout that lived in the tank.

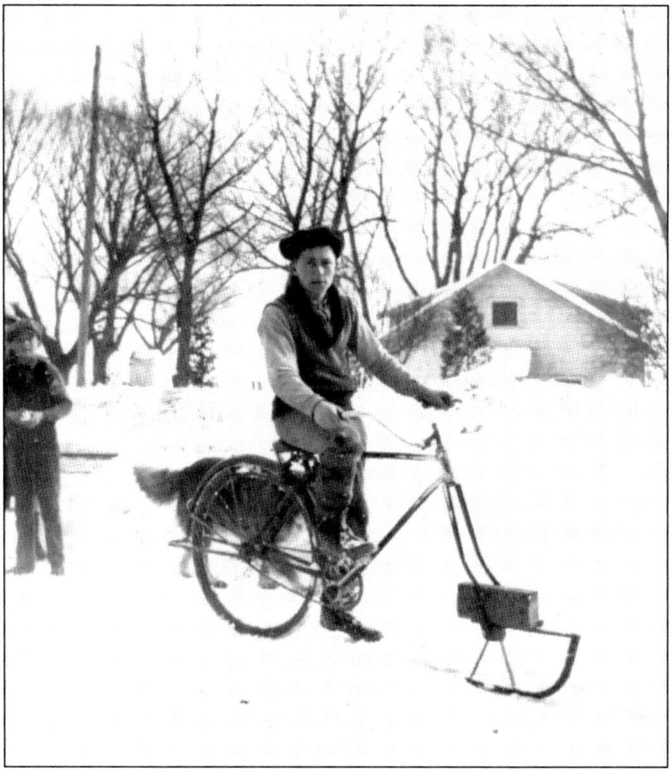

Good old American ingenuity and a block of wood were all the ingredients necessary for this young man to have hours of enjoyment during the winter of 1923. The roar of snowmobiles and a thirst for speed have replaced the simple joy of a homemade snow-cycle. A boy in the background is seen holding a snowball at the ready.

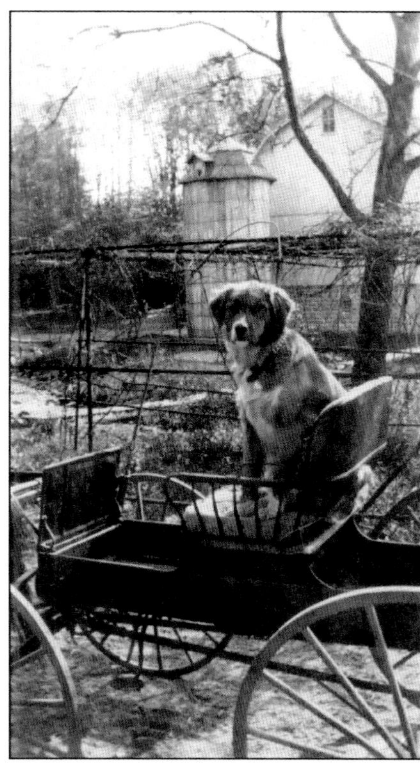

In 1923, Ted the mail dog was seen almost daily carrying his basket on his appointed rounds. Ted boarded the New York, Ontario and Western Railway passenger car to retrieve his master's suitcase when he came home from high school in Oneida. Ted also liked to chase cats, and one time, he spilled his basket, which carried cookies. It is said he picked up every cookie and did not eat one.

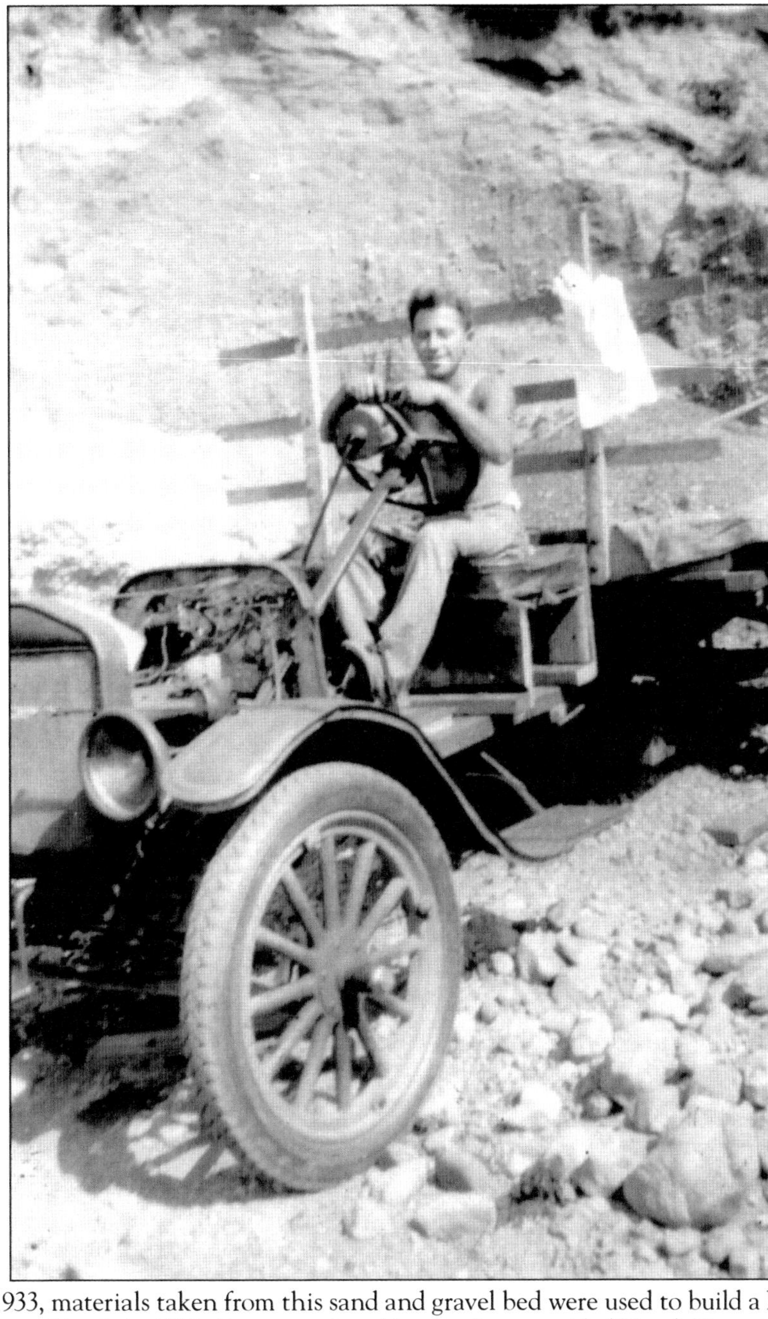

Shown in 1933, materials taken from this sand and gravel bed were used to build a hydroelectric dam on Murray Brook in 1920. Power produced by the dam provided North Bay with electricity. During the winters, the H. R. Phelps factory made cinder blocks, and in 1933, those blocks were used to build the first firehouse. Previous to that time, the fire truck was stored in a garage behind Johnson's Central Hotel. Located on West Lake Street, the garage was at the top of the hill, which was handy because they sometimes had to push the old truck down the hill to get it started. One time, there was a fire across the street and they could not get the Model T started, so they pushed it to the fire. The post office that is still in use today was built with Phelps's concrete blocks.

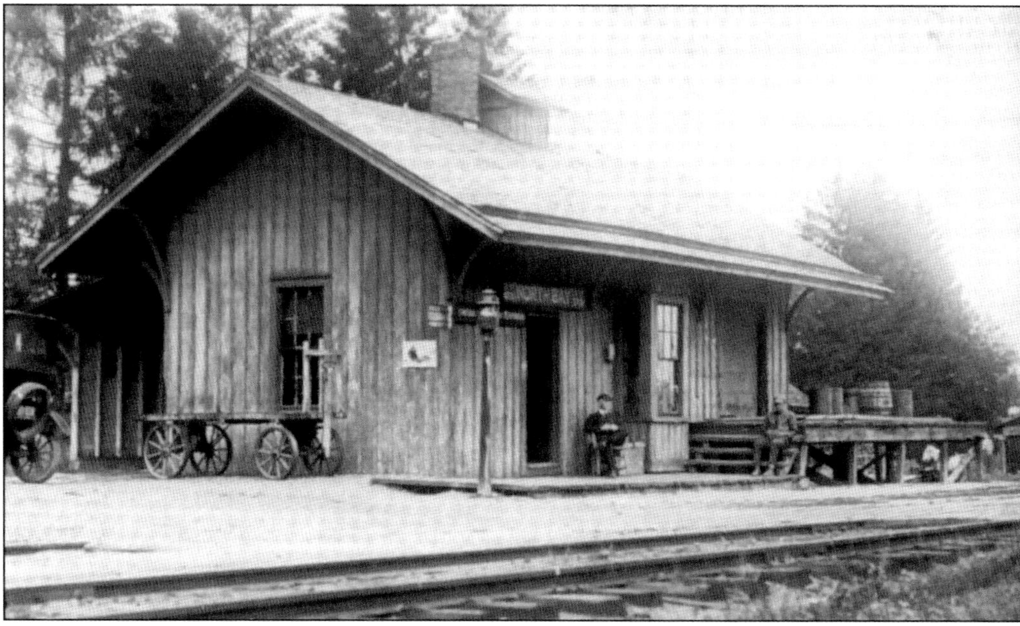

Completed in October 1878, this is the second station the New York and Oswego Midland Railroad built in North Bay. The railroad went into receivership in July 1873 and was sold on November 14, 1879, to a group of investors for $4.2 million. It was reorganized on January 21, 1880, as the New York, Ontario and Western Railway. The railway remodeled the station, adding a cupola and a bay window.

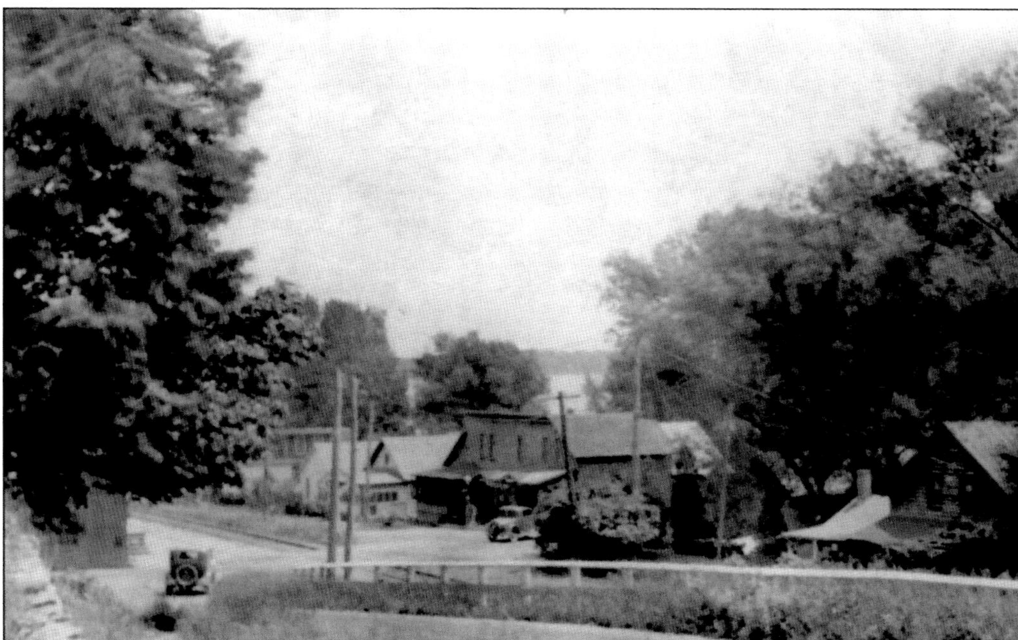

Initially a more important station than the developing Sylvan Beach area, the North Bay station served the resort, recreation, and picnic facilities that North Bay was noted for. By the time this picture was taken in 1927, Sylvan Beach had long since replaced North Bay as the place to go on a summer excursion by railroad or car.

The transport of milk was a mainstay of the New York, Ontario and Western Railway traffic. Dropped on a siding at the North Bay station, this wood-sheathed milk car, No. 2862, is a prime example of a steel framed, ice-cooled refrigerator car equipped with the latest Jenner couplers and Westinghouse air brakes. The Jenner increased rail safety considerably with its positive coupling action and reduced injuries and deaths on railroads nationwide.

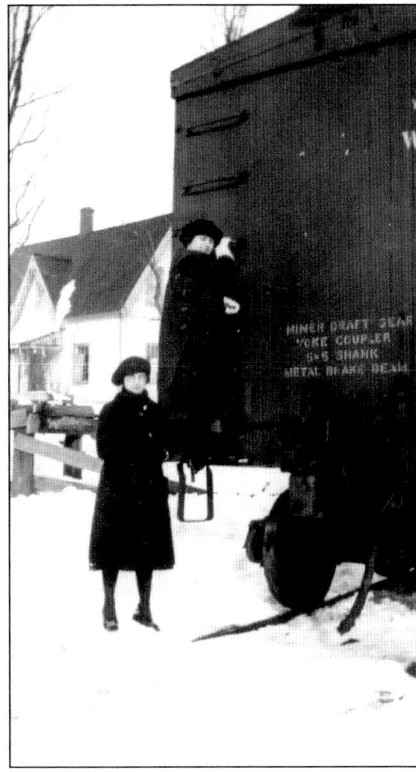

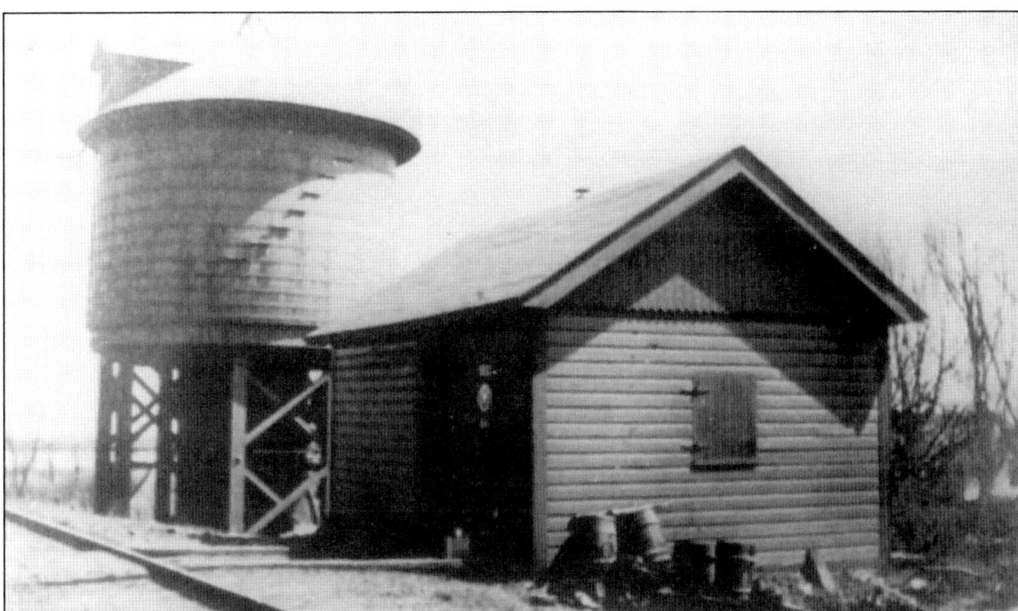

Located east of the North Bay depot behind Lloyd Hepburn's cottage, this water tank was designed with a feature unique to the New York, Ontario and Western Railway. The tank followed the basic design used throughout the East, but the New York, Ontario and Western Railway incorporated a gabled dormer on the roof and a standpipe to fill the engine's tender. After the station closed in 1930, the water tower was dismantled by Harley R. and Russell Phelps.

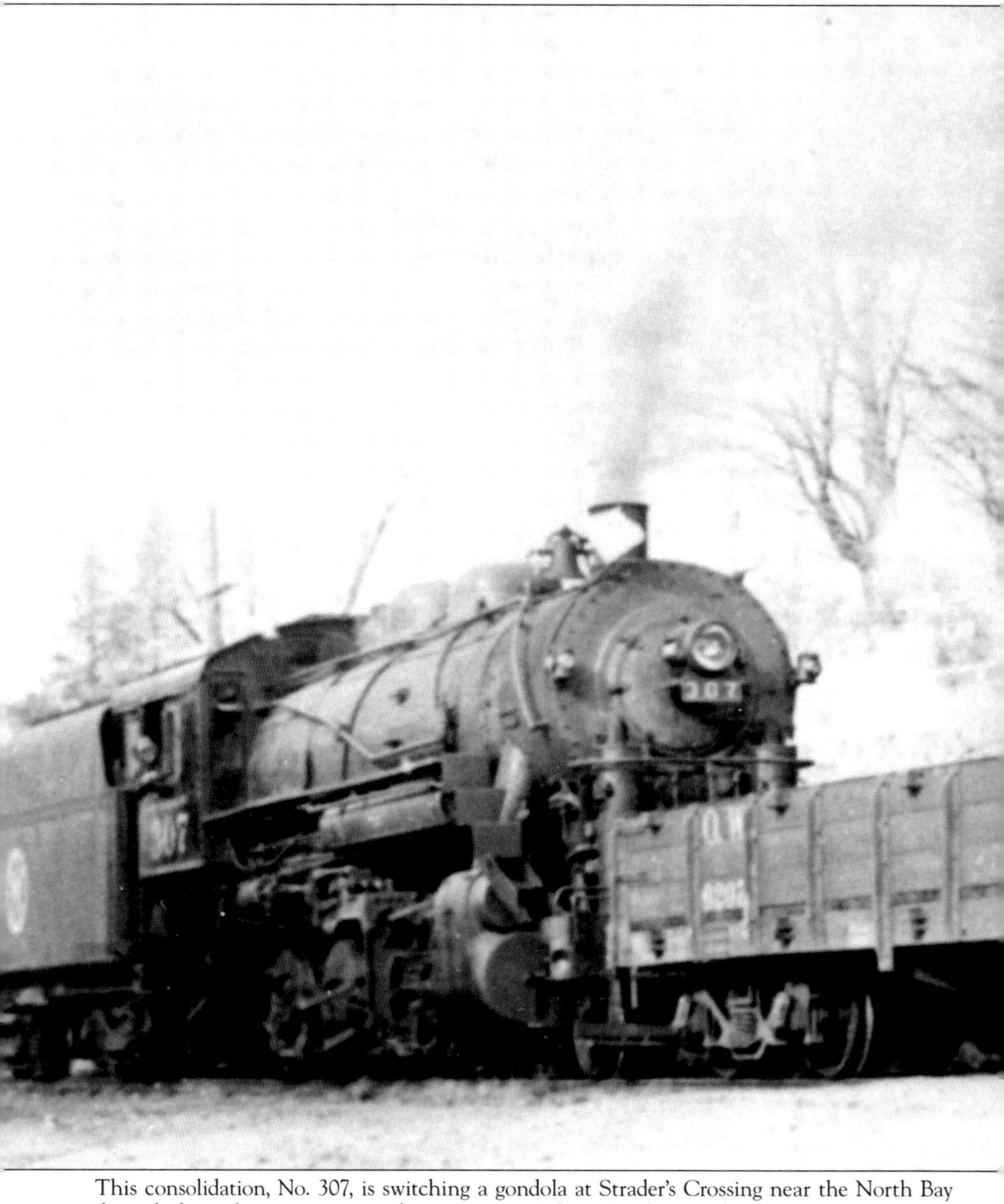

This consolidation, No. 307, is switching a gondola at Strader's Crossing near the North Bay depot before taking on water and returning to Sylvan Beach to pick up its eastbound train. Often the crew went to Strader's restaurant for lunch or to pick up a meal to be eaten aboard the caboose. A mainstay of the New York, Ontario and Western Railway, the consolidation's wheel arrangement provided high traction to maintain hauling capacity while reducing wear

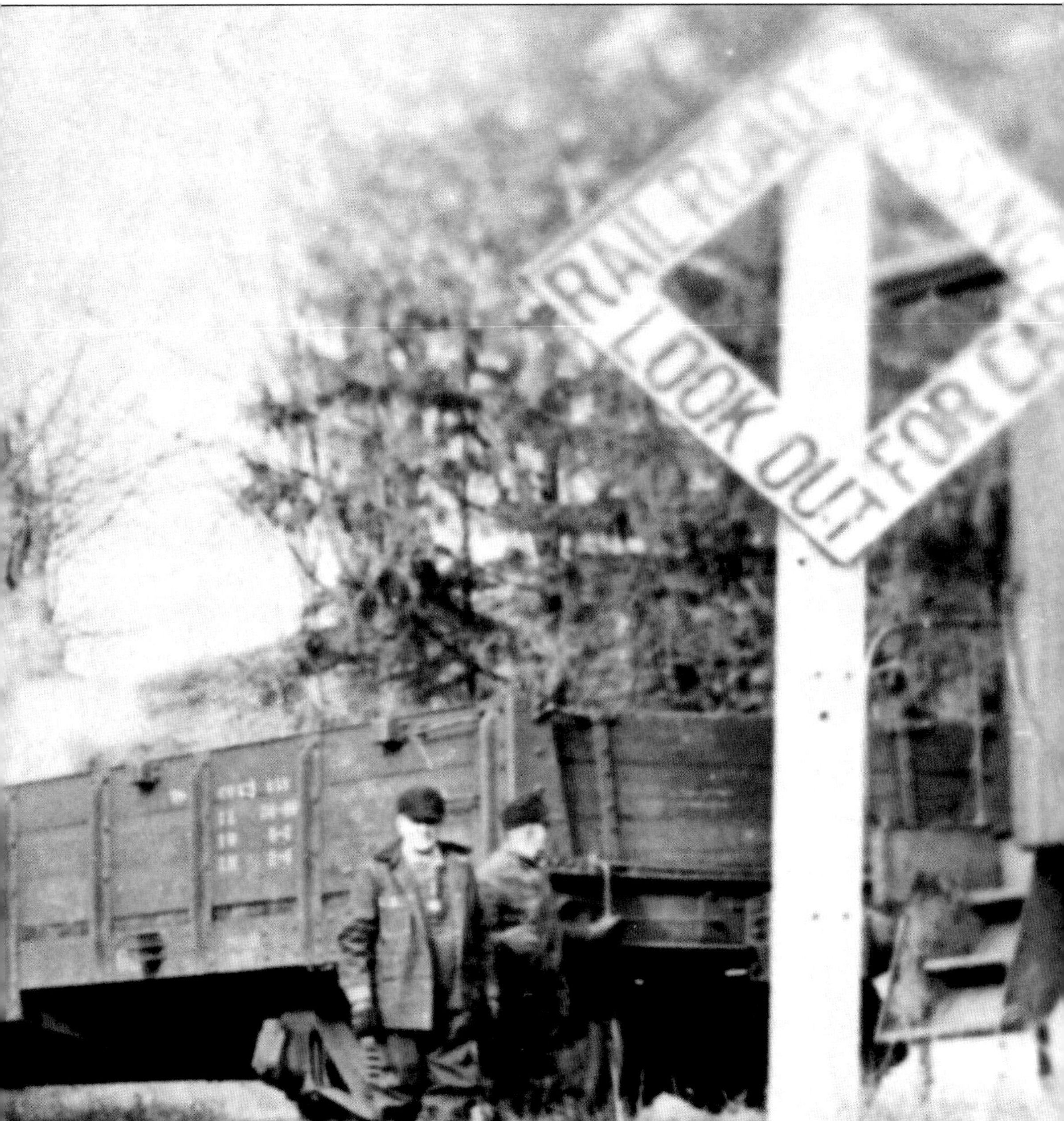

on the rail. The last of the heavy steam power, it was replaced by diesels in an effort to reduce operational costs for the railway, which faced financial difficulties from its beginning. In 1945, the New York, Ontario and Western Railway bought 18 Electro-Motive 1,350-horsepower freight engines and completed dieselization in 1948 with the purchase of ten 1,500-horsepower F3 road units and twenty-one 1,000-horsepower switchers.

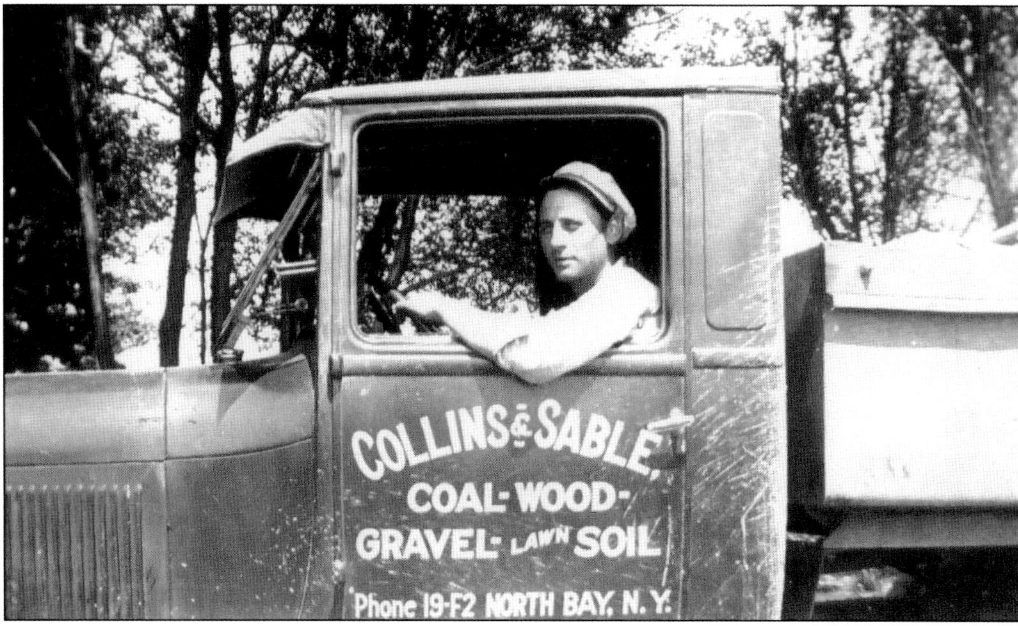

When the North Bay station closed on March 24, 1930, station agent John W. Jordan sold his coal business to the Collins and Sable Company. Walter Collins acquired sole ownership of the company. Assigned as the first caretaker of the depot, the New York, Ontario and Western Railway allowed him to use the depot scale to weigh his coal shipments. He married Emma Louise Rogers, who was born on the canal boat *Nettie Irene*, built in North Bay.

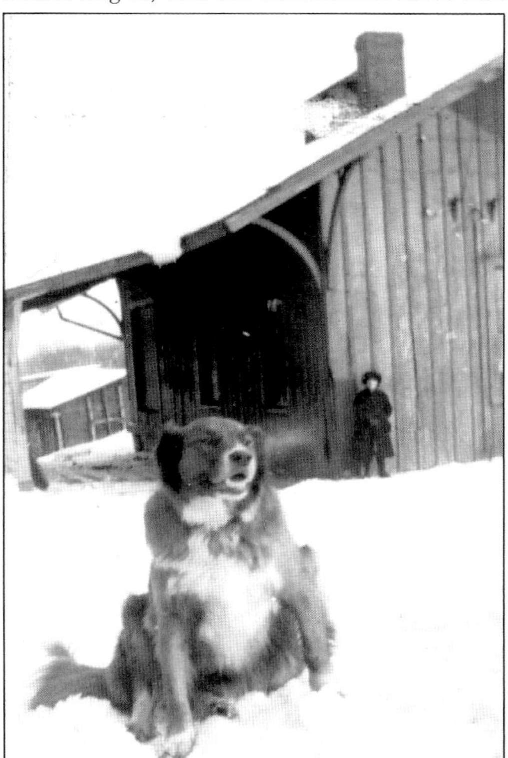

The advances in transportation made by the construction of the Barge Canal and the automobile contributed to the decline of the New York, Ontario and Western Railway. Referred to as the "old and weary" or "the old woman," its North Bay station was sold in 1953, and Russell Phelps was the last stationmaster. This photograph shows "Old Ted" waiting for the old and weary one last time.

Three

THE FLOOD

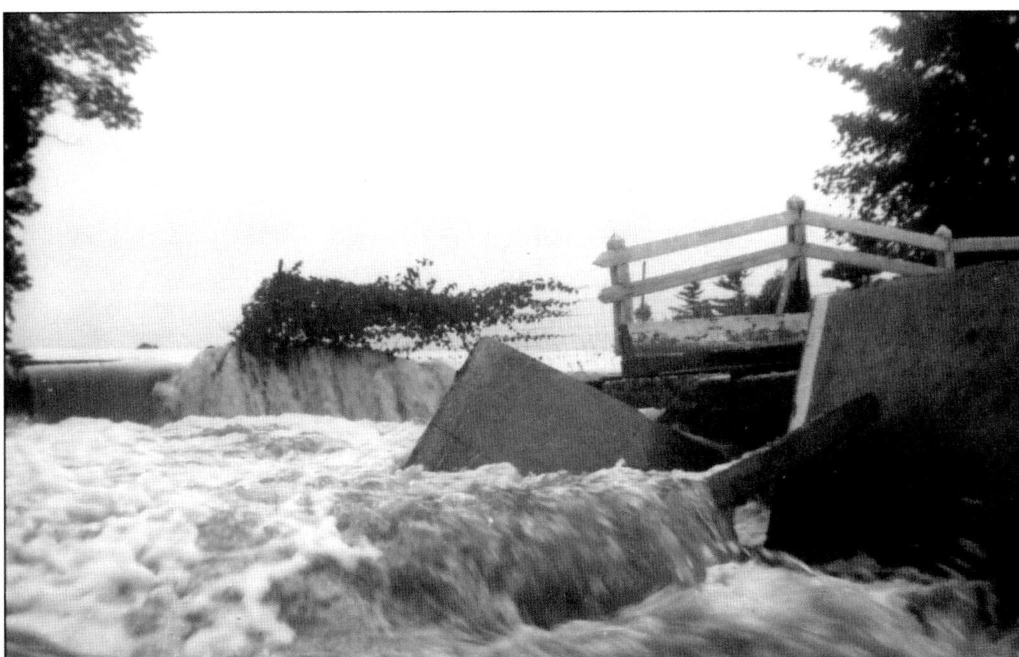

Late in July 1951, following an early-morning thunder and lightning storm, the area was pelted with a heavy rain for two and a half hours. These images were captured in North Bay when a natural resource people depended on erupted and caused unbelievable devastation. The swollen waters of Murray Brook and the debris it carried ate away at the embankment supporting the bridge on Route 49, and it collapsed.

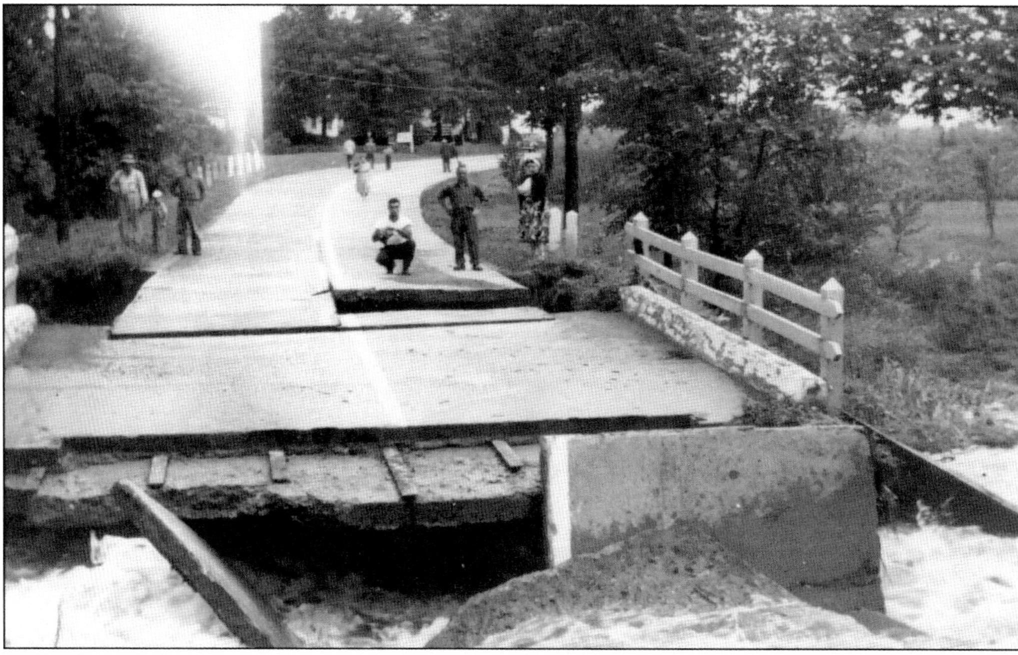

According to the New York State Department of Transportation (DOT), a bridge must measure at least 20 feet in length. Anything smaller than that is a culvert; therefore North Bay has no bridges, only culverts that cross the creek. The DOT measured the span that crosses Murray Brook on Route 49 to be 16 feet and referred to it as a box culvert.

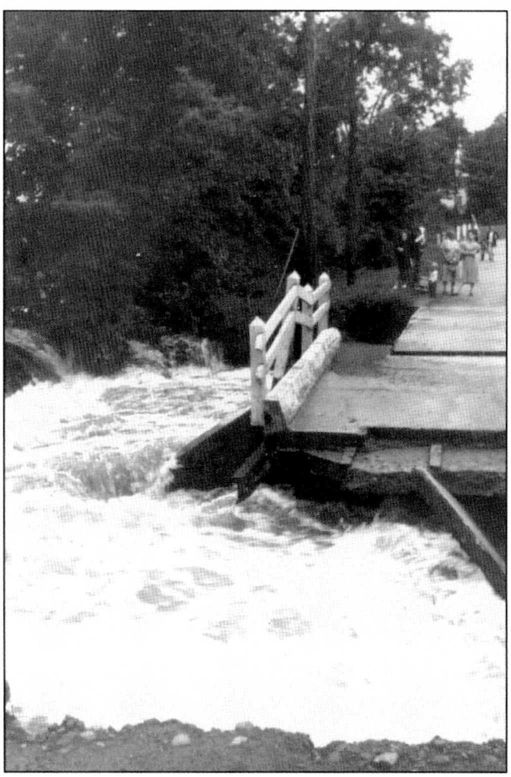

In October 1951, the DOT received orders to replace the culvert on Route 49 in North Bay, and it was built early in 1952. North Bay had two culverts connecting East Lake Street to West Lake Street, and until one of them was made safe, the citizens had to drive halfway to Camden to reach a street 16 feet away.

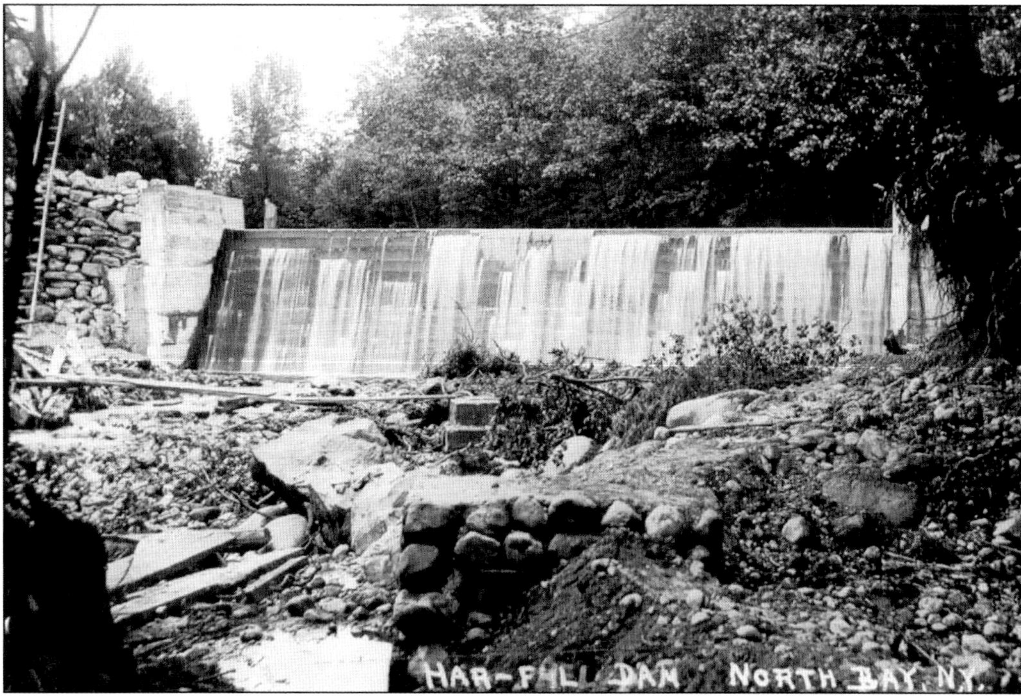

After leaving the bridge on Route 49 in ruins, the waters were confronted by the Har-Phel Hydroelectric Dam less than a half mile away. Built in 1920, the dam held, but the waters washed over the west embankment, quickly removing this earthen obstruction. The raging waters of Murray Brook created a new course around the dam, a path it continues to follow to this day.

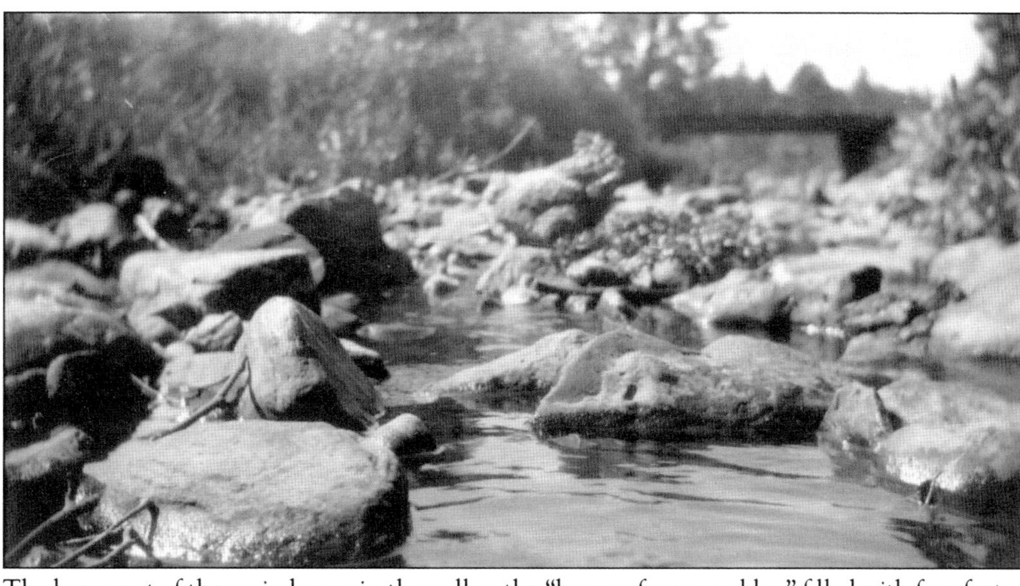

The basement of the main house in the valley, the "house of seven gables," filled with four feet of water; and canned goods floated among the ruins of items stored there. The bridge in the valley that crossed Murray Brook washed away, and for a time the two sides of the valley were separated by an impassable force. Shown is Murray Brook and the valley bridge from a gentler time.

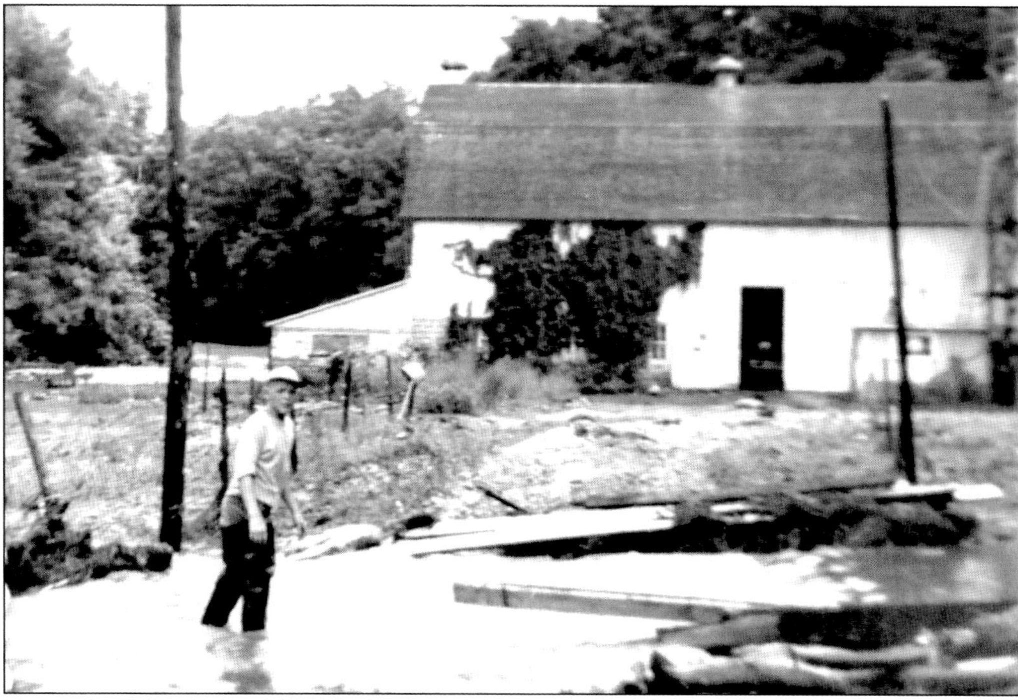

Now at high flood stage, the water continued its surge forward, spreading across the floor of the valley. Entering the barn, it put the livestock in peril. Quick measures taken by George Cook and his son Andy saved the calves. A few heifers were washed away, but they were all rescued. Francis Baker, shown here, was just one of the many townsfolk who pitched in to help.

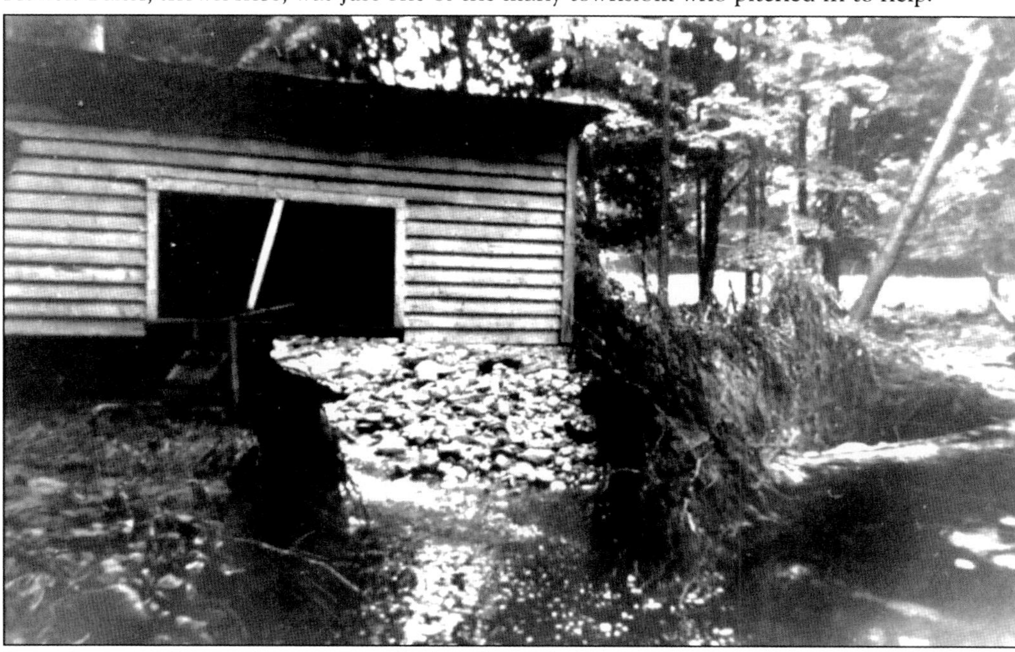

Directly across the creek, an empty chicken house belonging to Jessie Phelps hung precariously over an area that was once solid ground. The birds were removed a year or two before the disaster, so the only loss was an empty building often used by the children as a playhouse.

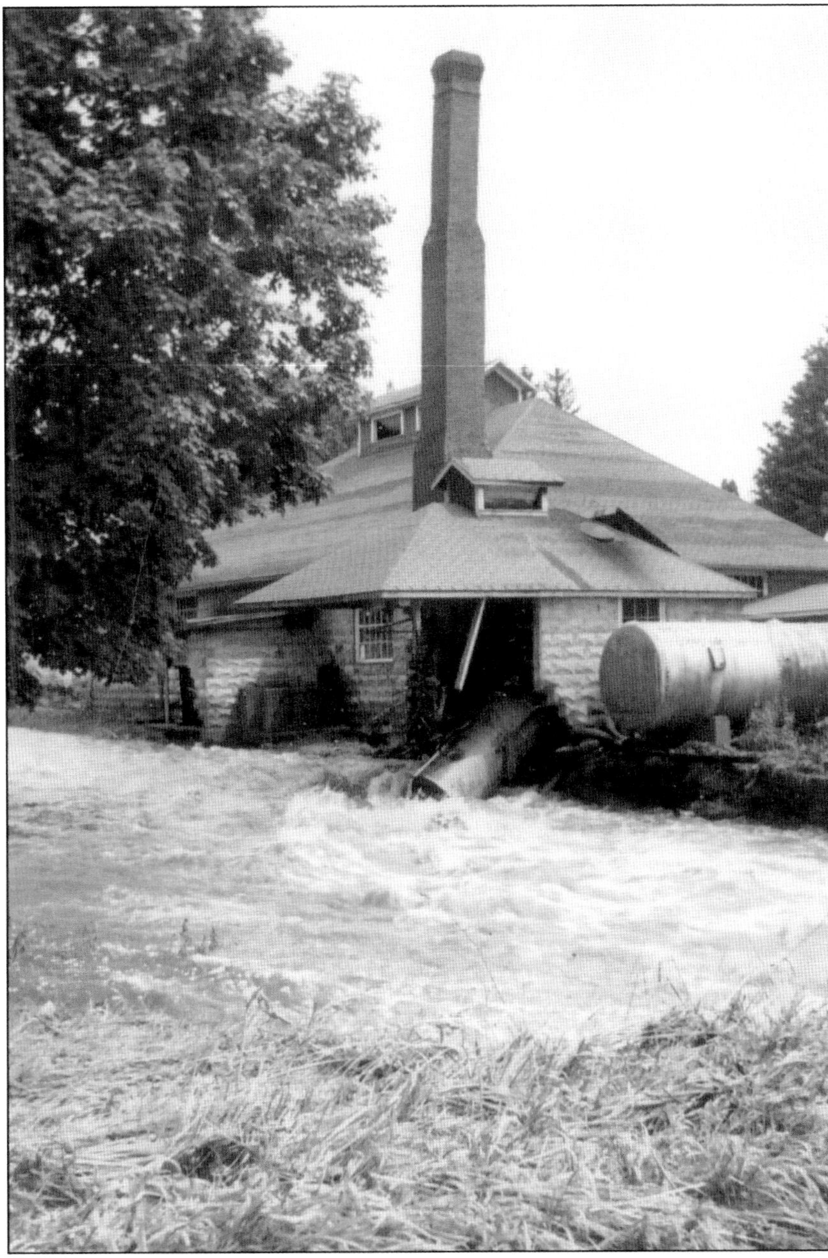

Around 150 feet down the creek from the main house on the opposite bank, the H. R. Phelps canning factory was assaulted by the flooding water. As the water rose in the factory, it carried away several items, adding to the debris already carried by the great wall of water. A portion of an addition on the back wall of the building collapsed, exposing a restroom and a small storage area. The back wall of the concrete factory powerhouse was washed away, its concrete blocks strewn about like marbles. A new oil-fired boiler used to power the machines in the canning factory lay on its side at the edge of the stream, and a yearling (cow) floated by struggling to reach the shore. Two days later, the cow came wandering home, and Russell Phelps put the canning factory back together well enough to finish the canning season that year before closing it down for good.

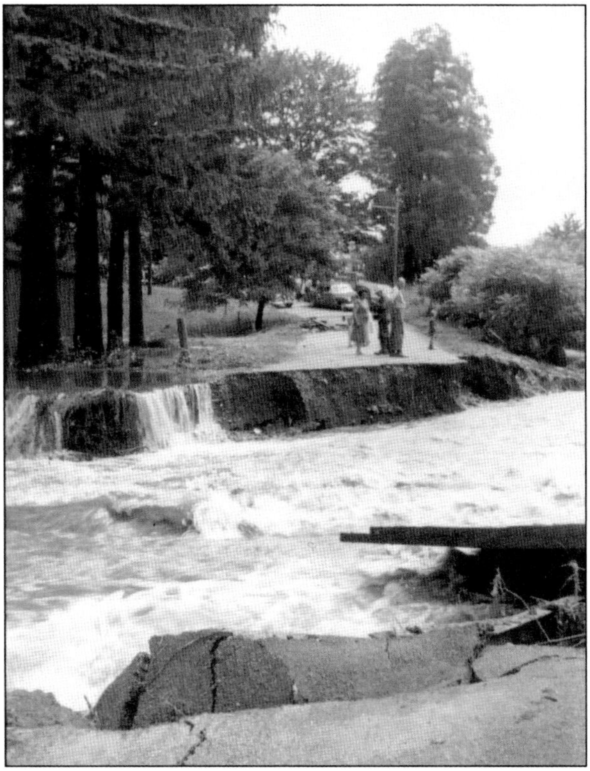

With in a few feet of the canning factory, East Lake Street meets West Lake Street at a bridge over Murray Brook. The bridge gave little resistance against the raging river that had replaced the quiet little brook. It tossed the roadbed and girders aside like toys. Here people on East Lake Street view the destruction.

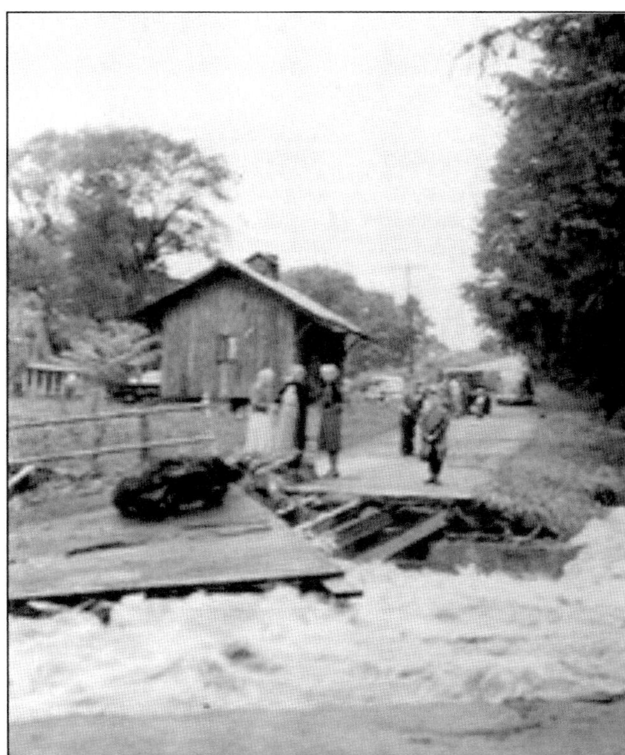

West Lake Street, only a matter of yards from East Lake Street, was still separated by high water the next day. A section of the bridge lies to the side pointing south, and when the water receded, it was on dry land. Visible in the background, the old New York, Ontario and Western Railway station was a familiar landmark from October 1878 until 1953, when it was removed.

The railroad bridge held but was badly weakened. Still it provided a convenient avenue for observers to view the dubious path chosen by the forces of nature. Here the tracks and railroad ties hang suspended in midair. Girders and pieces of concrete create a jumble of wreckage from the bridge visible in the foreground.

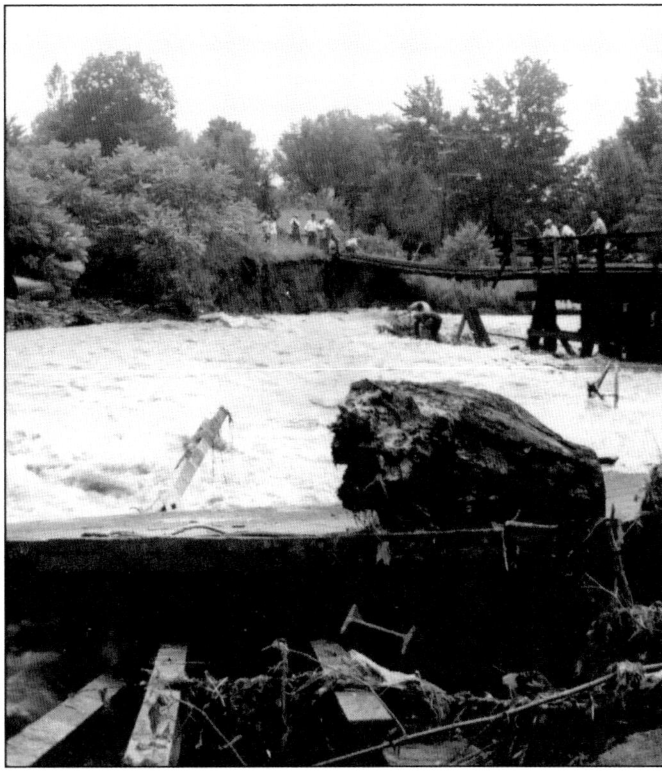

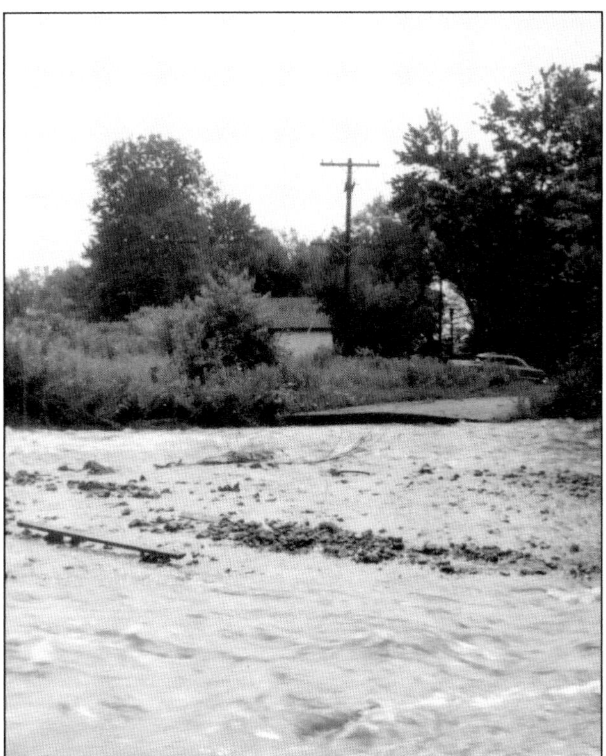

In its eager rush to reach Oneida Lake, the water created a new path flowing across the railroad bed and down Lakeshore Drive. A single span of railroad track is left behind ready to resume its job, only now it goes nowhere.

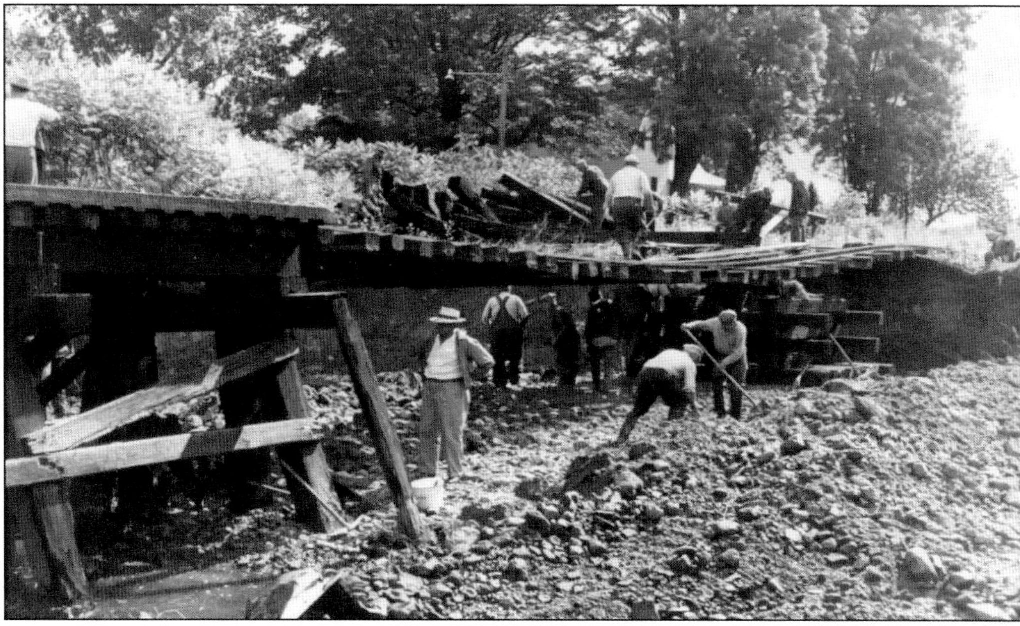

As a result of the flood, service was disrupted on the New York, Ontario and Western Railway tracks through North Bay. Here men work to remove debris and start the repairs. It took several weeks and several loads of gravel and rock to build a whole new railbed. A culvert on Lakeshore Drive was quickly repaired, and for a time, it was the only avenue connecting the two sides of the community.

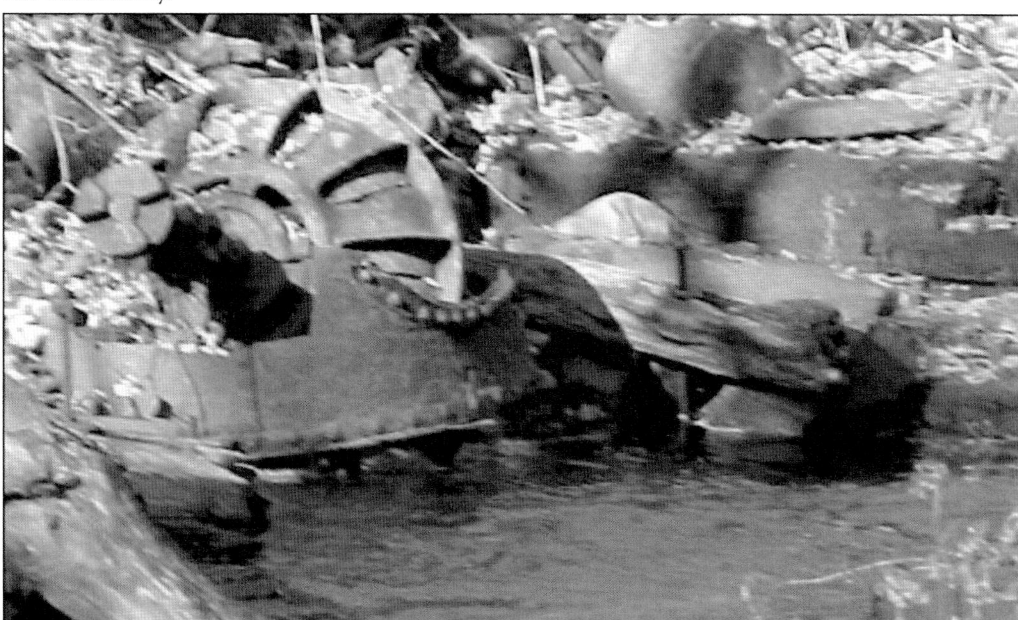

With no power, bridges gone, and no means of communication, North Bay was isolated from the rest of the world. Workers began to repair the damage almost immediately. Most of the signs of the community's greatest disaster have been removed, but up Murray Creek near the old dam, a turbine lies on its side washed there by the flood, a reminder of the fury of nature.

Four

THE GOLDEN YEARS

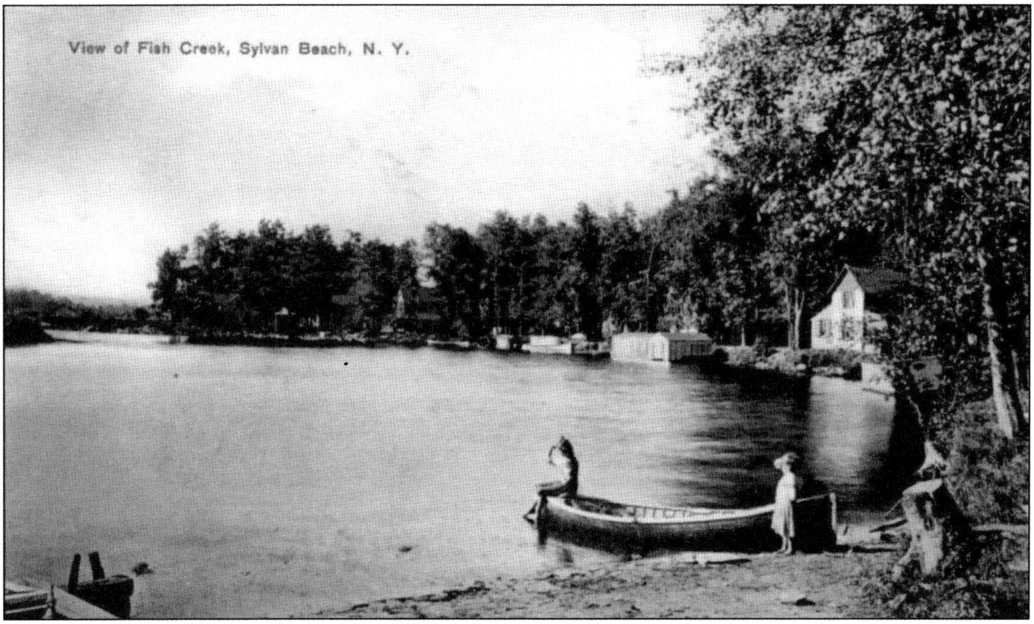

The popularity of North Bay as a picnic and resort area demonstrated the viability of developing a premier resort around Oneida Lake, and it all started at the Fish Creek depot. The junction of rail and water formed a natural location of debarkation, and the key was location. James Spencer owned the perfect location, 260 acres on the eastern end of Oneida Lake, which was a portion of tract No. 9 of Scriba's patent.

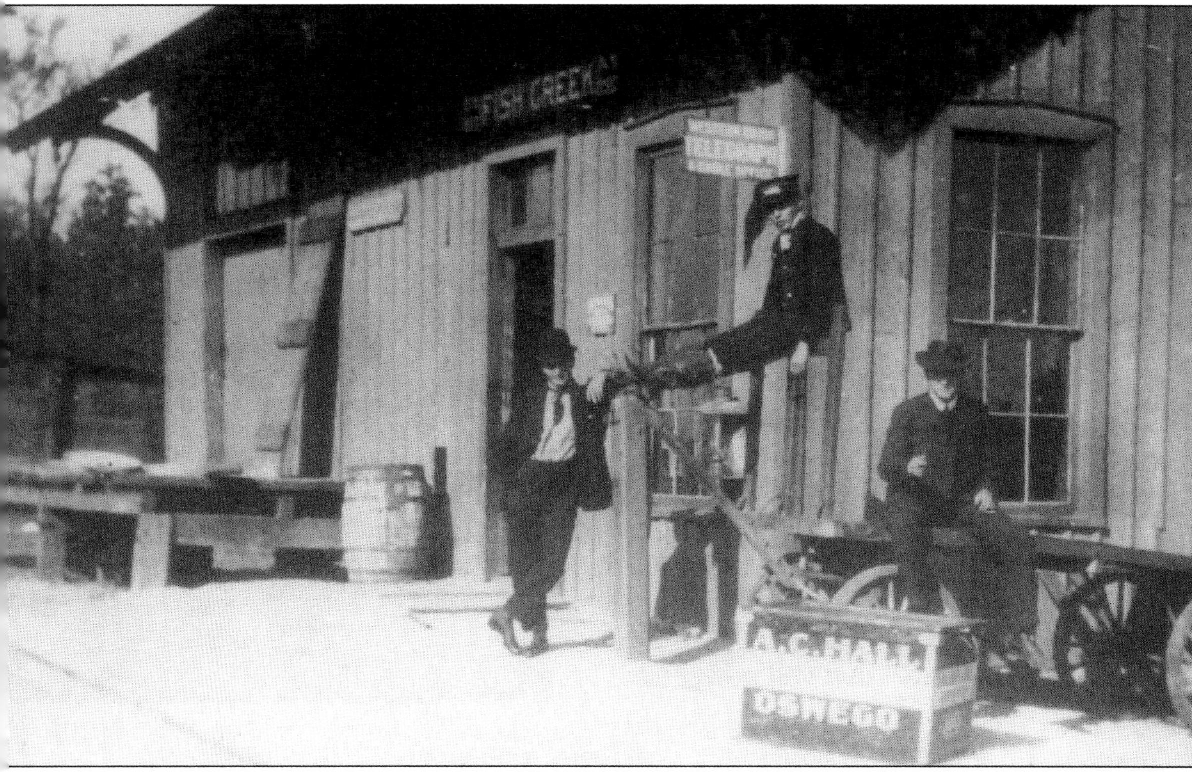

Before there was a Sylvan Beach, the entire area was known as Fish Creek. It was first settled by George Haskins, and he was soon joined by brothers George and William Covell, who left Massachusetts in 1807. Prior to 1850 and the construction of the Rome, Watertown and Ogdensburg Railroad, the only local railway station was the Midland Railway Depot in Fish Creek. As much as two million board feet of lumber a year was transported from this location by rail and Durham boat. As the area near the lake began to blossom and grow, it became a subdivision of Fish Creek. Known as Joppa for a time, the name of the little hamlet changed many times. Beacon Beach, Roberts Grove, and Spencer's Grove are but a few of the other names used. When the New York, Ontario and Western Railway entered the "beach" in 1886, it was called Sylvan Beach, and the name stuck.

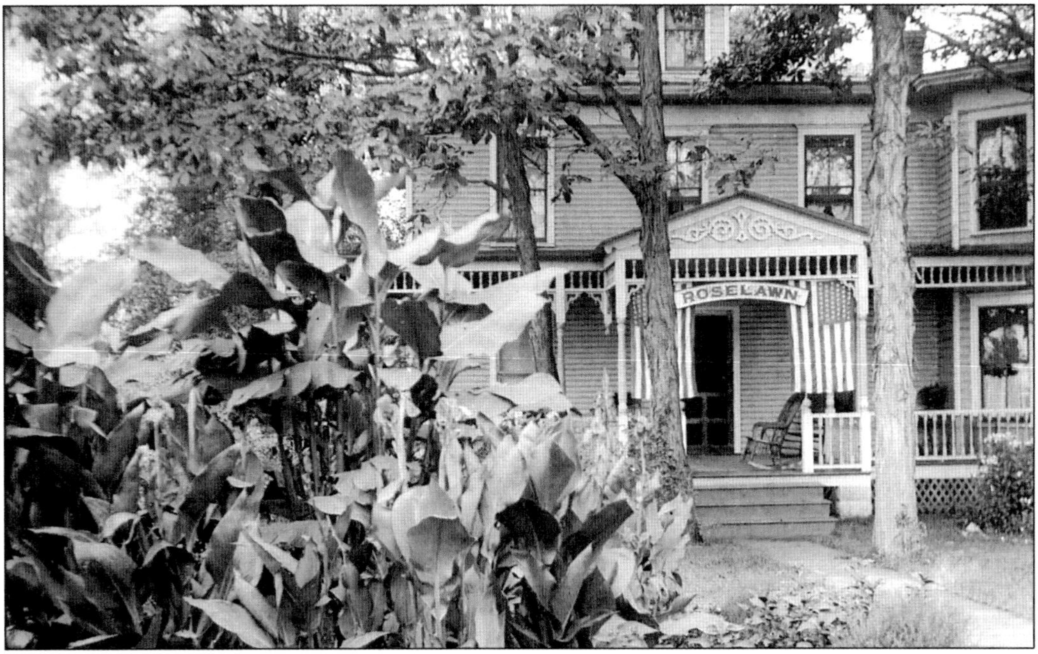

James D. Spencer, considered the founder of Sylvan Beach, was born in Amsterdam, New York, on December 27, 1813. In the 1840s, he moved his large family from West Monroe to the hamlet of Fish Creek, and together they built their home. A plain, honest man, he was active in real estate, and between 1847 and 1877, he obtained 660 acres of tract No. 9 of the Scriba Patent.

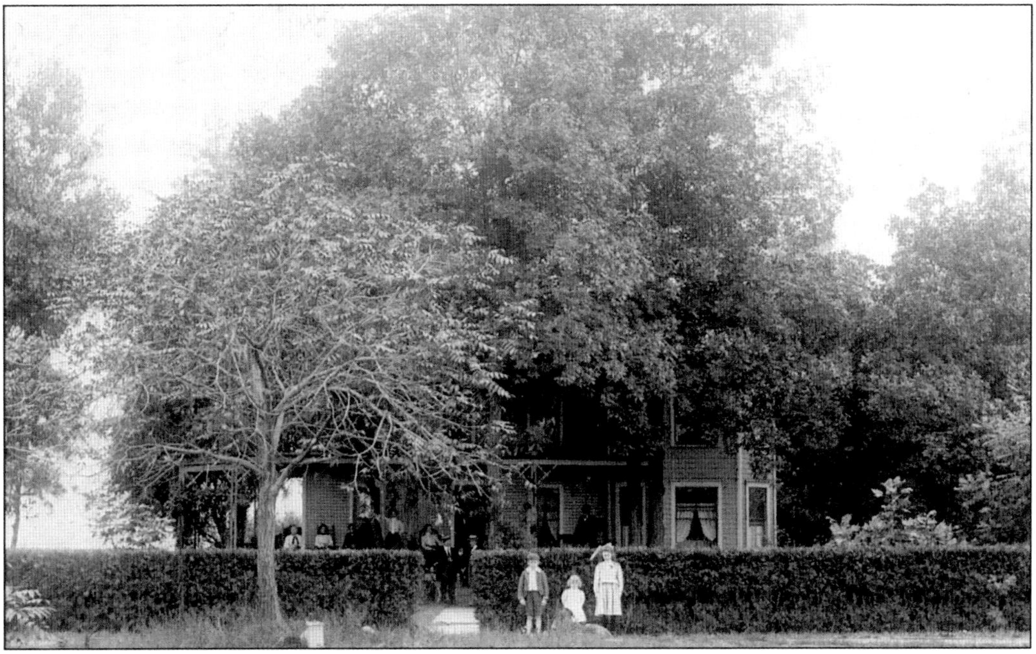

Pictured at Rose Lawn is Spencer (center, on the sidewalk) and standing in front of the hedge are three of his grandchildren, Hattie, Marian, and Lyman. The Spencer family was instrumental in the development and growth of the area. Ultimately their achievements led to the establishment of the only village in the town of Vienna, Sylvan Beach.

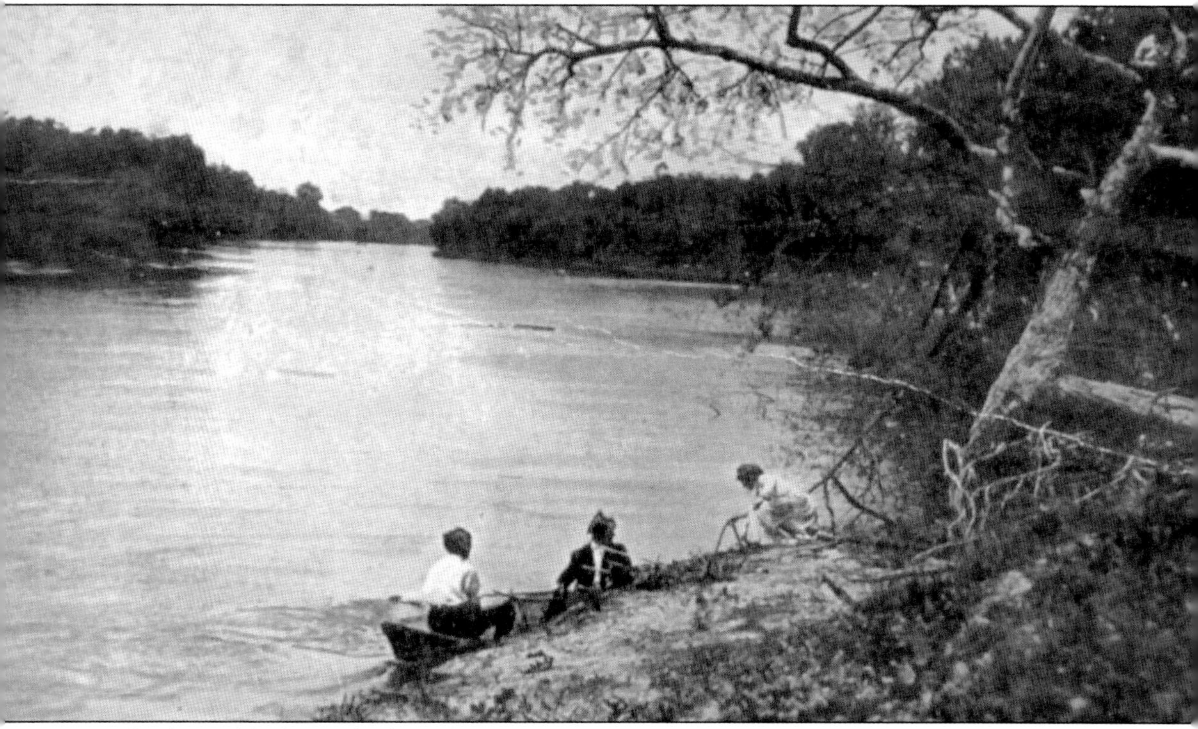

The first public house built in the area was Spencer's Forest House Hotel. Built by the Spencer family around 1870, it was diagonally across Jug Point Road from the Fish Creek depot. Jug Point is where Fish Creek and Wood Creek meet, forming Wood River a mile from Oneida Lake. However, Wood River curled snakelike north and south, so the distance by water was doubled. In late 1872, the religious group Oneida Community leased a section on Oneida Lake from the Spencer family for $25 a year. They built a plain, two-story building to be used as a retreat and named it Joppa. They were the first to return each summer season to enjoy the peace and seclusion. So the area between the Fish Creek railroad station and Oneida Lake became known as Joppa.

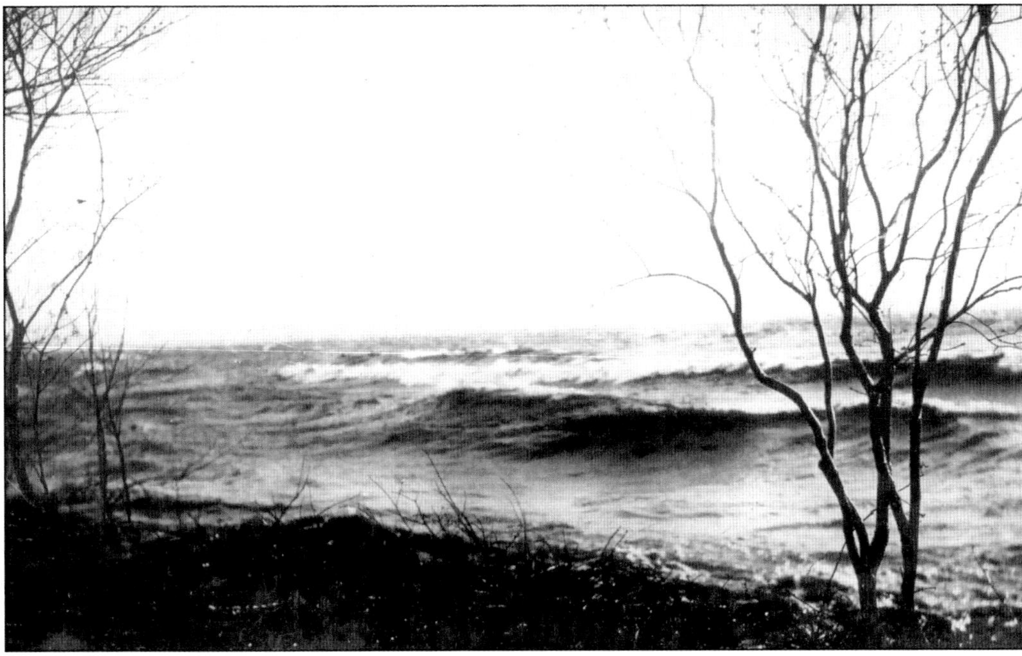

Meanwhile the activity in the bay aroused the interest of the Roberts brothers in Fish Creek. They built a picnic park between the New York and Oswego Midland Railroad and Wood River. First known as Roberts Grove, it was later called Sylvan Glen. During the same period, Spencer began work on the property he owned along the east shore of Oneida Lake.

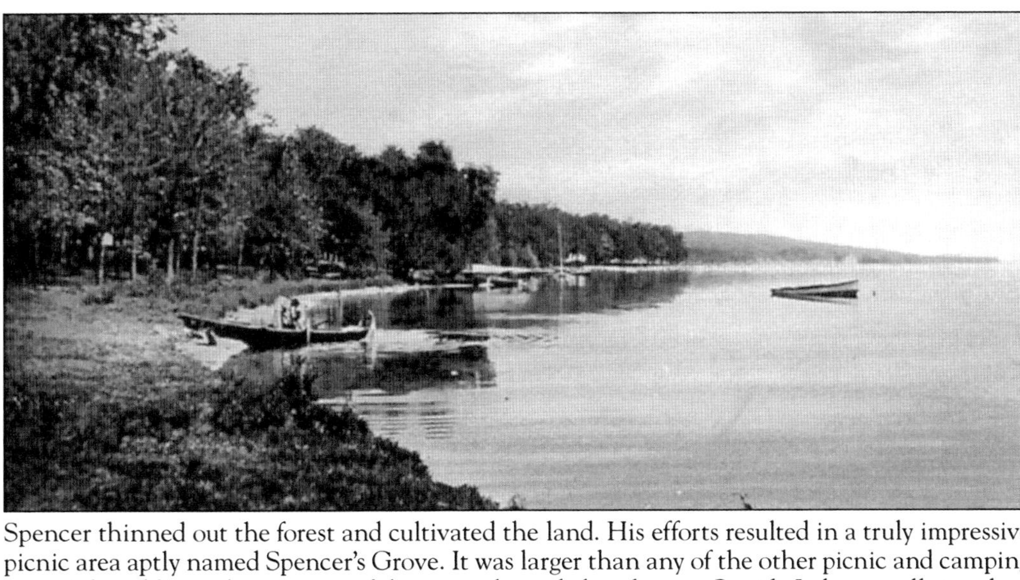

Spencer thinned out the forest and cultivated the land. His efforts resulted in a truly impressive picnic area aptly named Spencer's Grove. It was larger than any of the other picnic and camping areas. The additional attraction of the natural, sandy beaches on Oneida Lake was all it took to draw vacationers from the valley in North Bay and Roberts Grove.

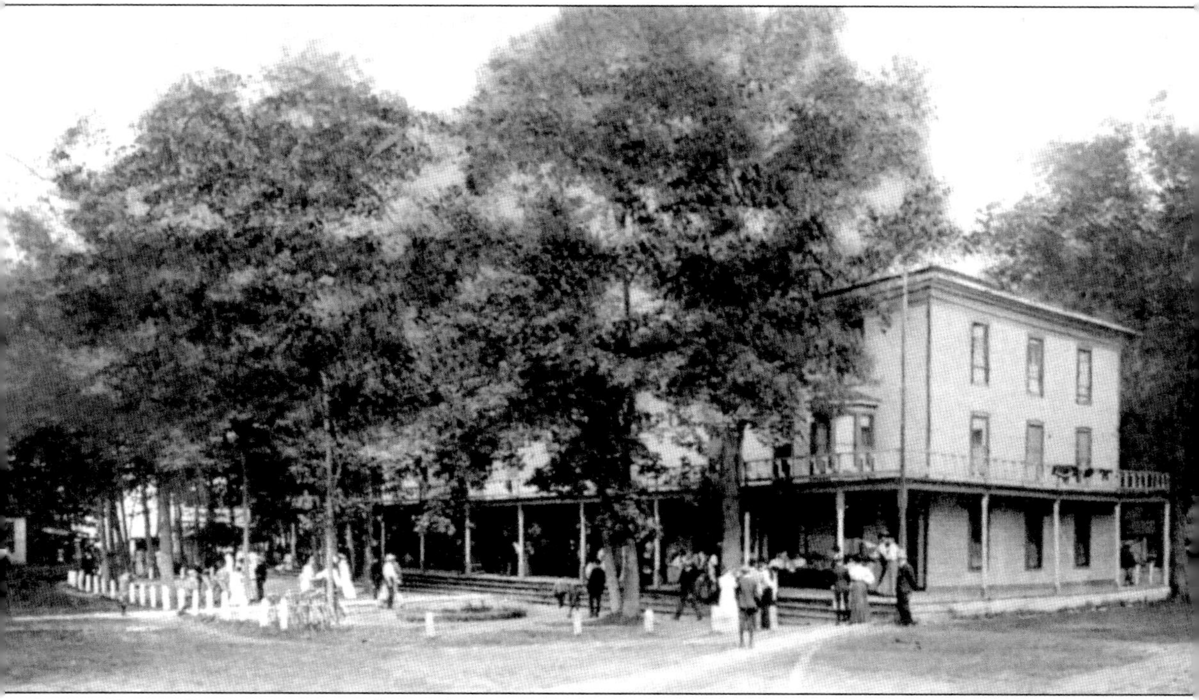

James D. Spencer went beyond just creating the grove. He drew the attention of the public, and through his influence, the New York, Ontario and Western Railway entered Sylvan Beach. One of his first major achievements toward his goal to create a popular summer resort was his arrangements with the Hop Growers to hold its picnic in Spencer's Grove on August 7, 1878. Located beside the beautiful blue waters of Oneida Lake, the grove offered ideal conditions for sports and relaxation, and the Hop Growers made Sylvan Beach a yearly tradition. In 1879, the Hop Growers made their headquarters at Spencer's Forest House Hotel, and on August 7, 1879, they hosted their second annual Hop Growers picnic. Tragedy struck on August 23, 1879, when the Forest House Hotel burned to the ground. That same year, Spencer's son Lyman built the Forest Home Hotel closer to Oneida Lake on Wood River.

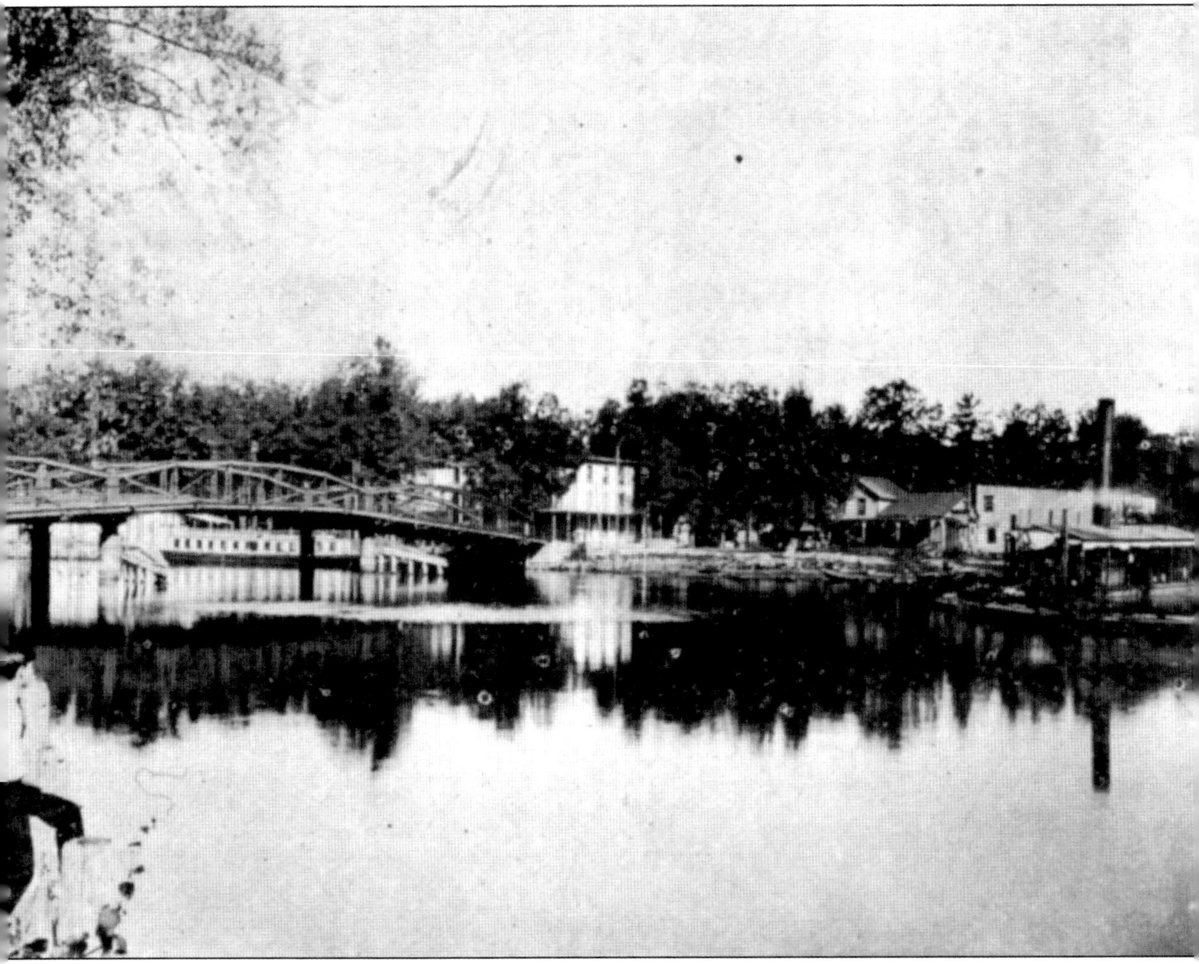

In 1887, the number of rail passengers attending the Hop Growers picnic was so great the New York, Ontario and Western Railway was forced to use freight cars along with its passenger cars to transport people. In 1888, purported to be the greatest year ever, 93 railroad cars loaded with passengers arrived on the New York, Ontario and Western Railway, and 46 cars were on the Elmira, Cortland and Northern Railroad, making a total of 139 railcars. Verona Beach was separated from Sylvan Beach by Wood River until the pedestrian/wagon bridge was built in 1889. Made up of three sections, it was 270 feet long and 16 feet wide. Pedestrians were afforded sidewalks on both sides. Prior to its installation, the only way across the river was to swim or go by boat. The Forest Home and the Algonquin Hotels operated ferries, each having a maximum capacity of eight persons.

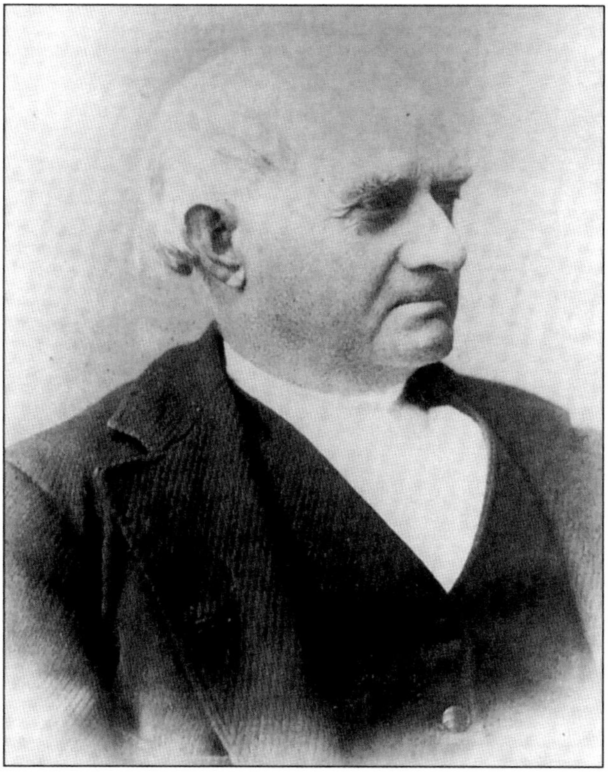

James D. Spencer made the Forest Home Hotel his residence. In the image below, notice the beautiful bay window on the second floor and imagine him standing in that window looking at the results of his years of hard work. He died in 1899; however, he lives on in the village he loved.

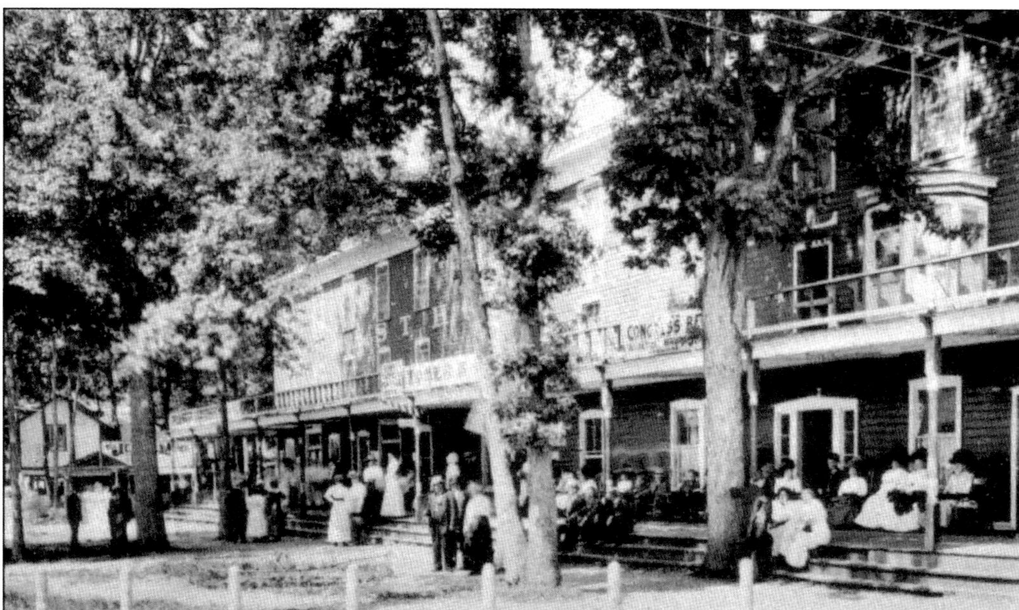

Built in 1879 by Lyman Spencer, the Forest Home Hotel was later run by his son-in-law F. B. Randall. The hotel had a capacity for 100 patrons, and it provided ferry service across Wood River and a steamer from the Fish Creek depot down the river. Accommodations included a boathouse, a dock, a bathhouse, a restaurant, a photograph service, and access to "5 miles of the finest beach in the world."

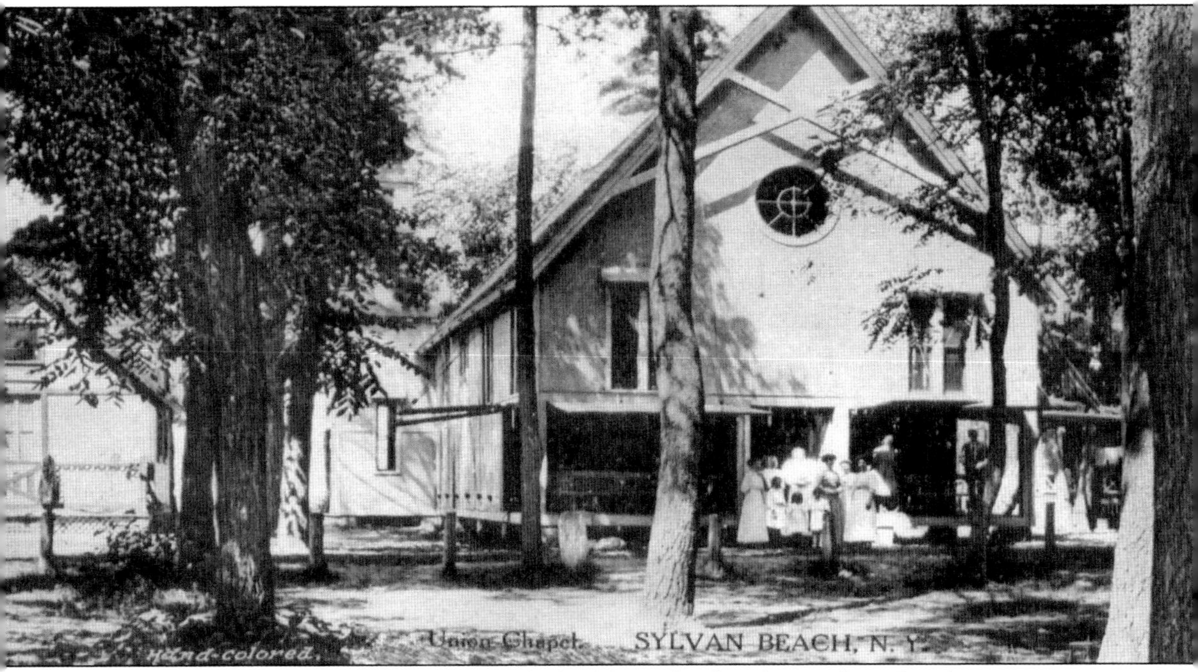

In 1886, Ruben Spencer donated a site for the building of a church in Sylvan Beach, wanting it to be open to all Orthodox denominations. On May 14, 1887, a committee met in the parlor of the Forest Home Hotel, and plans were made to build the church. The New York, Ontario and Western Railway provided free transportation to the members of the building committee for the meeting. Construction began on May 23, 1887, and the first service was held on July 10, 1887. The building is 60 feet long and 30 feet wide, with a seating capacity of 350. The seven lower feet of the two sides and one end can be lifted, thus allowing those seated or standing around the church to hear the services going on inside. During the summer months, local churches take turns holding Sunday service in the Union Chapel on Park Avenue in Sylvan Beach to this day.

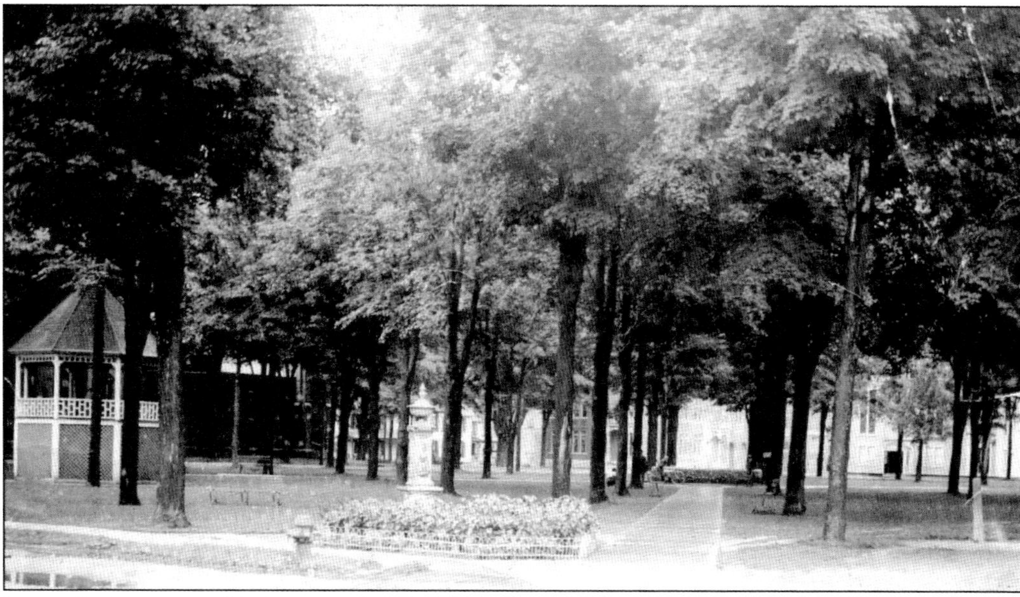

James D. Spencer sold the parcel of land between Railroad Avenue and Park Avenue to the Village of Sylvan Beach for $1. He intended for the property to become a huge, wooded village park, thereby retaining for all time a portion of the peace and beauty of his resort on the lake.

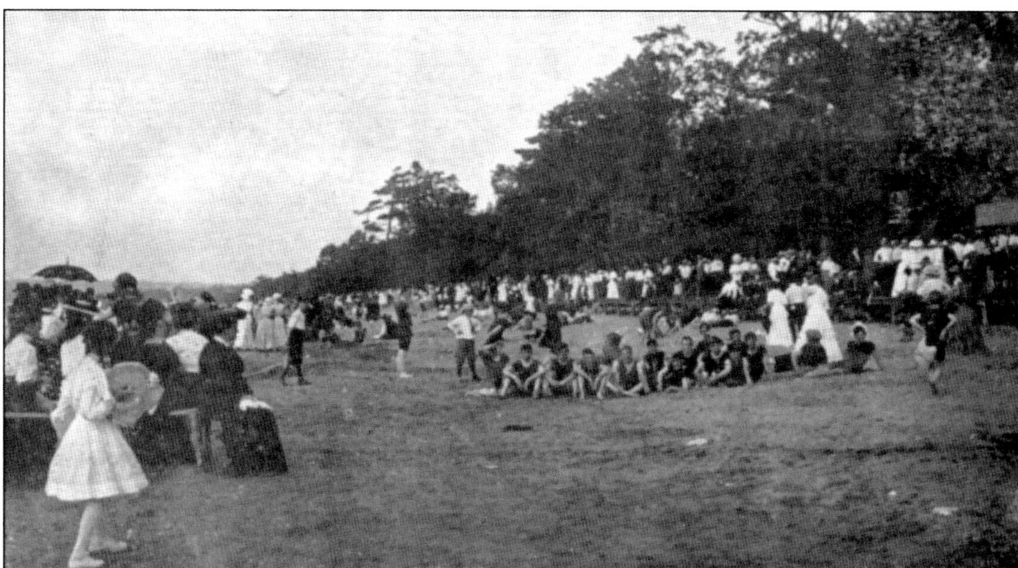

The annual Hop Growers picnic returned to Sylvan Beach from 1878 until 1892. After the 1892 picnic, a dispute developed between the association and the railroads concerning the payment of a commission to the association by the railroads for each passenger carried. No apparent record exists with the terms the two parties eventually agreed upon, but the Hop Growers returned to the beach for its picnic in 1894.

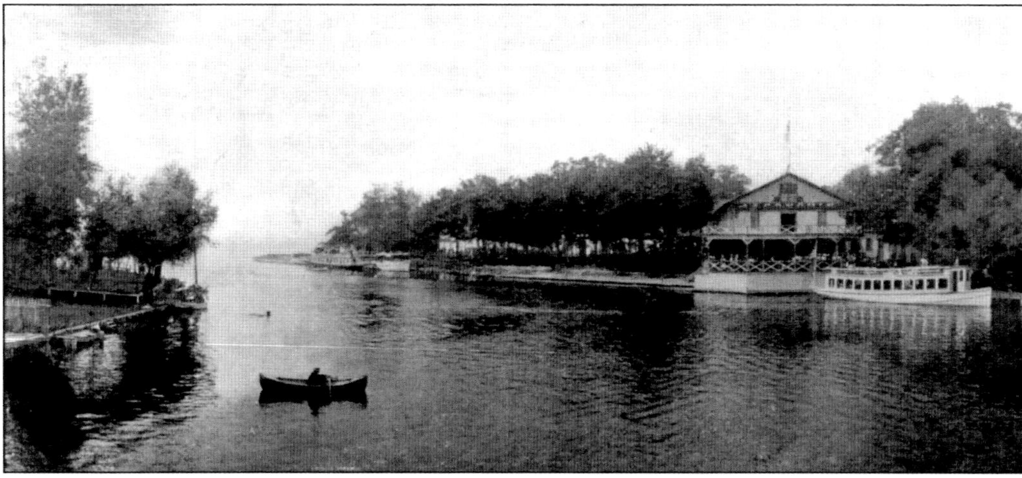

C. G. W. Stoddard and Anthony T. Garvin contracted William Rubles to build the Algonquin in 1884. It offered unobstructed access to both Wood River and Oneida Lake and advertised 1,000 feet of verandas. It offered 125 guests a cafe, ice cream and lunch for $2 a day or $8 to $10 a week. The Algonquin burned to the ground on February 27, 1904.

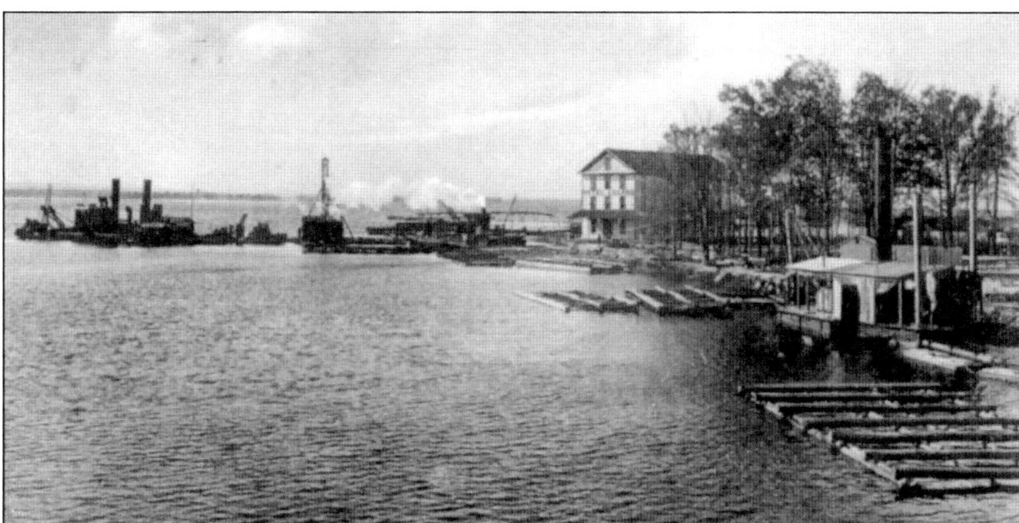

In 1896, Charles Scovile opened the Hotel Leland on the point of land at the mouth of the Wood River where it enters Oneida Lake. It was a large hotel capable of serving 75 tenants. Many of the hotels owned steamers to transport their visitors down Wood River from the Fish Creek depot and for excursions on Oneida Lake. The Hotel Leland owned and operated the steamer *Lottie*.

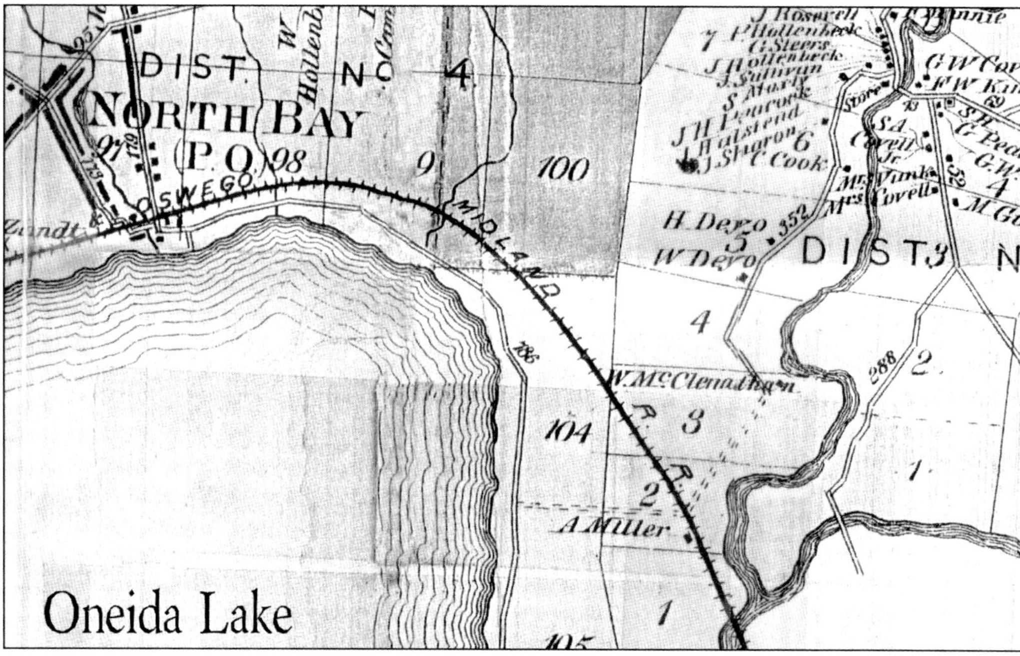

Time and progress determine the worth of land. Sometimes it works out well for an investor, but sometimes it does not. Such was the case for George Scriba, who acquired 500,000 acres in 1794. His patent stretched from the north shore of Oneida Lake to the southern shore of Lake Ontario. Never realizing his dream, he died a pauper.

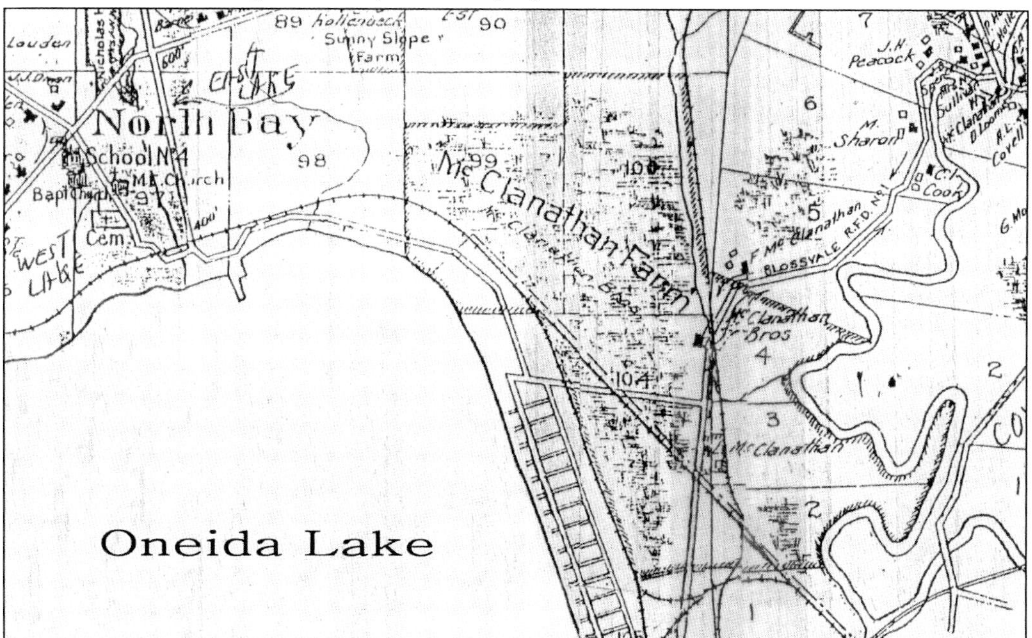

James D. Spencer had a dream and 260 acres of land on the east end of Oneida Lake. Between 1878, when he held his first picnic, and 1907, when this map was completed, Sylvan Beach grew from a wilderness into a well-developed entertainment center. Everything seemed to fall into place; it was the right time and progress included steam, the railroad, and the electric motor.

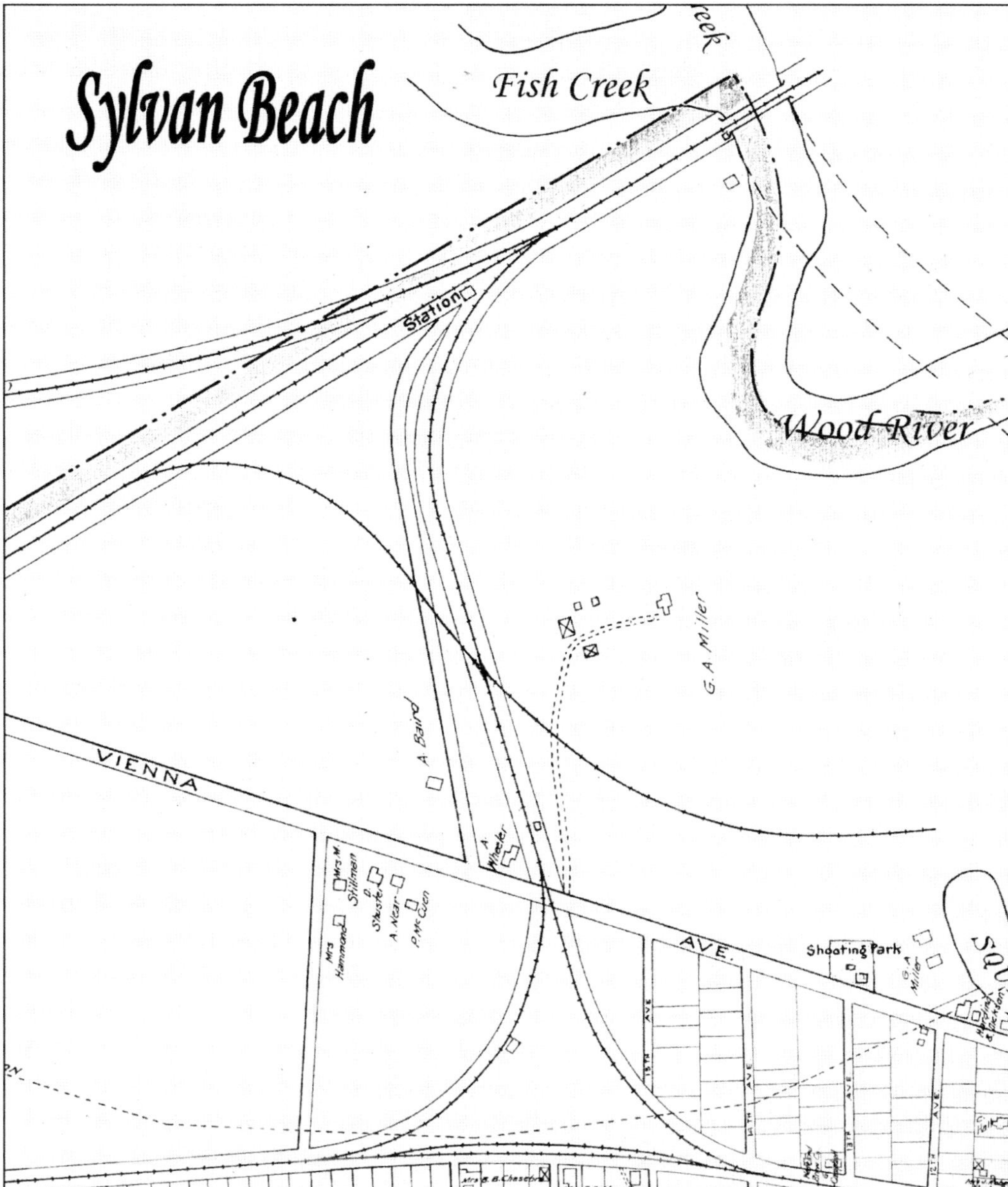

The loop and the 40-lever SX (Sylvan Crossing) tower were masterpieces of engineering, allowing 20 different routing combinations. Commonly referred to as the "loop," or the "Sylvan Beach loop," the track plan was a closed return loop to the north and an open loop to the south with the addition of two wyes. Incorporating the two wyes, the southern loop allowed all trains, under order, to back down to the Sylvan Beach station. With the construction of the new Bridge No. 367 in 1906 over Wood River, a switch tower was built at the north end of the span. Designated SX for Sylvan Crossing, the switch tower incorporated a new interlocking system to control the 40 switches involved. The 40-lever machine controlled 20 routings on the main lines and the entrance to the Sylvan Beach south loop. The building of the new interlocking system had an added benefit to the New York, Ontario and Western Railway because it allowed them to use the Sylvan Beach loop as a year-round route.

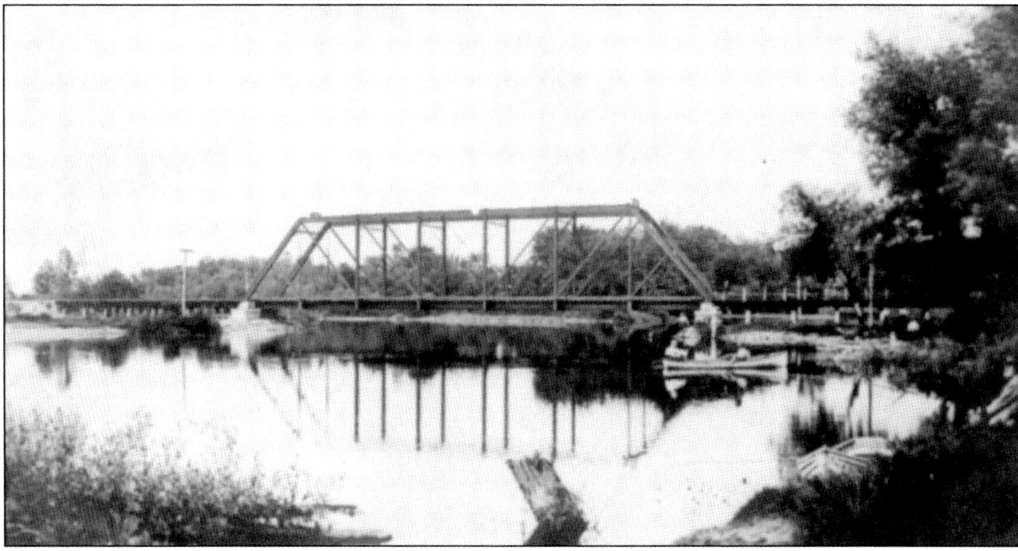

The New York and Oswego Midland Railroad built the first bridge across Wood River in 1869. The wooden bridge was replaced by this metal bridge in April 1887. Bridge No. 367 and the trestle approaches were a joint project of the New York, Ontario and Western Railway and the Elmira Cortland and Northern Railroad. The cost to build the 147-foot span was $12,664.73, equally shared by the two railroads.

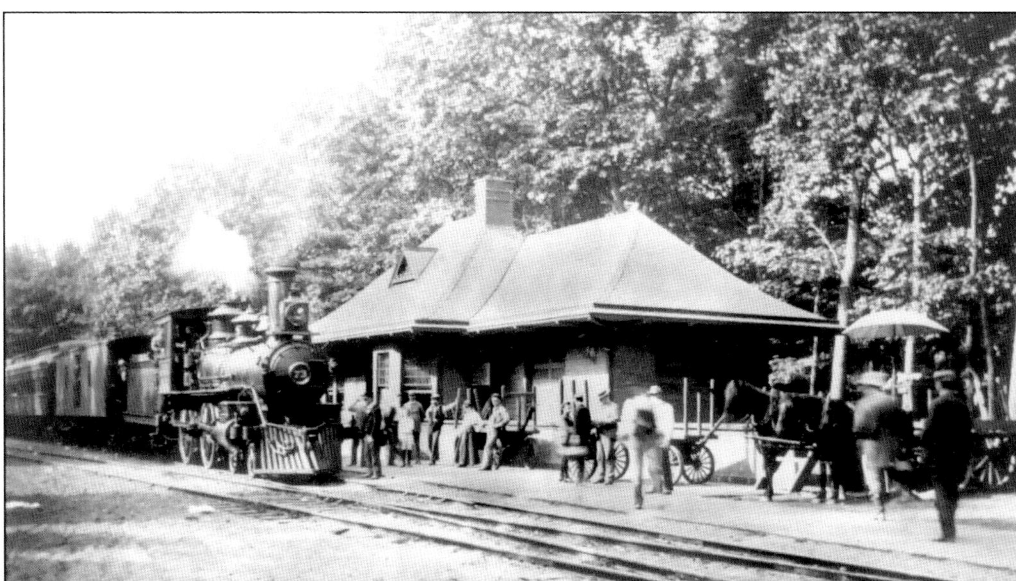

In the early years, the New York, Ontario and Western Railway most often used this type of locomotive for the Sylvan Beach trains. The four ponies (wheels) in front carried some weight, but their actual purpose was to guide the locomotive into the turns. Generally it was a much easier riding engine because the front did not "hunt" on the track. An excellent duel-service locomotive, it was a fast passenger or good light-freight engine.

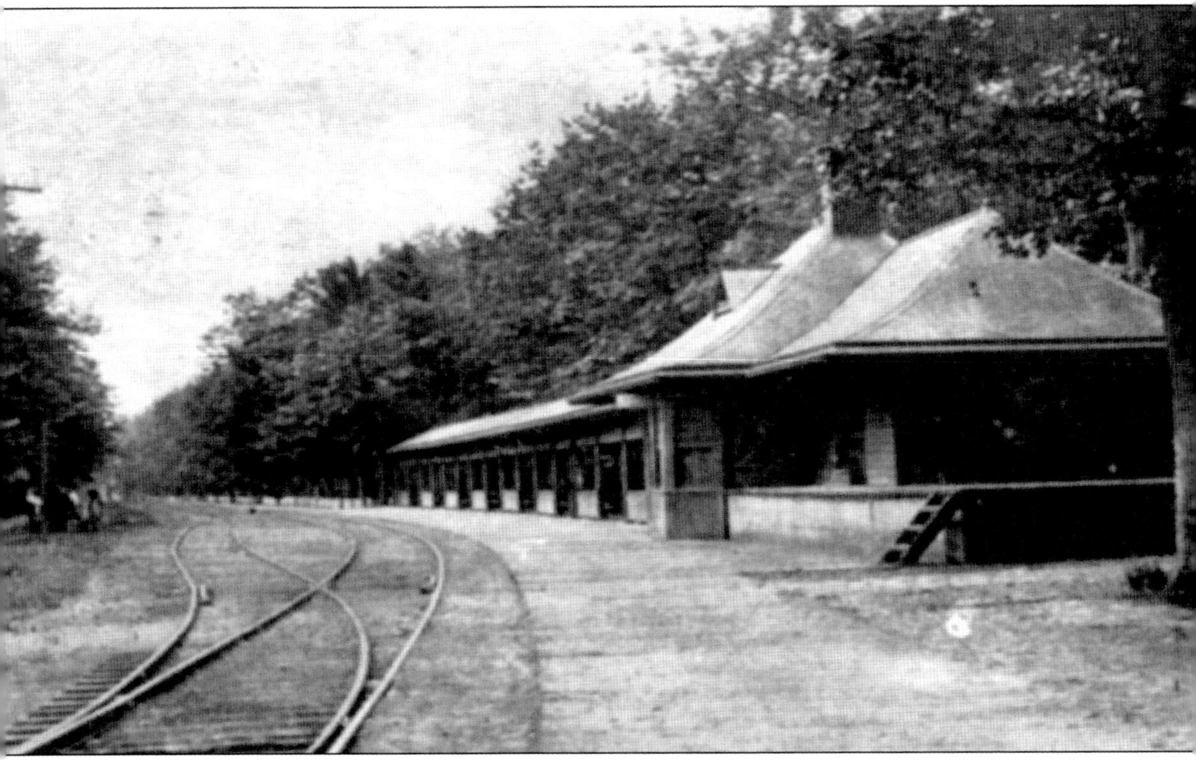

Facing south on Railroad Avenue, the New York, Ontario and Western Railway's Sylvan Beach Grove depot is on the right. It was located at the northeast corner of Spencer's Grove, and the covered platform opened onto the beautiful wooded picnic area. Just beyond the grove were major resort hotels, and to the south was Luna Park. The turnout or switch is easily seen in this picture. It was used to direct the passenger trains onto the correct spur when arriving or departing the station. It was a simple switch with only two guardrails that put pressure on the outside wheels, forcing them to follow the track. In more advanced switches, several guardrails were used close to the frog to lessen the chance of derailment as the wheels passed through it. The frog, where the tracks crossed each other, had a groove that directs the wheels onto the desired track.

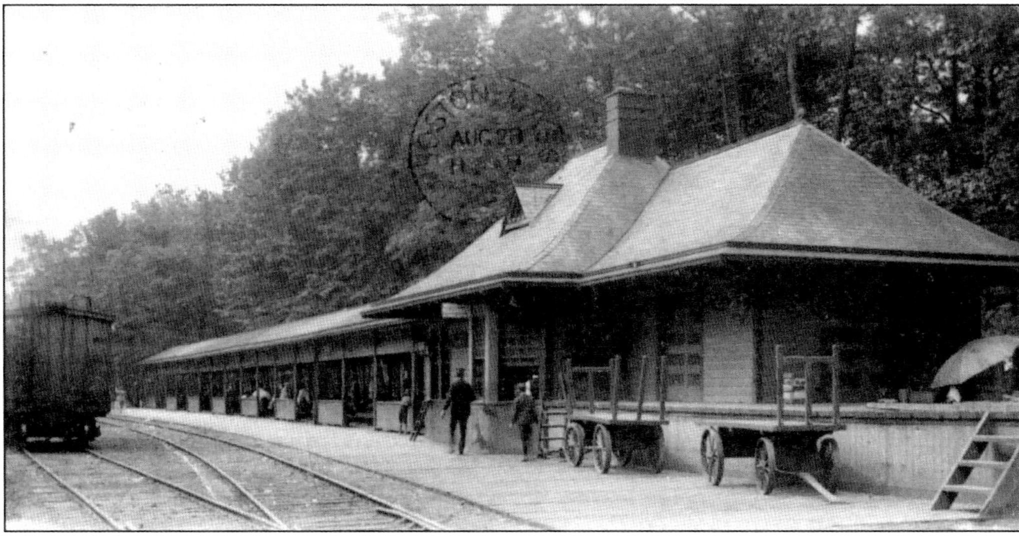

The New York, Ontario and Western Railway station in Sylvan Beach was moved four times; the first station was built in 1886. This station was named the Grove station because of its location in Spencer's Grove. In 1892, the Grove station was moved within the north loop and became the Sylvan Beach Platform station to be used for freight. During the same month, a second station was built in Spencer's Grove.

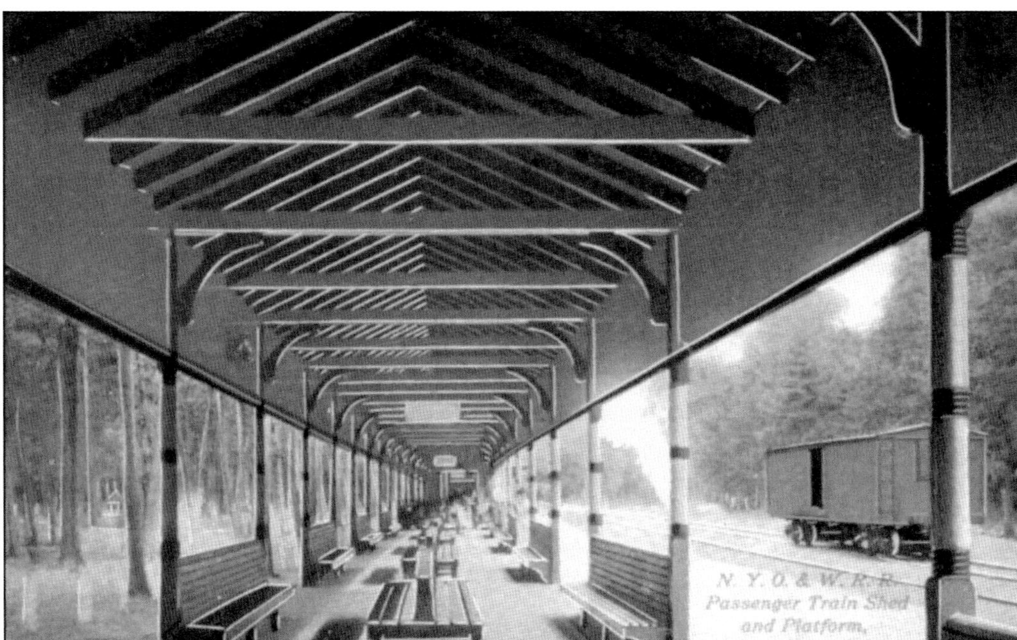

This version of the two stations erected at the Spencer's Grove site in Sylvan Beach was the most impressive, with a 256-foot-long covered seating area. It afforded the waiting passengers shelter from inclement weather. This was the last location the New York, Ontario and Western Railway occupied inside the village. The building was moved to the north loop in 1924, and the railway discontinued service to the beach on September 1, 1934.

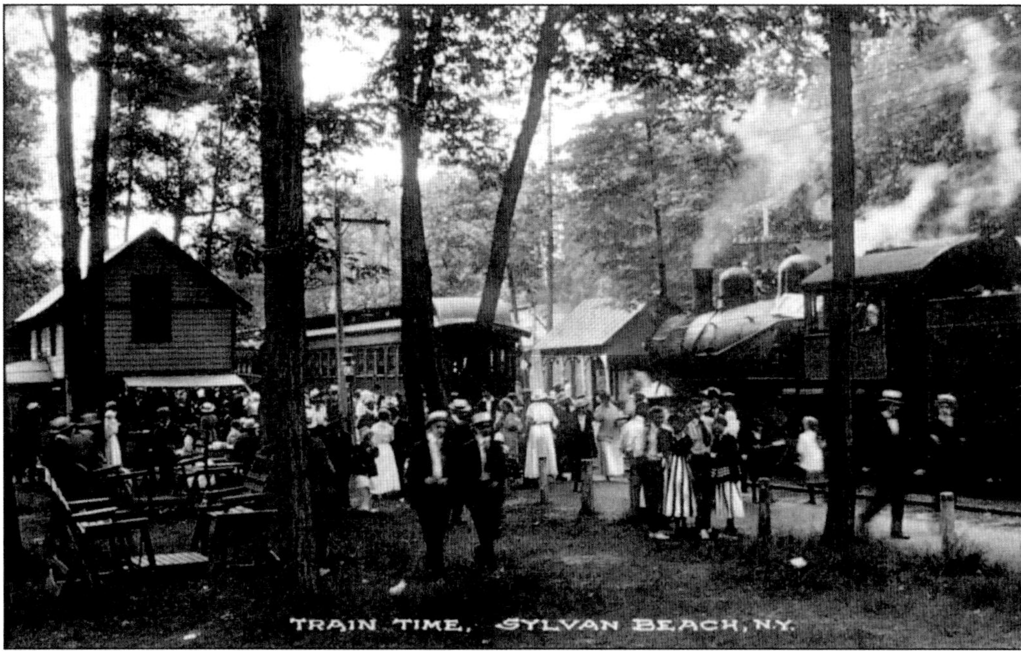

Vacationers eager to share their fun with friends and family back home frequented souvenir shops. On a pleasant summer's day, the shop owners near the depot enjoyed a surge of business when the railcars arrived. Perhaps it is difficult to believe, but between 1908 and 1917 when the railroad and steamship companies enjoyed an overwhelming business, there were times when the station seemed too small.

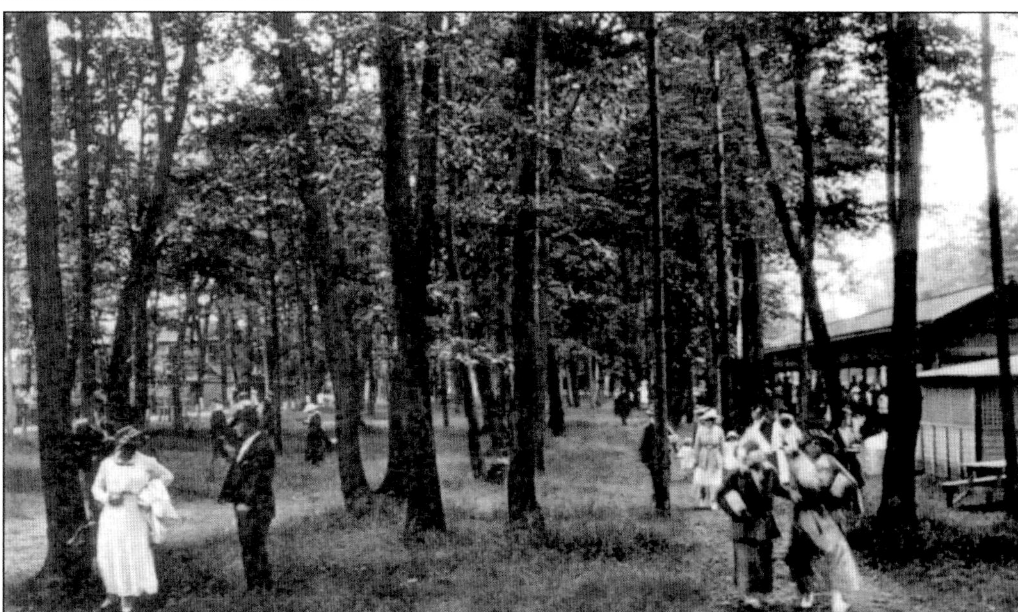

The area behind the 256-foot station was smooth for walking and well groomed. The shade trees and a cool breeze from Oneida Lake added to the wonder of it all. Vacationers entered another world far away from their everyday life where hard work was often required to make it another day.

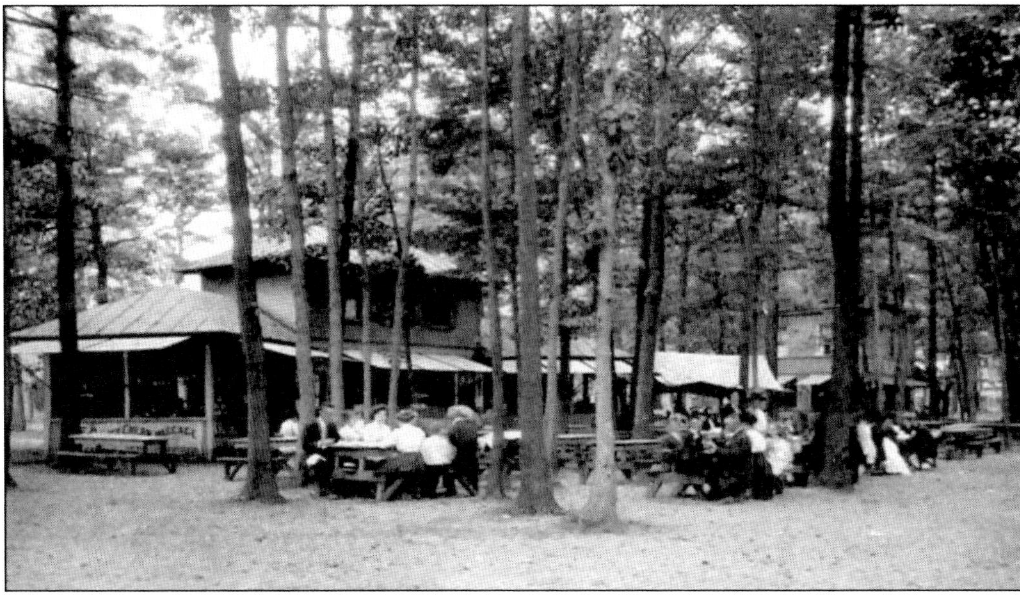

Located in Spencer's Grove near the rail station, the two Vienna Villas offered lunches, delicious ice cream, coffee, and tea. Sixty picnic tables were provided to visitors for lunches or leisure. In addition, vacationers were allowed to check their baggage until plans could be made for a place to stay. Every type of housing imaginable was available in Sylvan Beach in every price range.

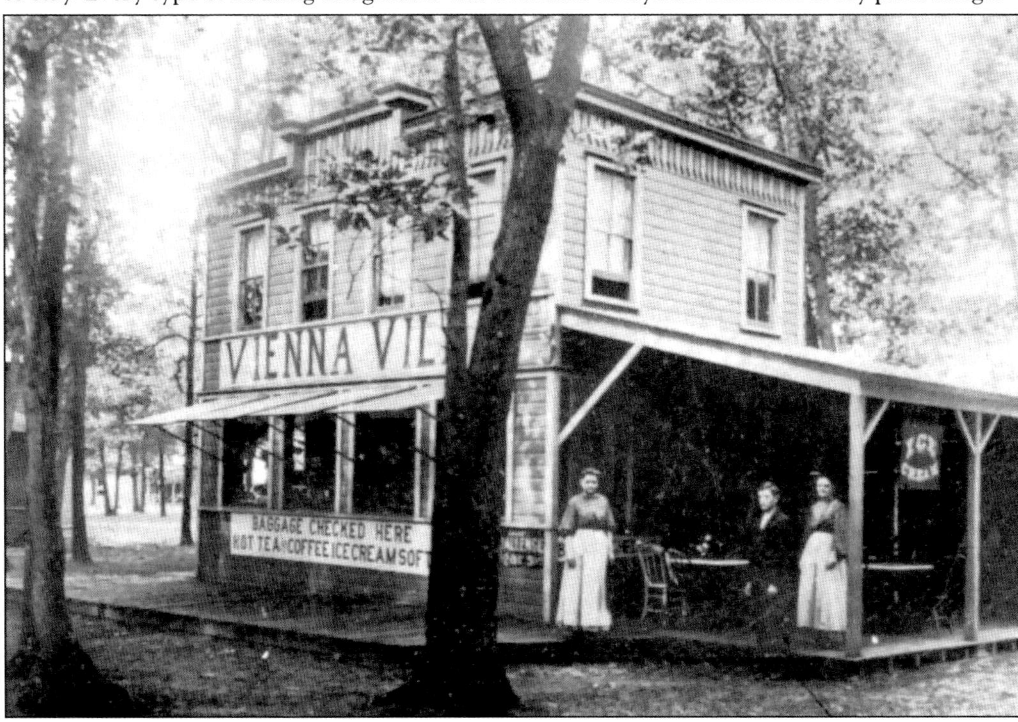

This photograph from about 1910 of one Vienna Villa exhibits a help wanted sign. Schoolchildren found summer employment in Sylvan Beach. However, during harvest time, there was often a greater demand for their time at home. With a carnival type of atmosphere, the work provided warm memories on a cold winter's night.

Dr. Martin Cavana arrived in Sylvan Beach from Oneida in 1891. An entrepreneur, he was a strong influence in the area for the next 33 years. Immediately elected a member of the trustees of the territory, he served in that position until 1901 when he was unanimously chosen president. Vast improvements were achieved through his efforts, including the addition of a police justice, a police court, an assessor, and changes in health and sanitation.

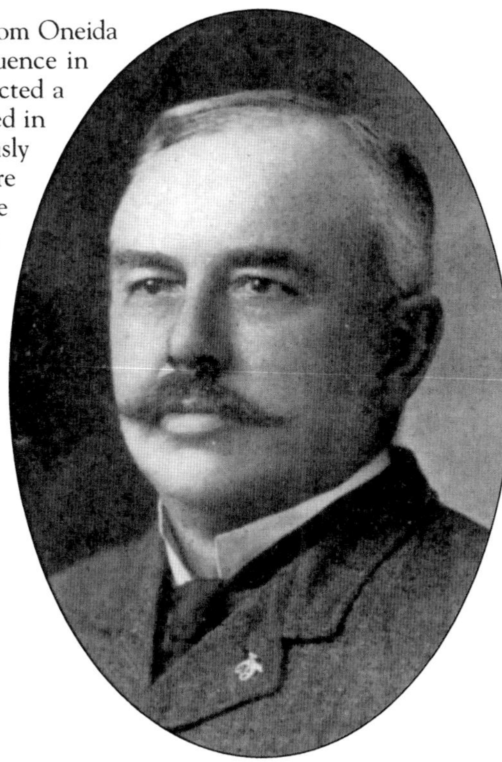

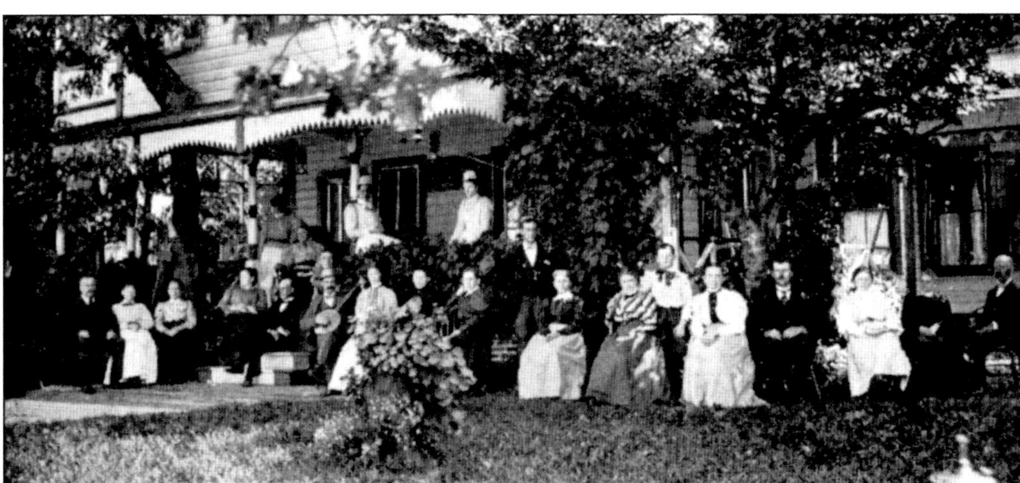

In 1891, Cavana opened a sanitarium for the treatment of chronic diseases, and eventually the facility reached a capacity of 45 patients. Conveniently located on the lakeshore a short distance north of the railroad depot, the hospital also served as a school of nursing. Cavana was involved in acts of public improvement, and he pioneered the creation of lawns, cement walks, and a seawall.

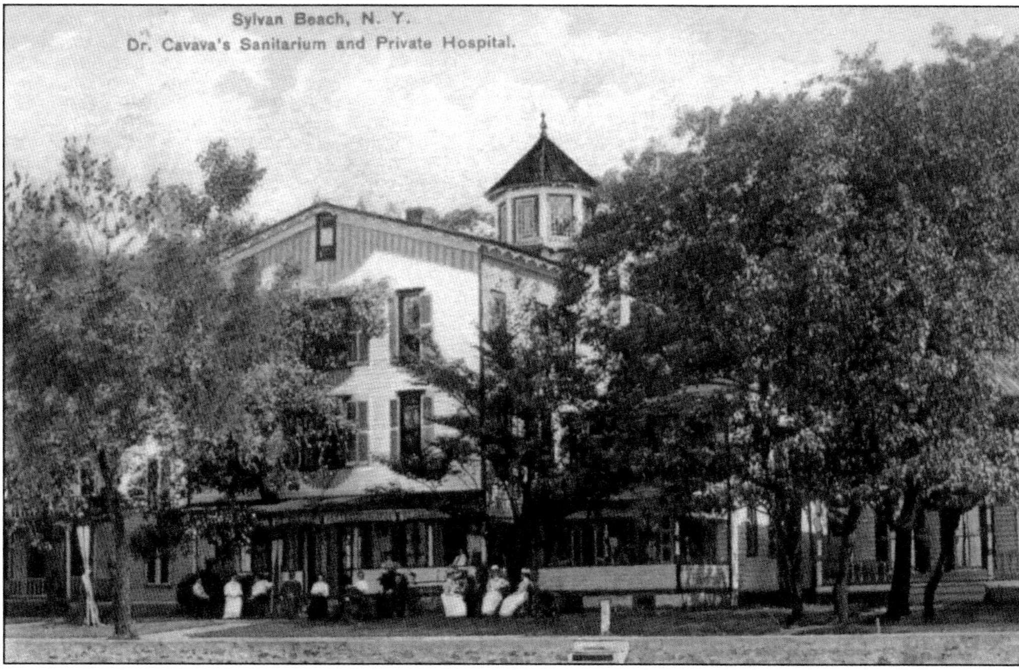

Dr. Martin Cavana was a compassionate man. He saw the talents as well as the needs in his fellow man. Often he applied his wit and his financial backing to improve the world around him. Around 1882, he convinced William Bowman, formerly of Vienna but then living in North Bay, to move his newspaper to Oneida. Bowman opened the *Oneida Post*, and it was a great success.

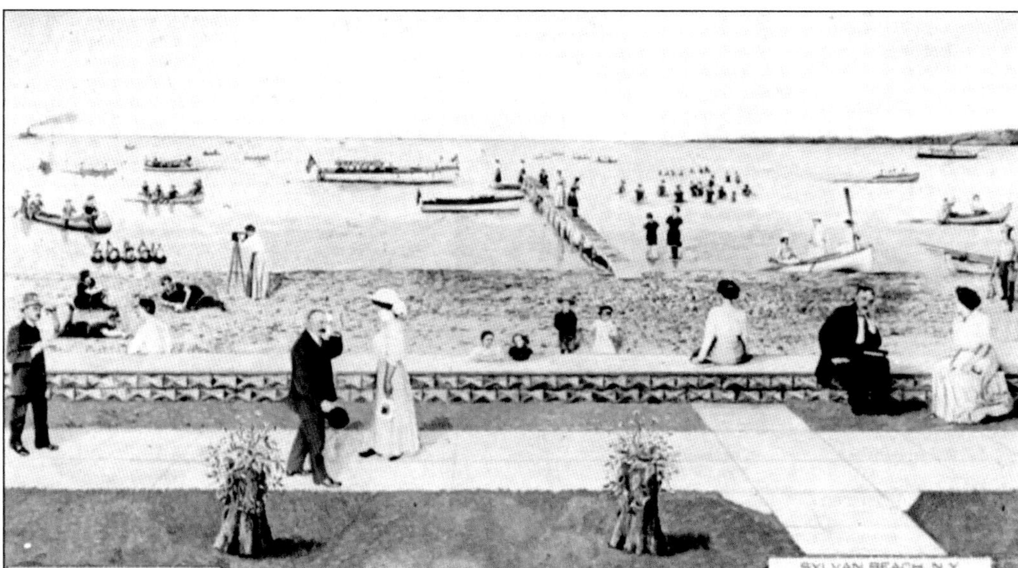

A few of the positions held by Cavana included president of the civil service commission in Oneida, president of the police and fire commission in Oneida, president of the New York and New England Association of Railway Surgeons, and surgeon of the New York, Ontario and Western Railway. In spite of all this, he had a sense of humor. On this postcard, the gentleman seated to the right sporting a mustache is Cavana.

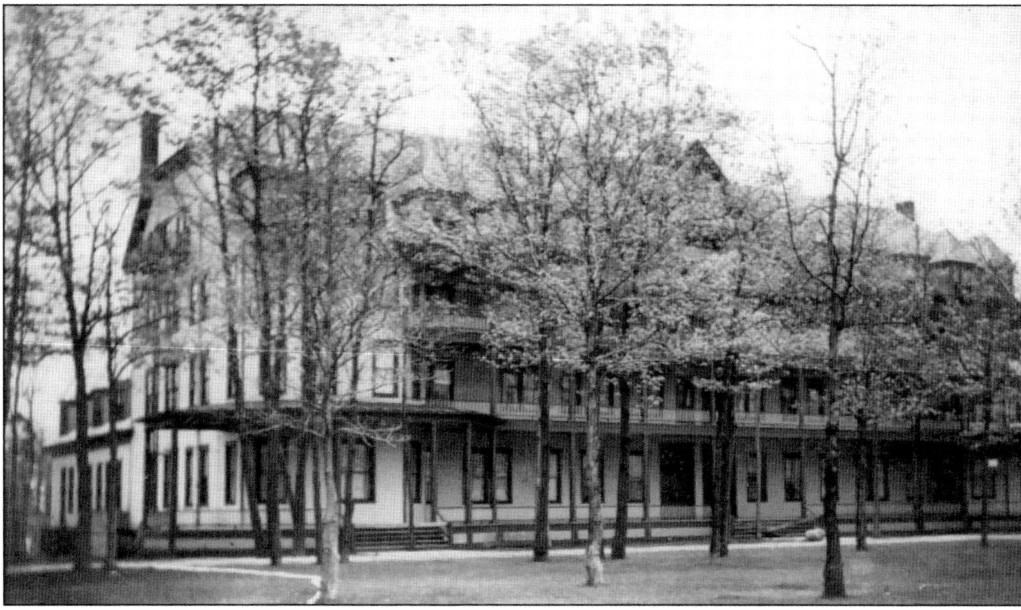

In 1893, Louis B. Cheesebrough built the St. Charles Hotel when the area was still a wilderness. It was the epitome of elegance 30 years before its time; no other hotel before or since has achieved that type of refined luxury. In 1899, Cavana and Cheesebrough purchased a block of 16 lots on the lakeshore in Sylvan Beach. They built several cottages along the 240-foot shoreline.

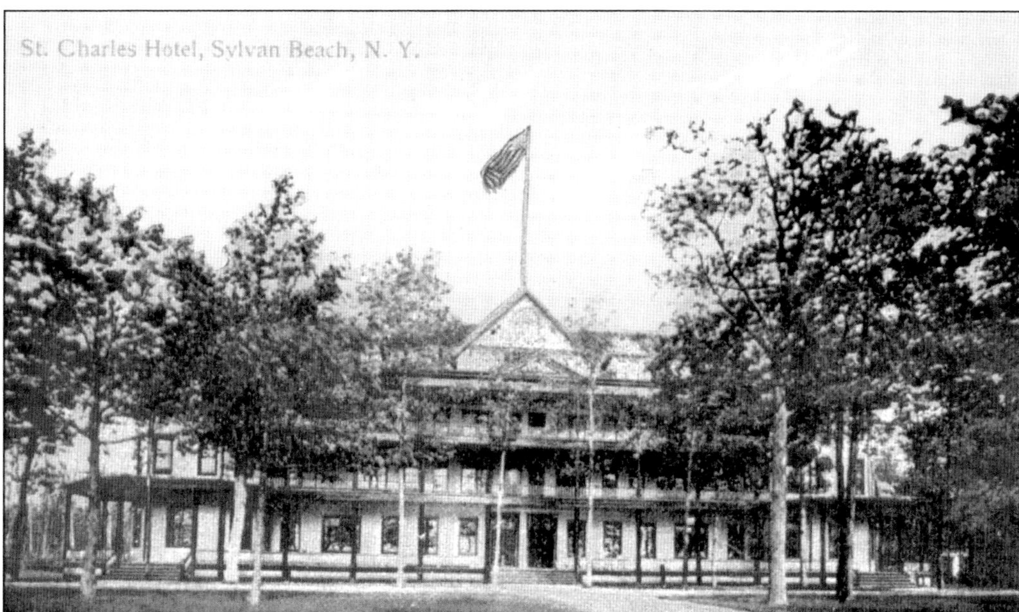

The St. Charles Hotel was a huge, glamorous resort with a capacity for 150 guests. A special coach transported guests from the train station. Expert chefs prepared mouth-watering delights, and talented dance orchestras played for the nightly balls. Built during a time when North Bay was still a popular resort area, the St. Charles was an addition to Sylvan Beach that drew attention and promoted its growth.

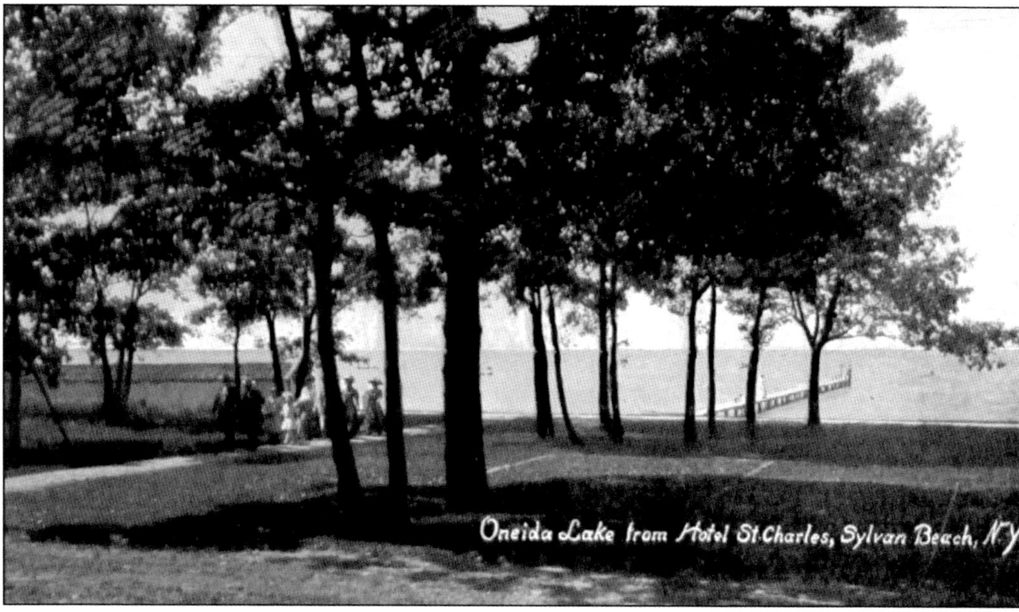

Louis Cheesebrough, the son of a wealthy New Yorker, was sickly and traveled the world looking for something that interested him. The peace and beauty of the sandy beaches on Oneida Lake in Sylvan Beach drew his interest, and he became a hotel proprietor. He died suddenly and unexpectedly in 1903, leaving an estate of $2.5 million. He was remembered for many of the improvements to the area that he sponsored.

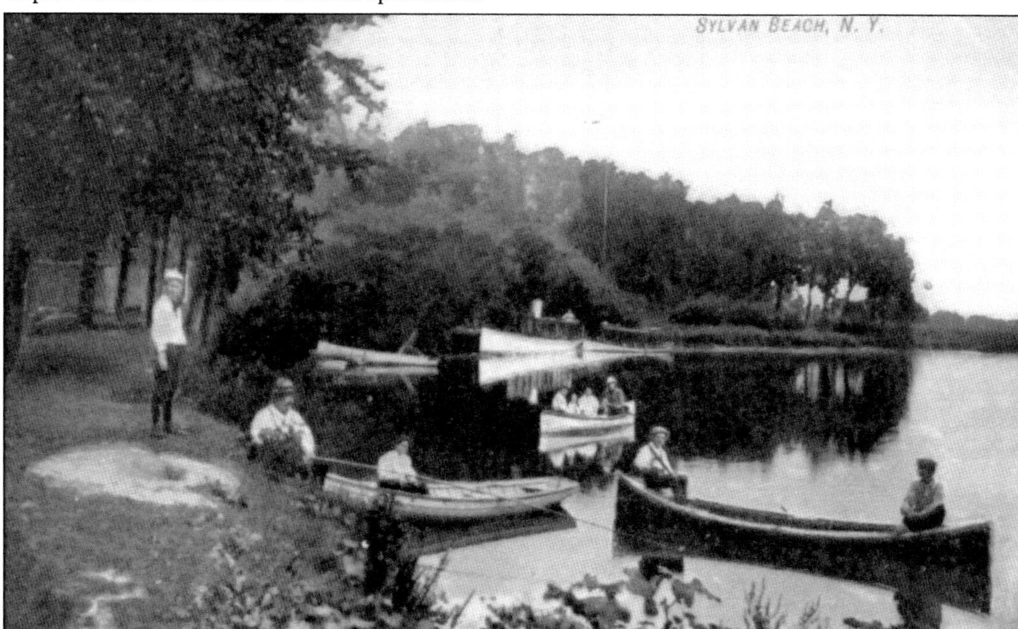

The staff of the St. Charles planned many amusements for the guests, including horseback riding and trips to Frenchman's Island. In the fall of 1914, the hotel was repainted. It is thought that oily rags caught fire during the night, and the grand hotel burned to the ground, ending an era. Cheesebrough's widow, Bertha, was not interested in rebuilding and went to live with her father-in-law on Long Island.

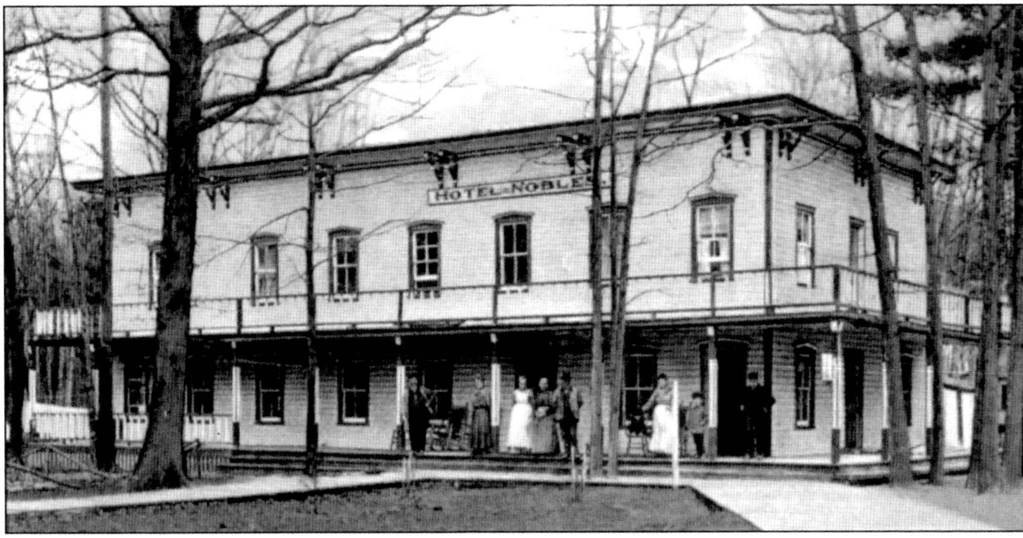

Diagonally across the street from the depot north of the four corners was Hotel Nobles. Eventually William Russell bought it and named it Russell's Danceland. Russell died in 1937, but the establishment continued to be popular. At times, Route 13 was lined with cars for a mile or more, and people were anxious to see the popular entertainers. In later years, it became Skateland run by Allen and Nanetta Jackson.

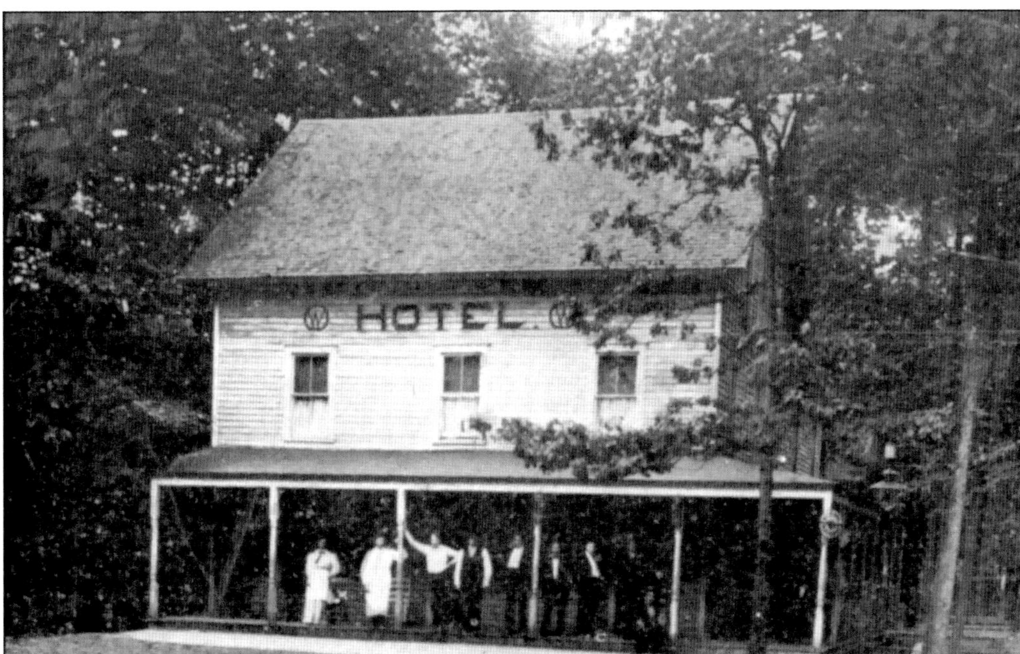

On the corner opposite the New York, Ontario and Western Railway depot was the Ontario Hotel. It bore the New York, Ontario and Western Railway logo on each side of its name printed above the door. Like so many of the smaller boardinghouses or hotels, the name of the establishment changed from season to season. Originally known as the Onyan Hotel, it became the Ontario Hotel and later the Noble House Hotel.

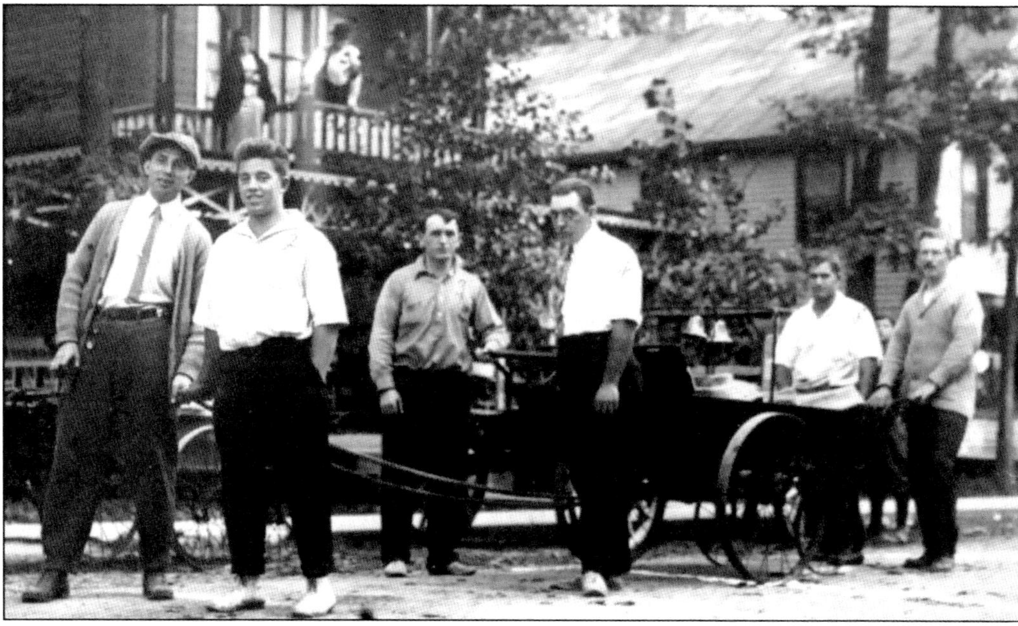

In the 1880s, the first volunteer fire department was organized in Sylvan Beach with two hand-drawn hose carts and the installation of fire hydrants. Two additional carts were added shortly afterward, and the four carts were strategically placed at different locations within the beach. Each of the four crews wanted to be the first responder to the fire alarm, which resulted in a healthy competition.

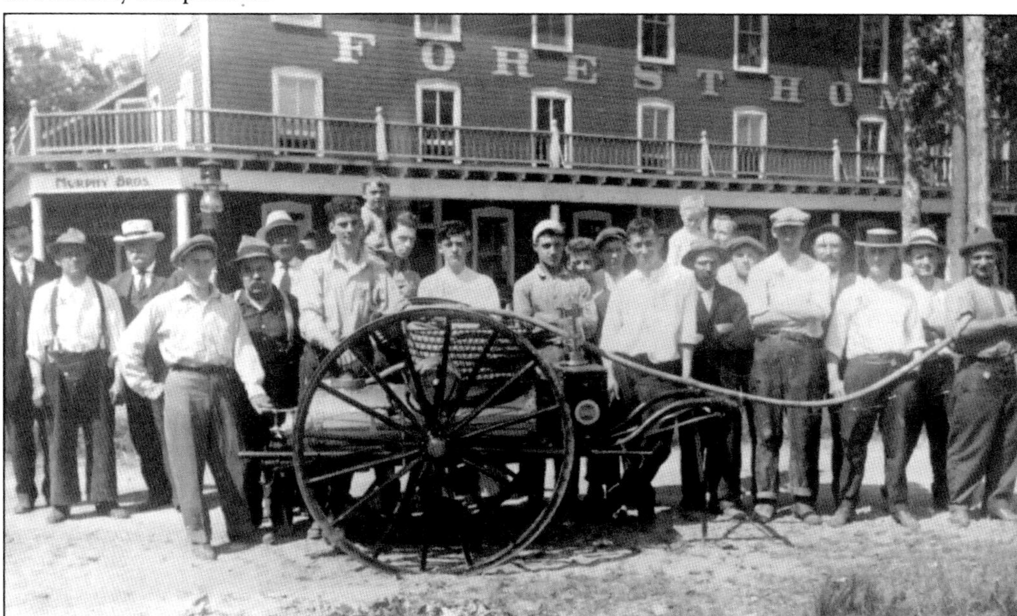

The Sylvan Beach Fire and Protective Association joined the Firemen's Association of the State of New York in 1914. Certified in 1915 with the department of state in Albany, they became the Sylvan Beach Fire Department. South of the Ontario Hotel on Main Street, a firehouse was built in 1930. A siren was installed; prior to that, the bell of the Catholic church was used to sound the alarm.

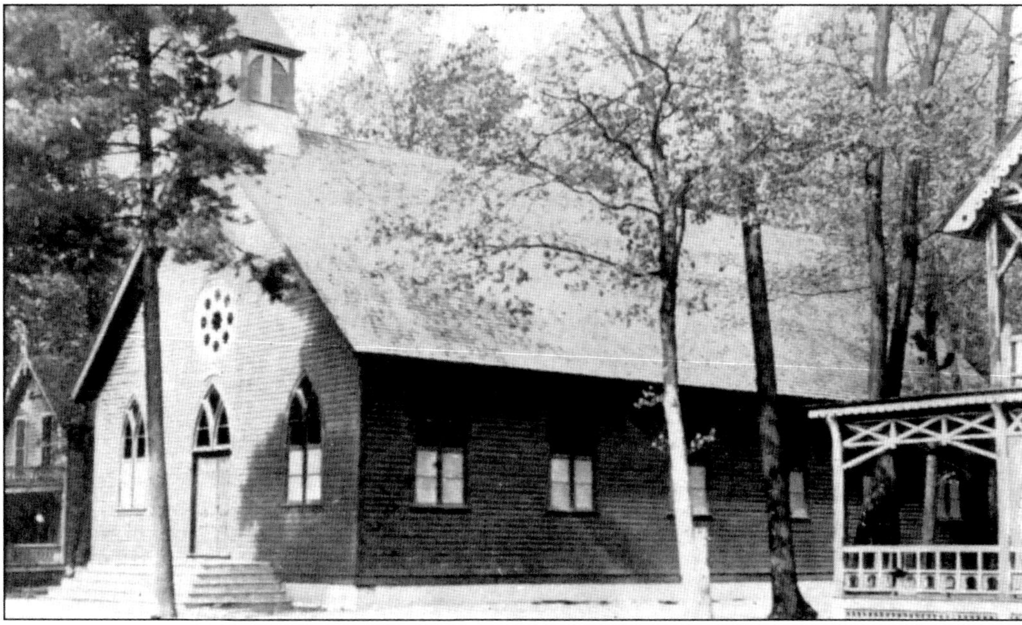

Continuing south on Main Street, the next building of interest was the Catholic church, St. Mary's on the Lake, built in 1899. It was the first permanent Catholic church in the area. Father Mertens, born in Brussels, Belgium, in 1861, was a key figure in founding the church and served as the first priest.

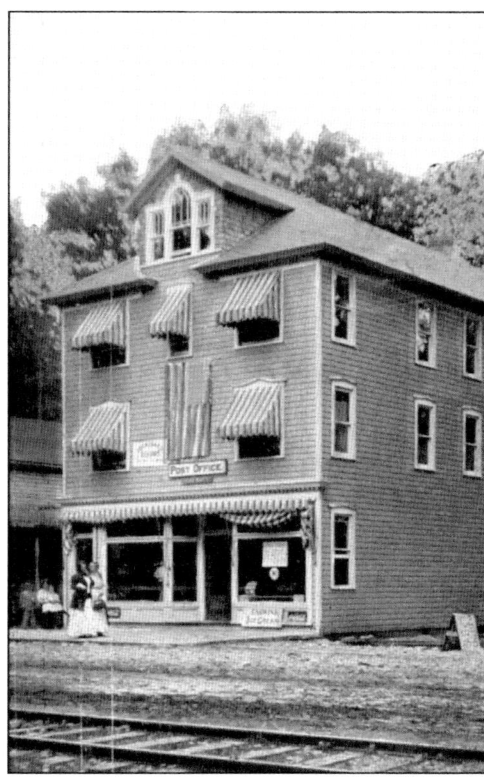

A little farther south there stood a store that also served as the post office. One of the early postmasters was C. C. Clifford. The structure of the building underwent a number of changes during the years. At one point, four Greek columns and three balconies were added, giving it a more Victorian appearance.

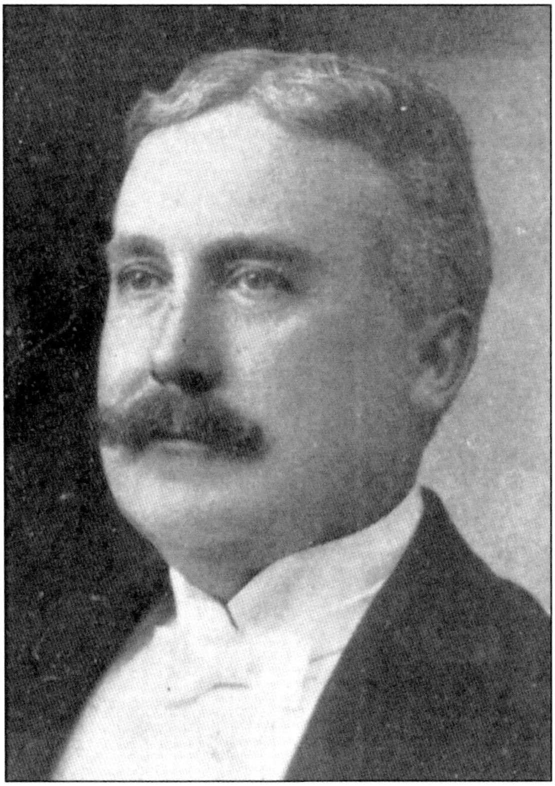

Charles Bell was the postmaster in Sylvan Beach for a few years. A member of the National League of Fourth Class Postmasters of New York, he was also a notary public in Oneida County. His store was the headquarters for Tuck's Beach Views, a top-quality postcard. He sold other items, including cigars, tobacco, and confectionaries.

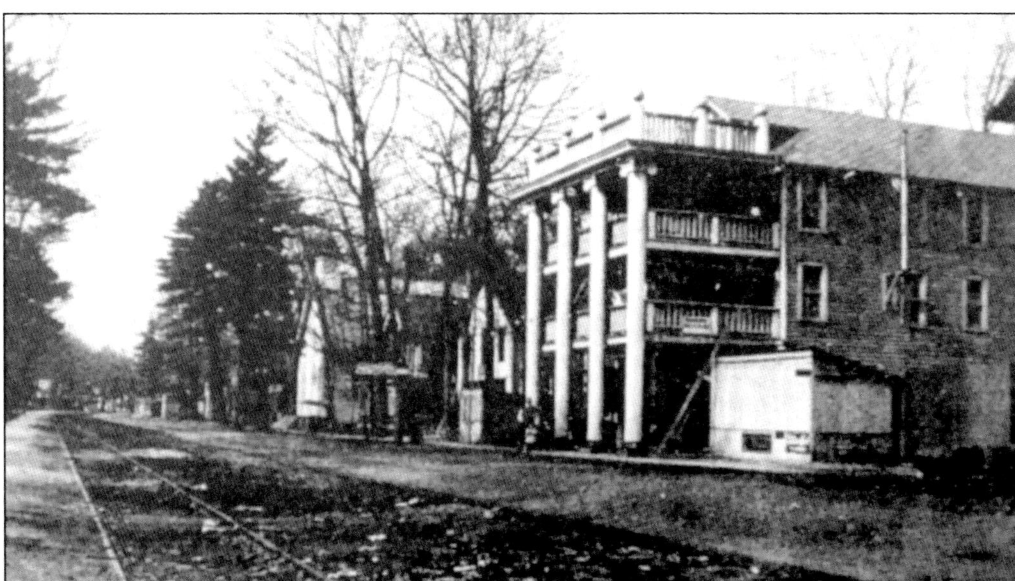

This picture, taken in the fall, shows the post office after the Greek columns and balconies were added. A few doors up the street is the Catholic church. A small concession stand, closed for the winter, is in the foreground. The beach was dotted with these stands that often changed owners. Sylvan Beach has prepared itself for the winter months and a quieter kind of life.

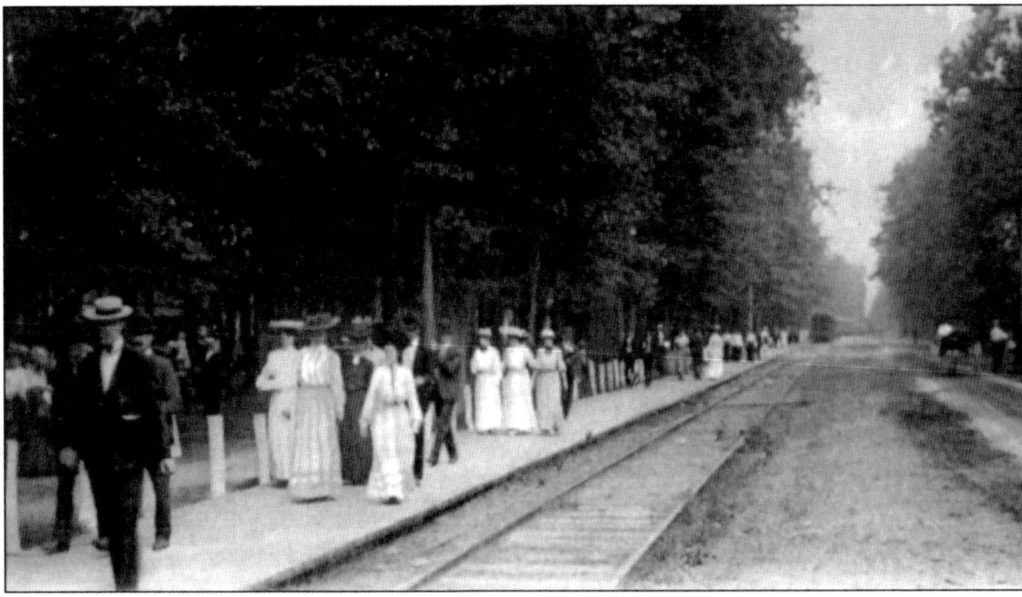

In 1916, unbeknownst to the community that had resisted the idea, the long spur, shown here, was extended to the Barge Canal in the dead of night. With the spur already in place, it was decided that the extension was needed to assist the block ice industry. A point of interest, all trains were required to back into the beach station, and the longer spur made it easier.

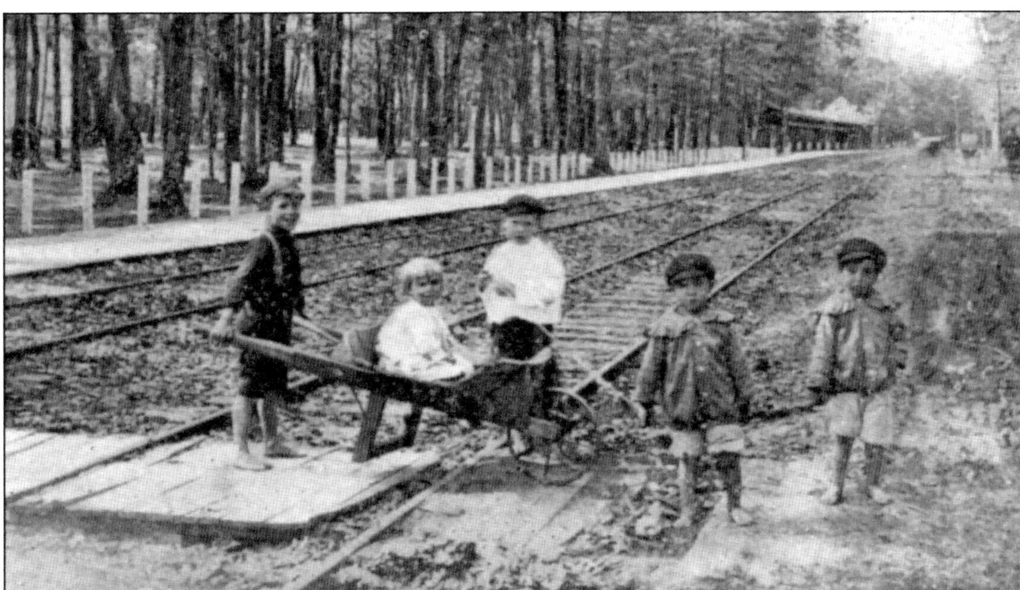

Sylvan Beach has always been a laid-back community that offered every type of entertainment imaginable. However, these children have found their own way to have fun. A photographer has frozen their images in time as they cross the tracks on Railroad Avenue. A child playing was a normal sight in the beach, but mirrored twins were a novelty.

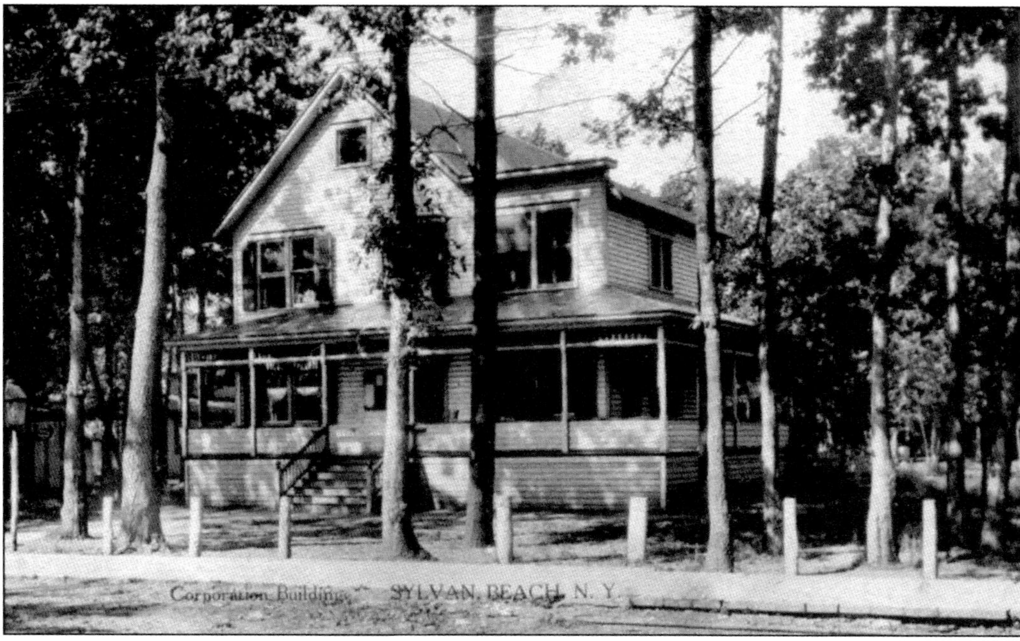

On the right at the lower end of the park was the corporation building. Through the efforts of Dr. Martin Cavana, Sylvan Beach formed a corporation in 1896. A lawsuit was brought against the town, and it was proven the population was not large enough to allow incorporation, and the corporation was therefore dissolved in 1911.

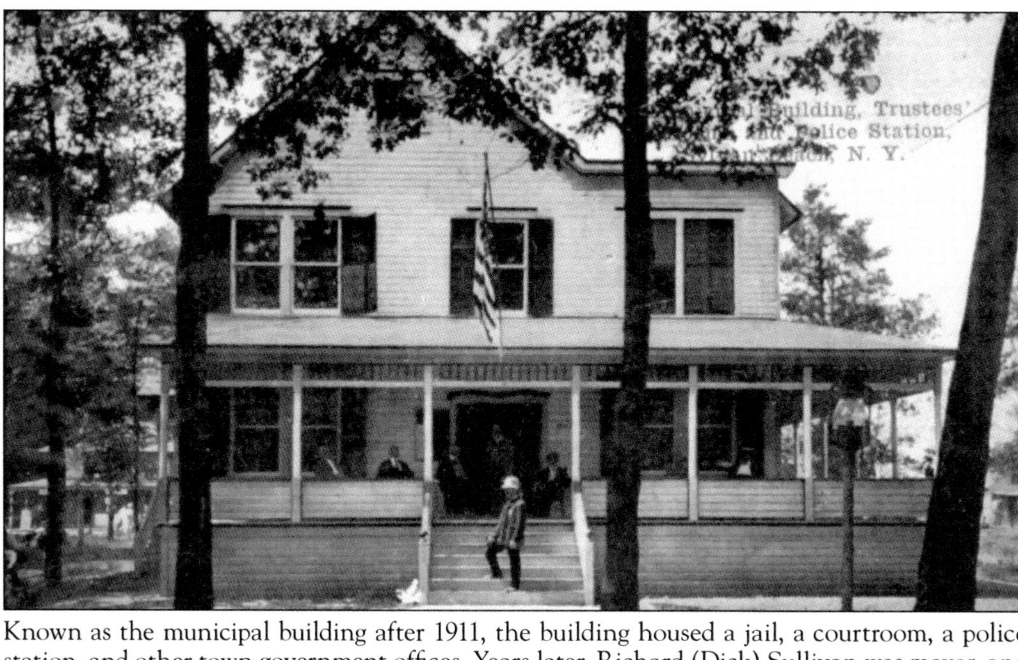

Known as the municipal building after 1911, the building housed a jail, a courtroom, a police station, and other town government offices. Years later, Richard (Dick) Sullivan was mayor, and through his efforts, the town was once again incorporated on March 27, 1971, making it the only village in the town of Vienna.

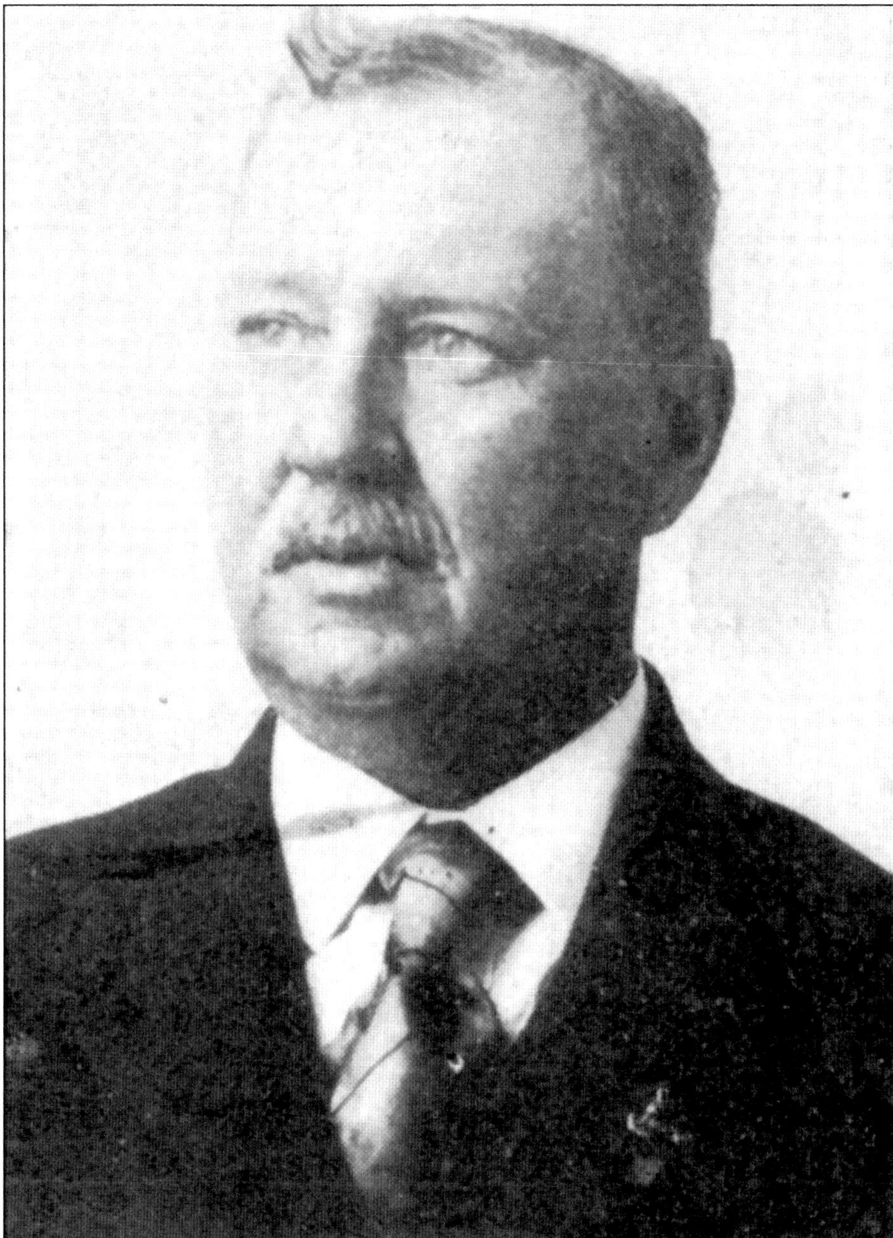

Thomas P. Bryant, born in Hudson on March 17, 1850, was chief of police for seven years when this photograph was taken. He was a cowboy for six years, and he joined the Secret Service in 1873. He then became a bonded officer as a New York State detective. Bryant was well liked for his friendly, efficient nature, and his past experience made him more than capable for the job. Wilber A. Palms (not shown) became chief of police in Sylvan Beach in 1919 after having served for nine years on the police force. Known as "the Chief," Palms was a clerk in 1893, but through diligence and hard work, he then bought a store and operated it until 1898. He was known as a likable person and was always on the alert for the safety and well-being of the residents. Today the state police have a station in the grove near the midway. The building is patterned after the old New York, Ontario and Western Railway depot.

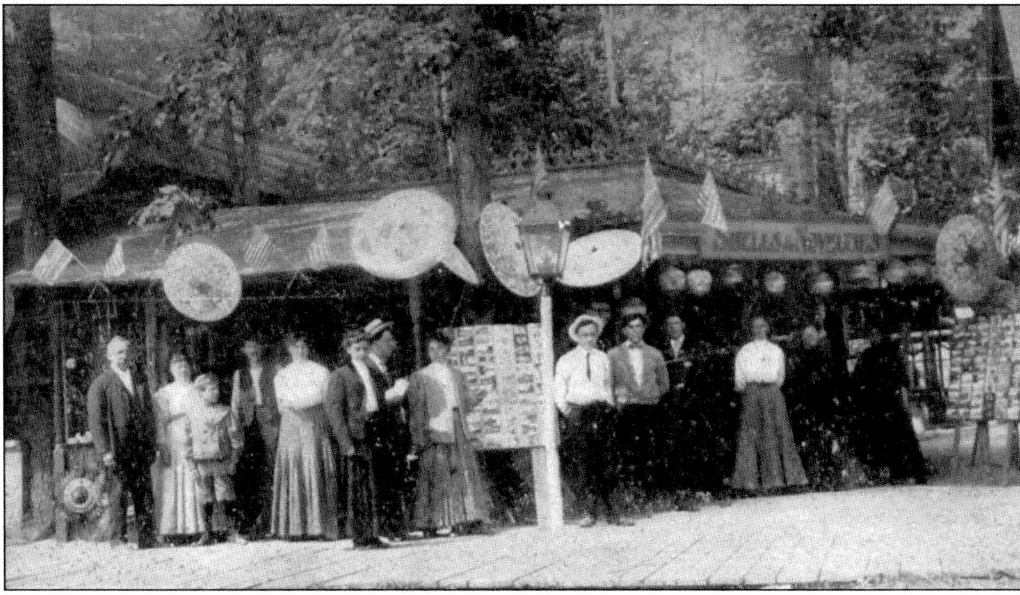

This concession stand was in the park next door to the municipal building. The sign advertises shells and novelties. Posters showing a variety of popular postcards for sale are strategically placed. Handmade items, along with Japanese paper umbrellas and American flags, serve as both sale items and pleasing decor.

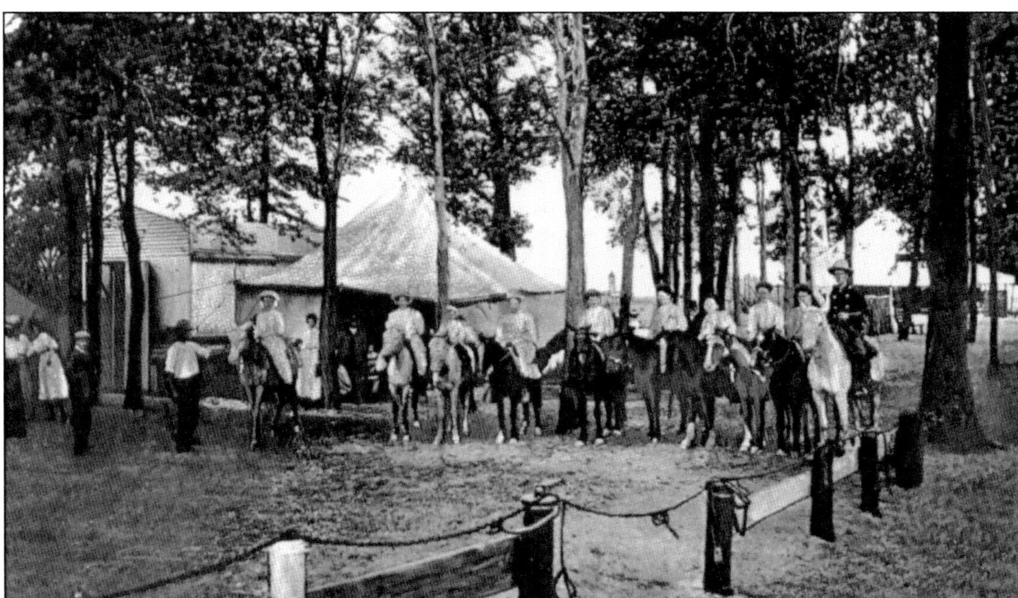

As evidenced by a number of tents in the background, this photograph was taken around 1908 during the reconstruction of the amusement park. At the south end of Spencer's Grove, Dr. Stevens rented his ponies, and much like the tour buses of today, he used a megaphone to tell the history and features of the various attractions as he led his patrons around the loop.

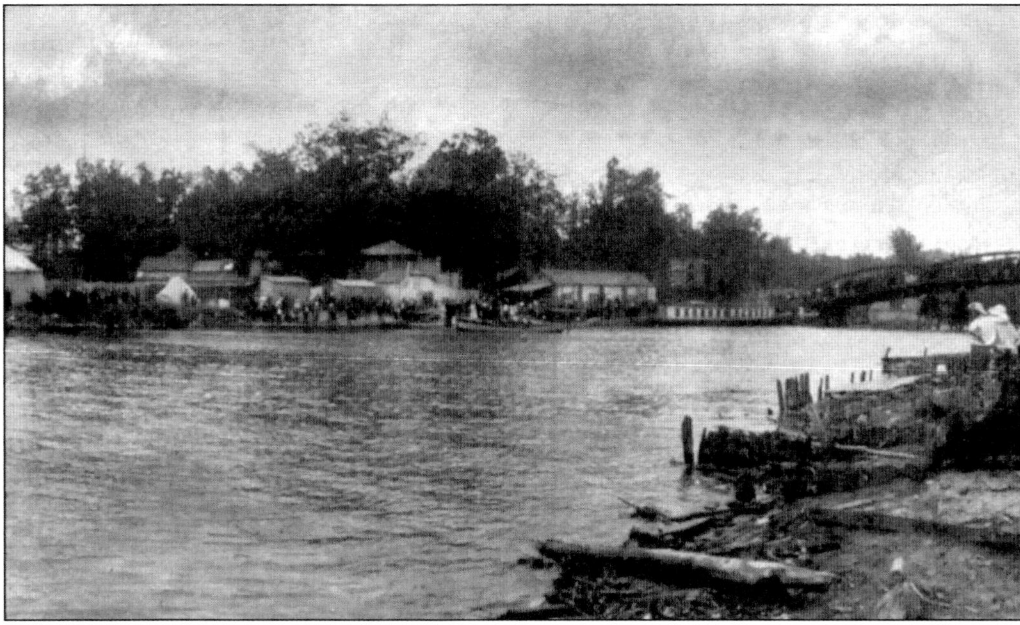

Luna Park, the midway of old, was built on a tip of land surrounded on three sides by Wood River slightly northeast of the Forest Home Hotel and the pedestrian wagon bridge. Wood River was a natural inlet on Oneida Lake, allowing for commerce and the arrival of steamboats loaded with vacationers. An additional popular pastime for vacationers was the excursions to Frenchman's Island out of Sylvan Beach.

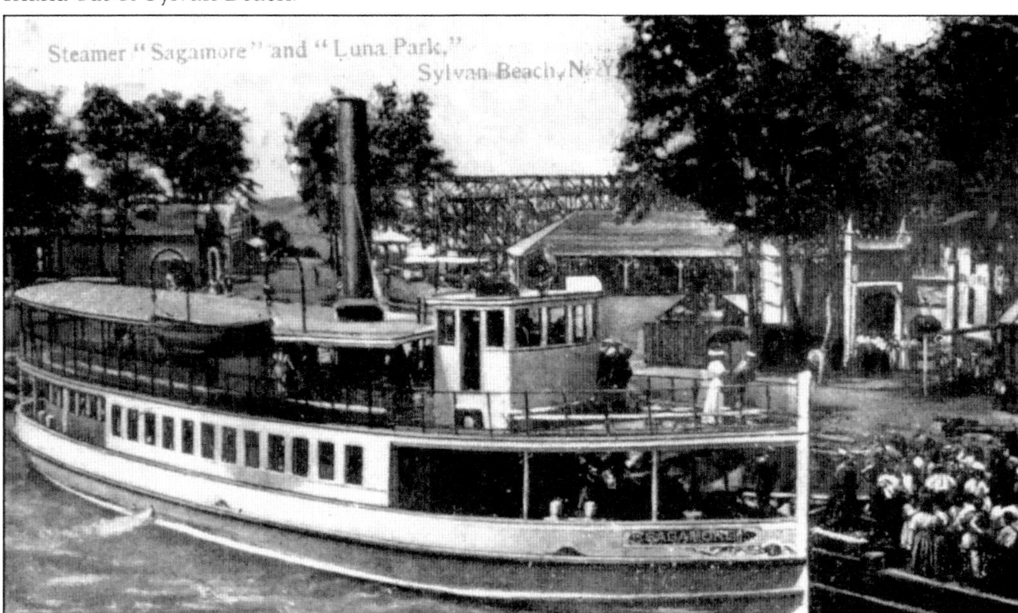

The Syracuse and South Bay Electric Railroad was a 10-mile trolley line that ran between Syracuse and lower South Bay. In 1908, it formed the Oneida Lake Transportation Company, which contracted the building of the steamboat *Sagamore*. Put into service the same year, it was 98 feet long and could carry up to 700 passengers the length of Oneida Lake in 1 hour and 45 minutes.

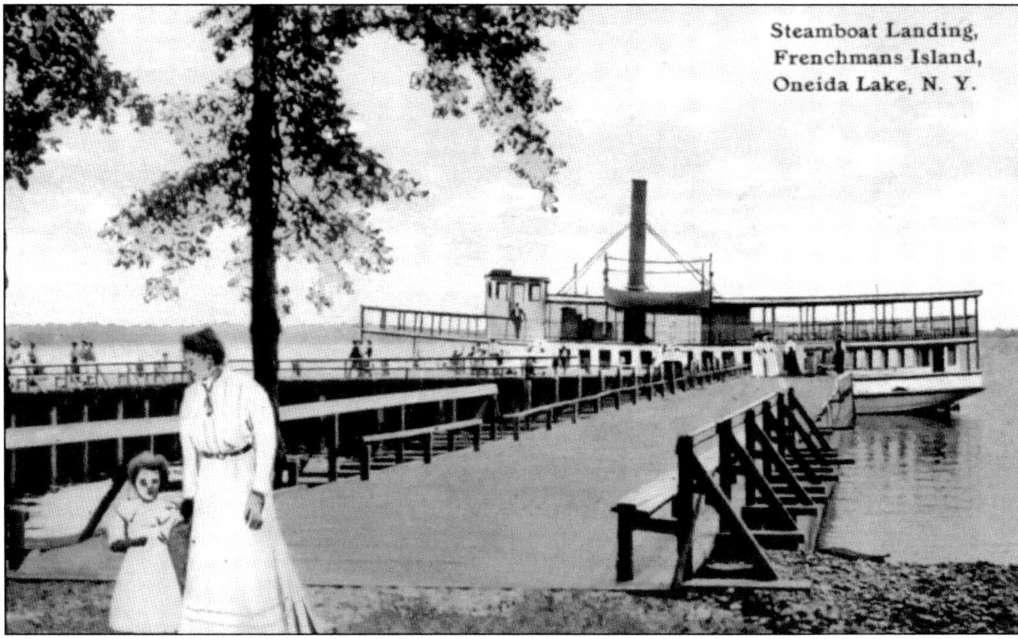

During the week, the *Sagamore* made two round-trips a day from lower South Bay to Frenchman's Island and "Lotus" or Dunham's Island. Legend says, "When the Great Spirit formed the world, His smile rested on the waters of the blue Oneida and Frenchman's Island arose to greet it. He laughed and Lotus Island came up to listen." The *Sagamore*, the "grand lady of the lake," remained in service until 1917.

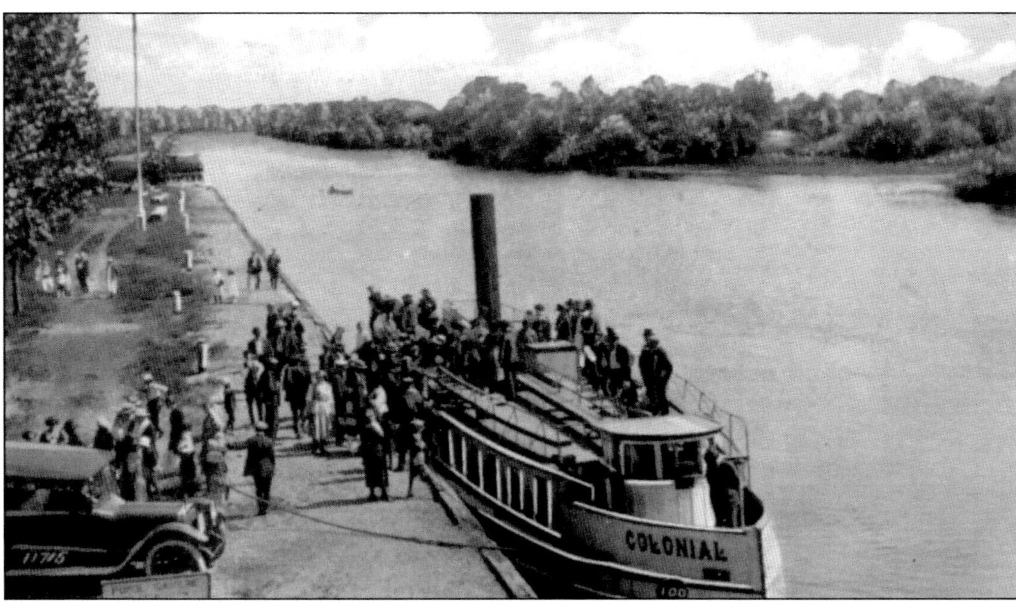

On weekends and holidays, the Sagamore made round-trips between lower South Bay and Sylvan Beach. Based in Rome, the excursion boat *Colonial* regularly steamed to the beach with a full load of tourists. In July 1910, 35 steamers licensed to transport passengers sailed the waters of Oneida Lake. Many of them were from Sylvan Beach.

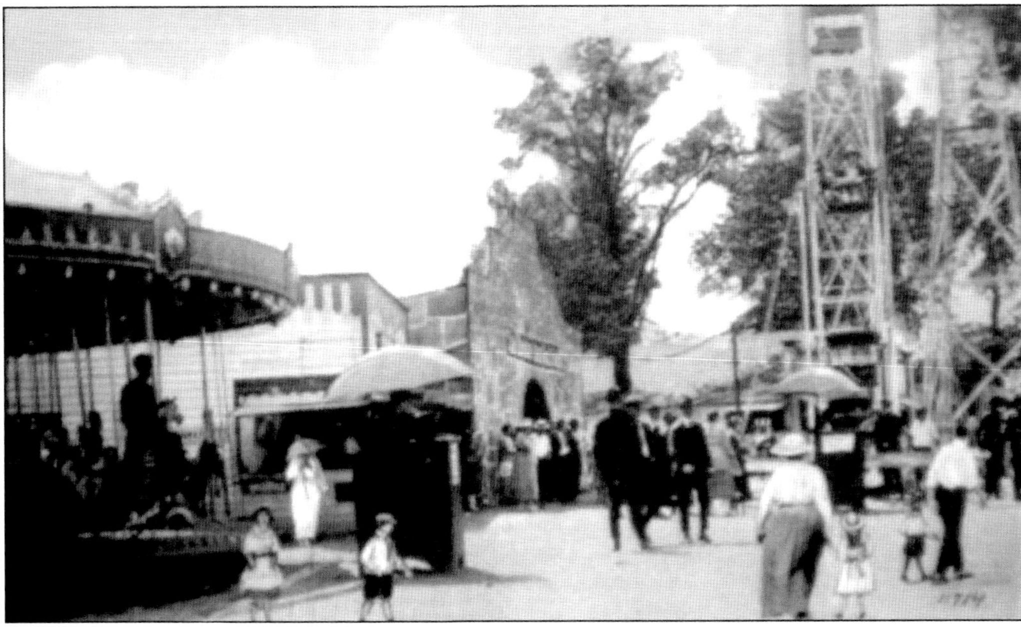

Evidence shows that Carnival Park was built while Luna Park was in operation. The carousel on the left is in Carnival Park. Joseph Cottman carved the figures in 1886. A German craftsman, he owned and operated the carousel and lived at the "Beach." The animals on the carousel have since been replaced with reproductions. The originals are in a museum in Tonawanda.

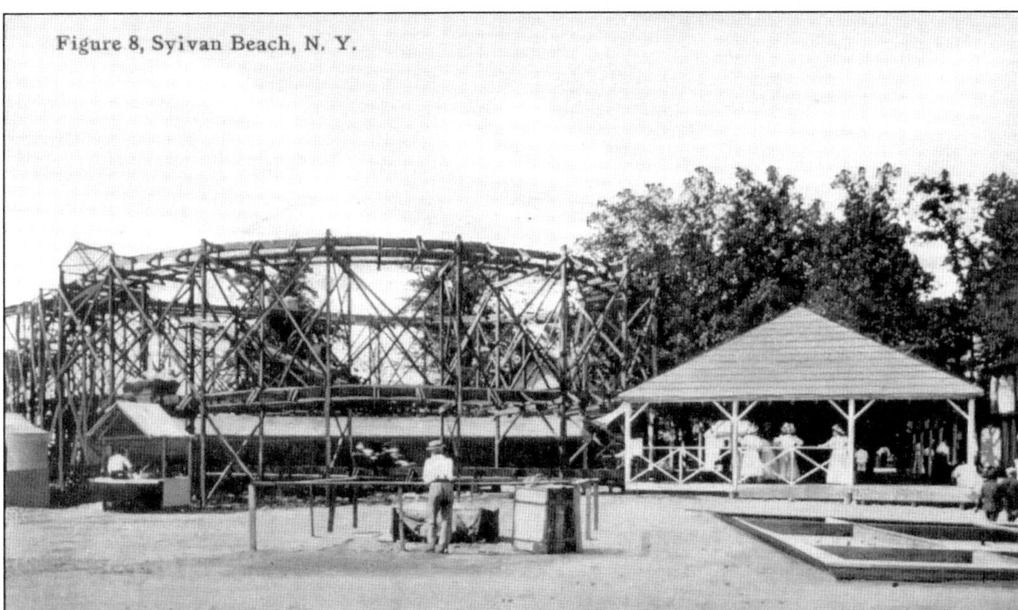

Seen here, the Figure Eight and the Japanese Bazaar were lost to progress. The timbers from the Figure Eight were used to frame a house built on the site of the former Algonquin Hotel. Marge Testa eventually bought the home and converted it into a restaurant. Jean Kowalski bought the restaurant from her mother and continues to offer a great meal at the Canal View Café.

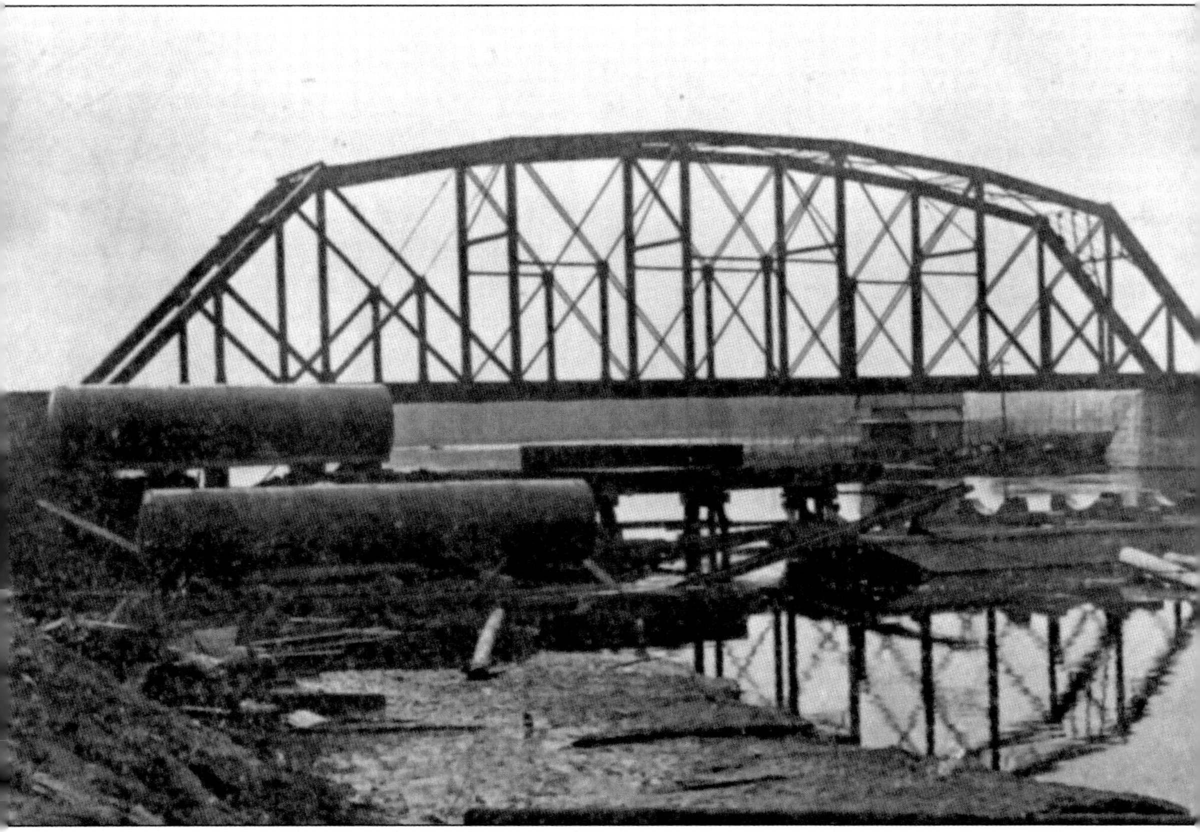

Built in 1887, the metal bridge was too short a span and too low to meet the specifications required for the proposed Barge Canal. To meet the specifications, an additional 14 feet of clearance was required along with raised approaches. Construction of the new Bridge No. 367 required the old bridge and main line to be closed on July 7, 1906. A temporary trestle was built to the west of its location in order to move the main line around the construction site. By November 1906, the replacement bridge was nearly complete, requiring only the dismantling of the old bridge and removing the construction equipment. New York State paid $250,616 for construction of the 212-foot steel span, the raised approaches, and the new interlocking system. However, the New York, Ontario and Western Railway owned the bridge, and the Lehigh Valley Railroad had trackage rights. Construction began in April 1906, and in December of the same year, the bridge was completed and put into service.

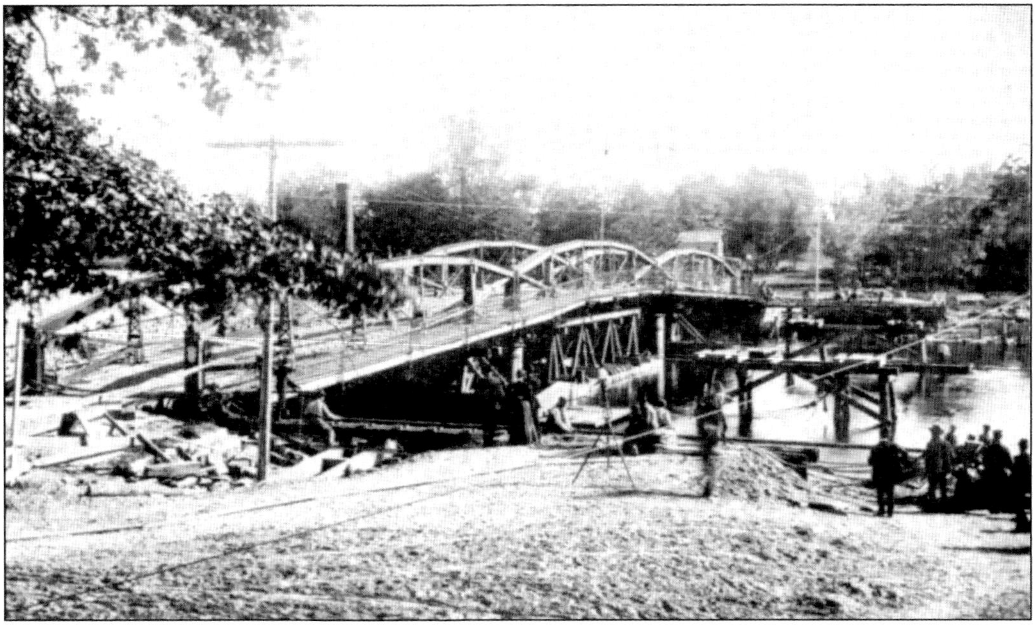

Built by the Empire Engineering Company of New York, the new Barge Canal bridge was opened to traffic in October 1908. The highway bridge was to replace the wagon/pedestrian bridge built in 1889. The former bridge remained in place until after the new bridge was completed slightly west of its location. The preliminary work is just beginning here with the driving of pilings under the surveyor's close supervision.

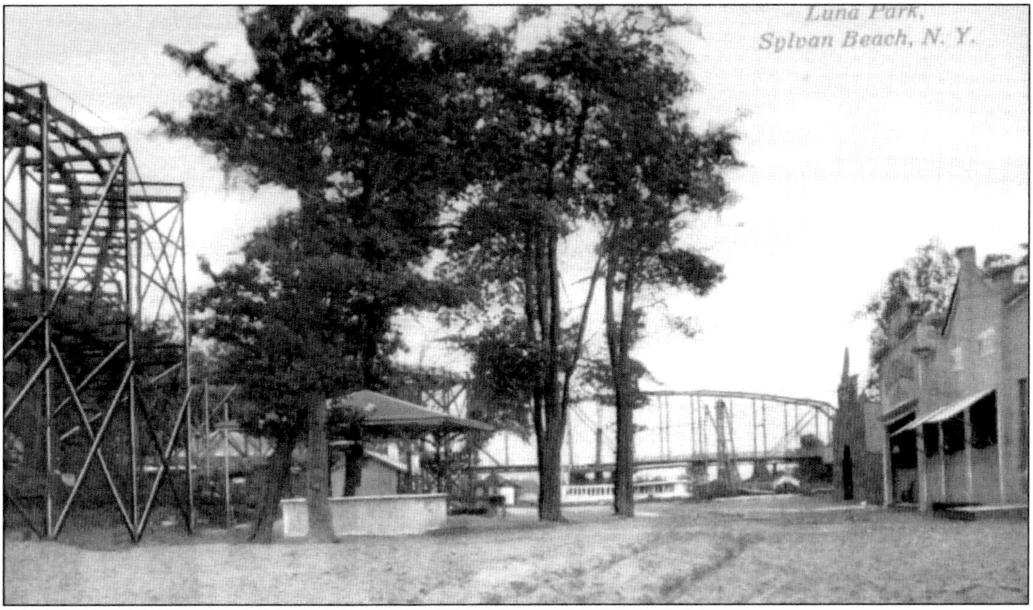

Once the highway bridge from Verona to Sylvan Beach was completed at a cost of $9,643, the Empire Engineering Company went to work digging the Barge Canal. This view shows the completed bridge and a dredge in place preparing to cut Wood River in three places, making the course to Oneida Lake straight. Luna Park, cut nearly in half, moved southwest, joining with Carnival Park.

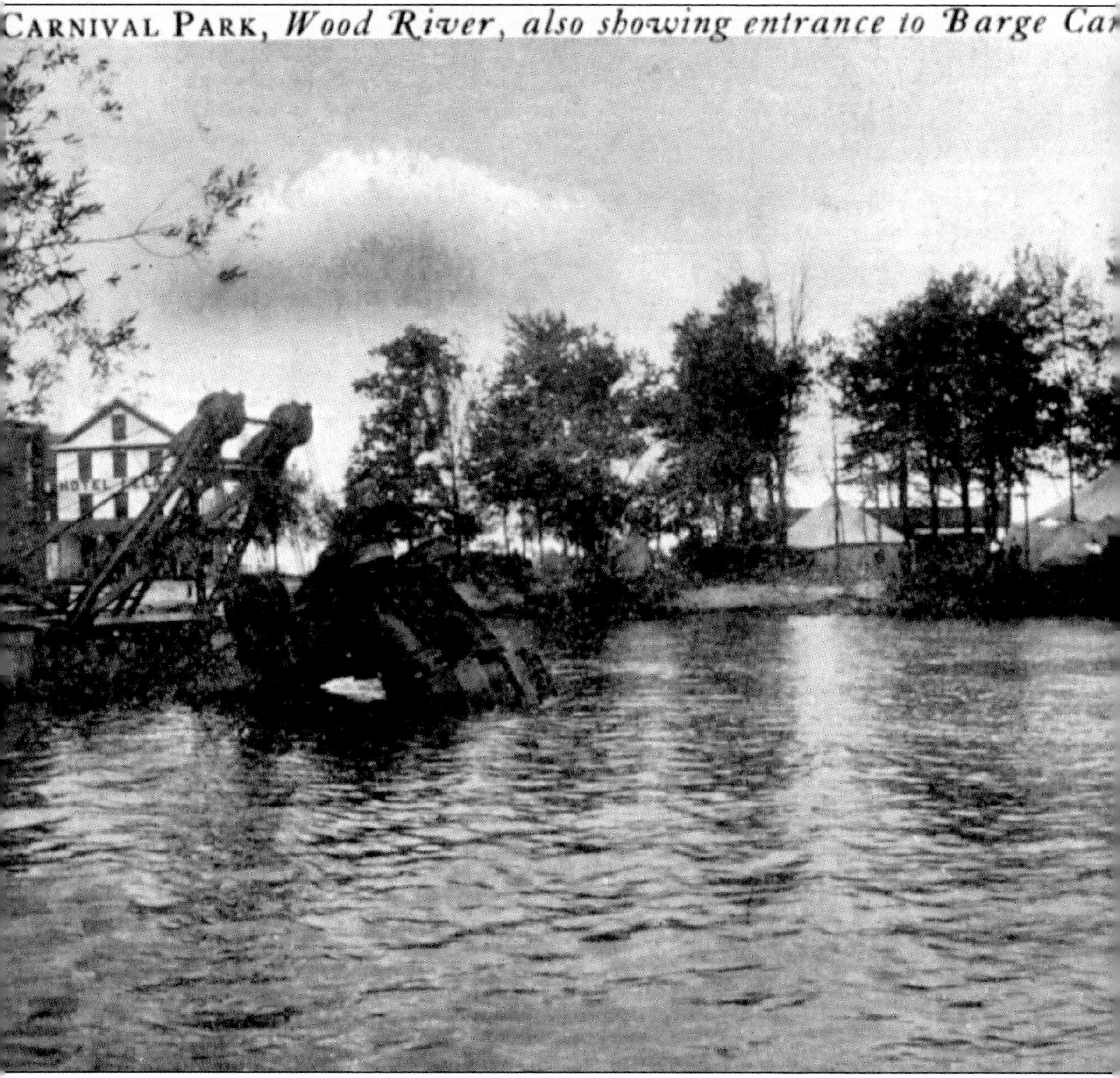

Luna Park and Carnival Park combined to clear the way for the Barge Canal, but as seen here, Sylvan Beach concessionaires did not skip a beat. During the summer of 1908, a lot of tents were used for games, souvenirs, and eateries until buildings could be moved or built to house them. The amusement area south of Spencer's Grove extended nearly to the lake and the edge of the

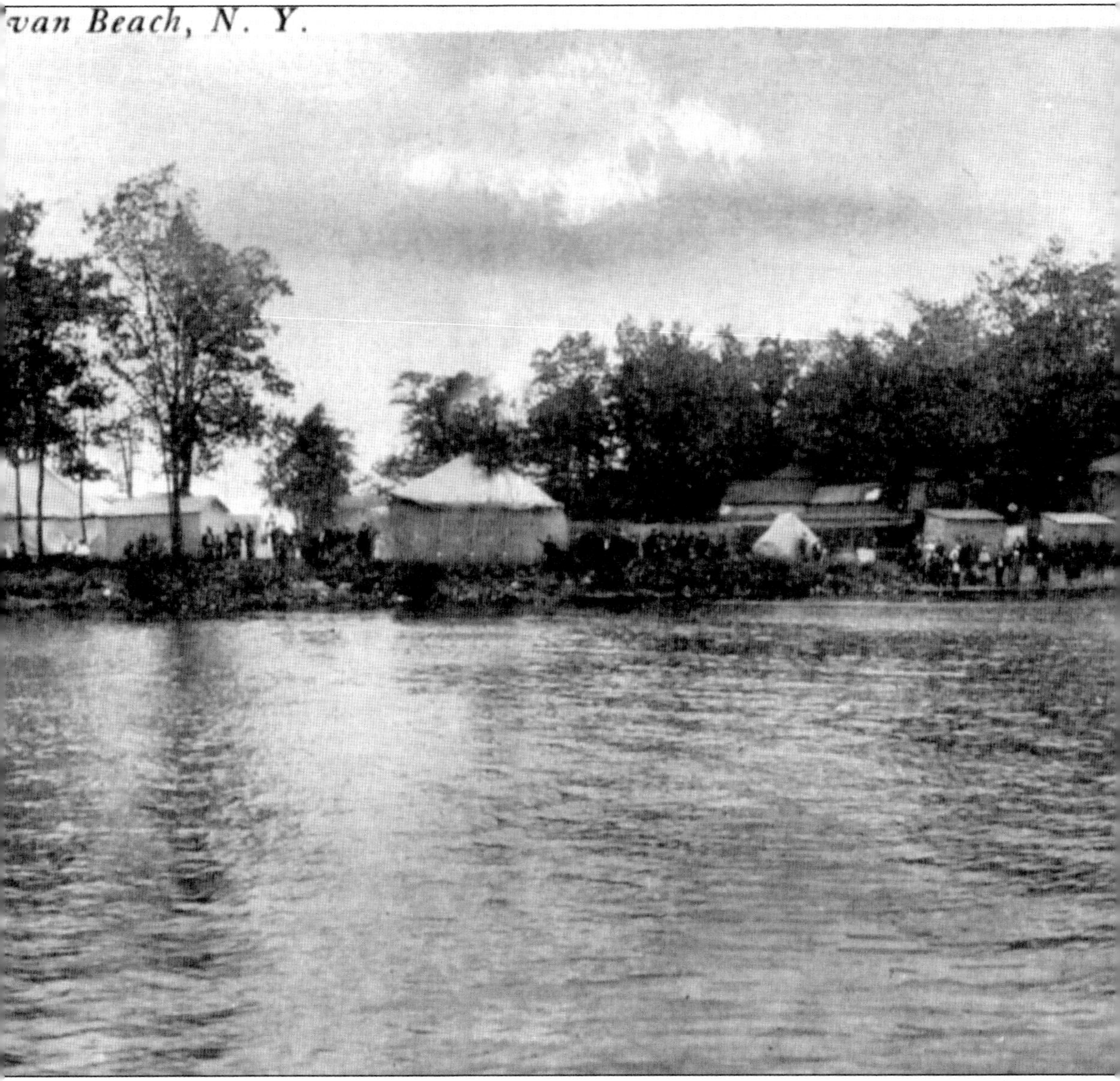

new canal. A large dredge is clearing the channel at the entrance to the canal. The Hotel Leland, established in 1896 by Charles Scovile, is pictured on the left behind the dredge and continued to operate in its original location until December 4, 1908. It was then sold to Peter Klippel, who relocated it to the site formerly occupied by the Algonquin and renamed it the Klippel.

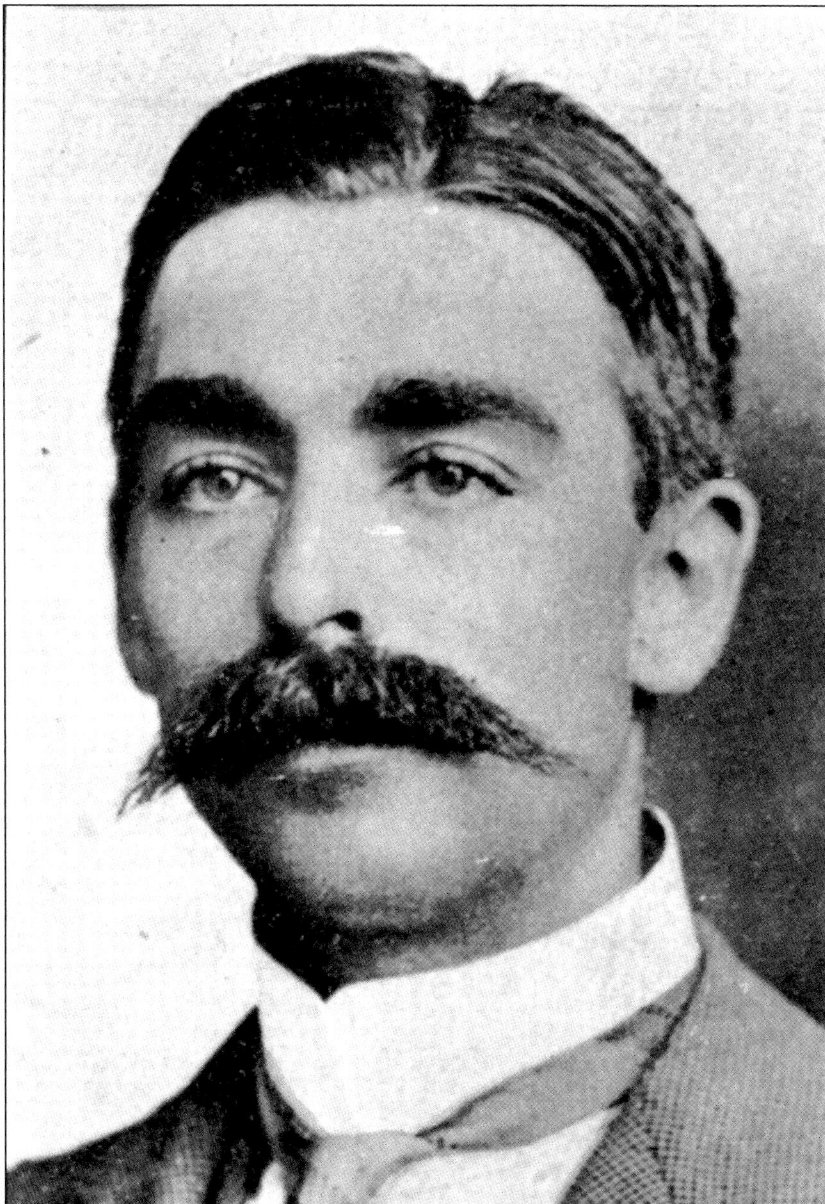

William G. Powell, a highly respected practical technician for the Empire Engineering Company, played a major role in the work done on the Barge Canal in Sylvan Beach. Born in Youngstown in 1874, he was highly thought of by all. His achievements were a result of his energy and perseverance. Powell was in charge of the pile driving and sinking of cribs for the breakwater at the mouth of Wood River where it entered Oneida Lake. He was one of the many excellent engineers, supervisors, and contractors who built the canal. When the project was completed, a celebration dinner was given at the Hotel Rochester. Frank Williams, the state engineer, rose to congratulate the men who worked so hard against seemingly impossible odds during a time of war. The words he chose revealed both pride and appreciation in a job well done: "Let not one of you regard lightly what he has done or the part he has played. Engineers and contractors alike, you have served the great cause perhaps better than you know."

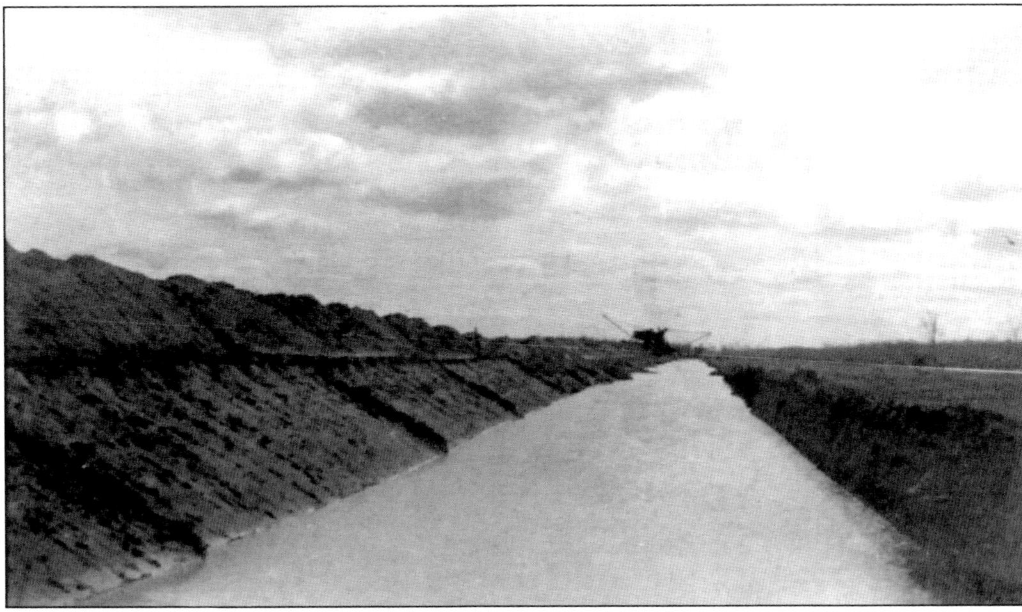

Constructed between 1904 and 1918, the Barge Canal has four sections, the Champlain, the Erie, the Oswego, and the Seneca-Cayuga. The section that includes Oneida Lake and runs through Sylvan Beach is the Erie. The huge task of building the Barge Canal is evident in this photograph. A large machine that ran on railroad tracks, this bucket dredge in Fish Creek cuts through solid ground.

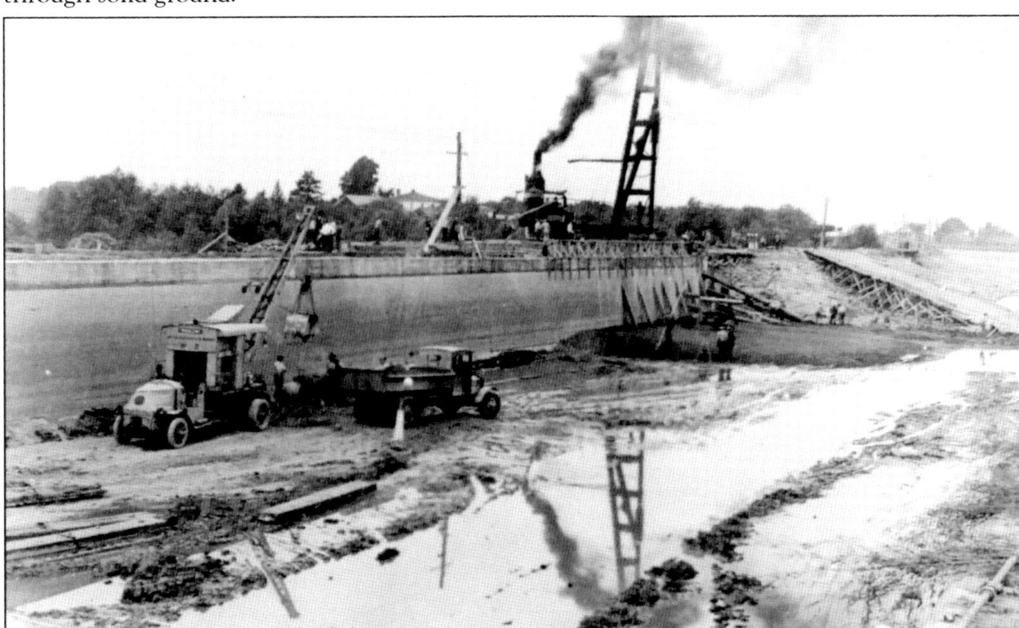

Machines and men working together accomplished the nearly impossible. Half a dozen novel mechanisms were invented to meet the difficult needs of building a canal during World War I. Constantly short of manpower, contractors had to depend on machines to increase productivity. On May 15, 1918, with the incoming water rising around their waists, the final work was done, and the completion date was met.

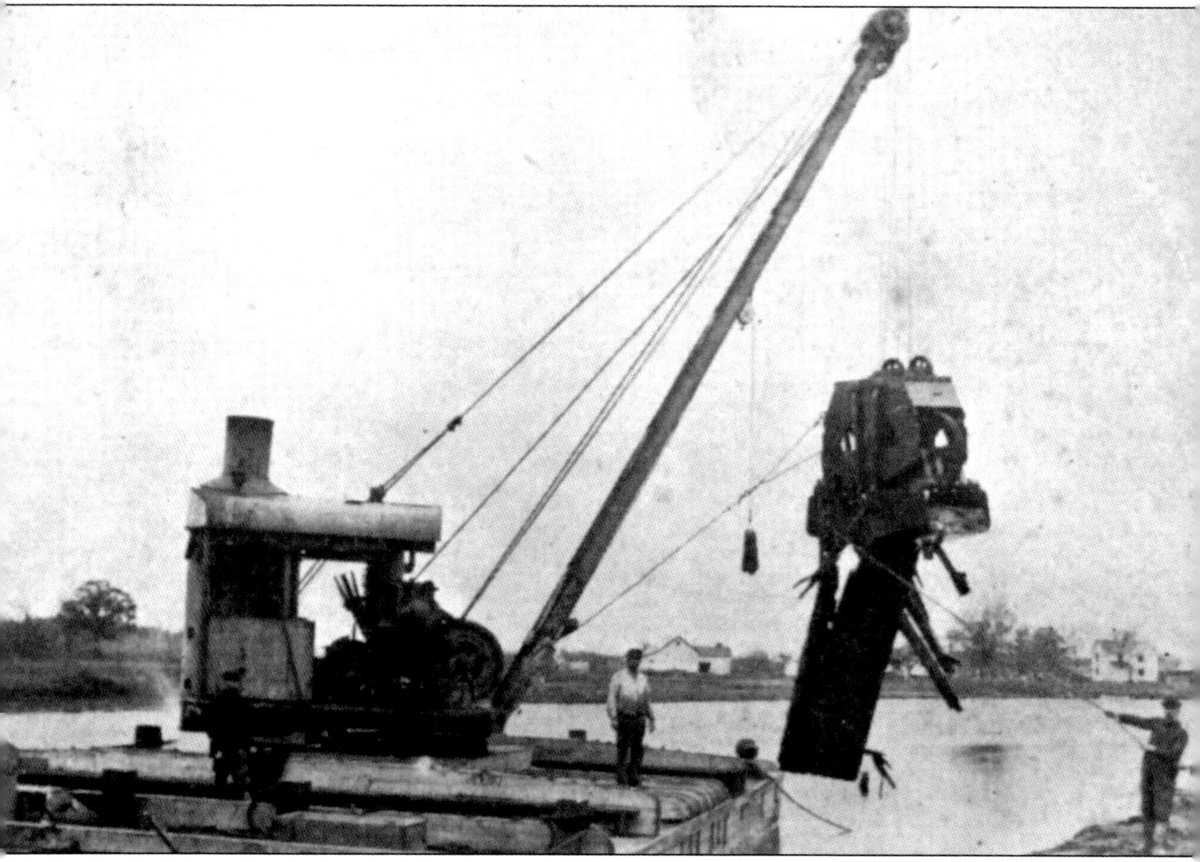

Once the highway bridge crossing Wood River from Verona to Sylvan Beach was completed, the Empire Engineering Company went to work in Wood River. The large dredges *Oneida* and *Oswego* were brought in sections by rail to the company's siding at Sylvan Junction. Reassembled and launched into Wood River, they cut the river in three places, creating a "true course" to Oneida Lake.

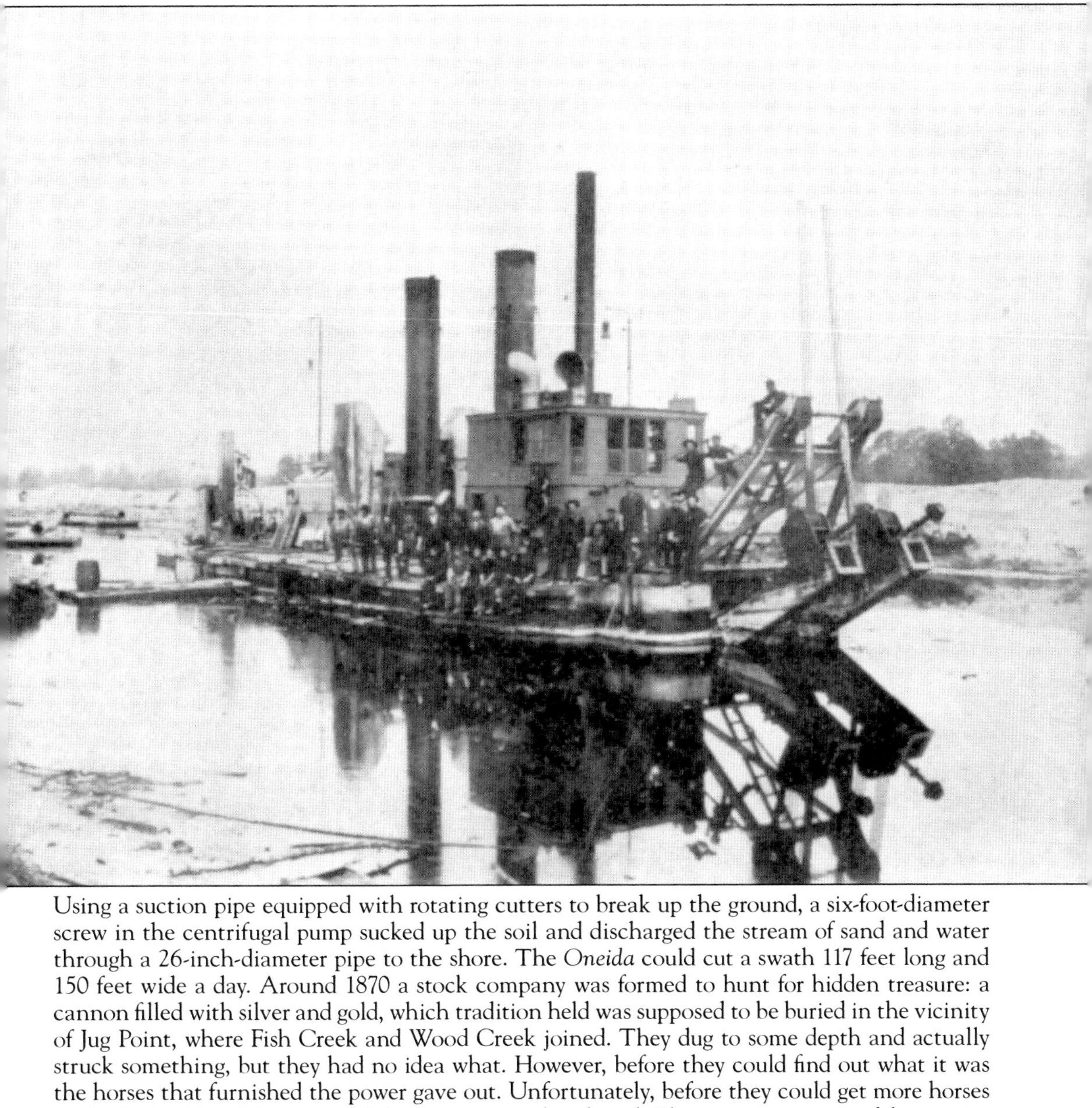

Using a suction pipe equipped with rotating cutters to break up the ground, a six-foot-diameter screw in the centrifugal pump sucked up the soil and discharged the stream of sand and water through a 26-inch-diameter pipe to the shore. The *Oneida* could cut a swath 117 feet long and 150 feet wide a day. Around 1870 a stock company was formed to hunt for hidden treasure: a cannon filled with silver and gold, which tradition held was supposed to be buried in the vicinity of Jug Point, where Fish Creek and Wood Creek joined. They dug to some depth and actually struck something, but they had no idea what. However, before they could find out what it was the horses that furnished the power gave out. Unfortunately, before they could get more horses the hole filled in with water and the project was abandoned. There are no reports of discoveries of treasure when the *Oneida* and the *Oswego* dredges burrowed through that area; perhaps the stories of buried treasure were just fantasy.

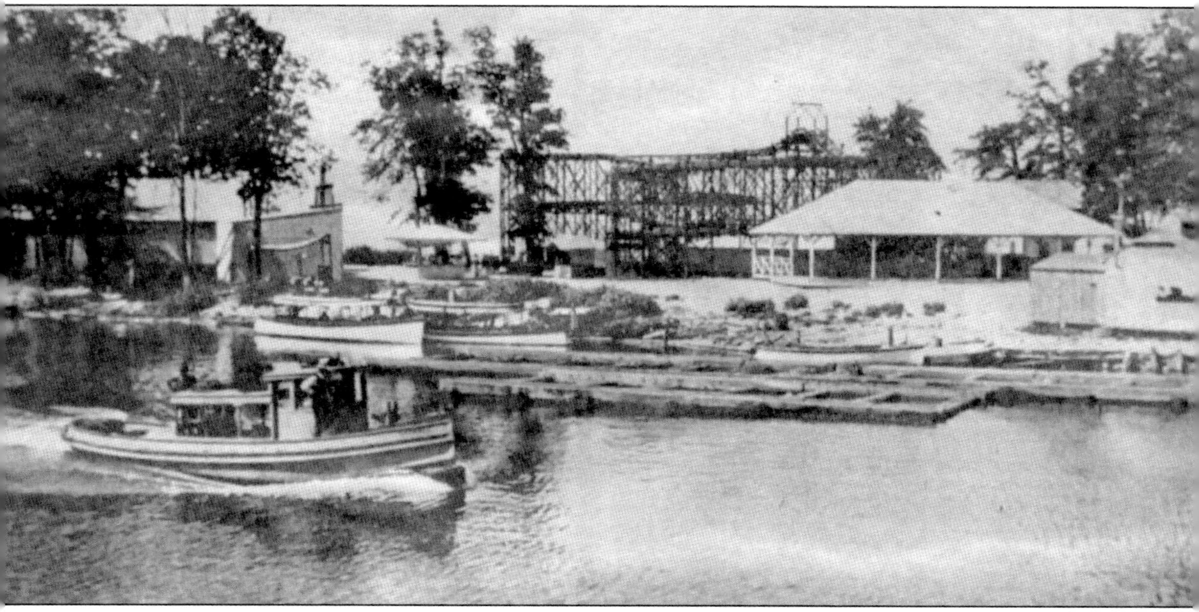

Building the Barge Canal was one of the most stupendous undertakings in history to be attempted by a corporation. Built during the early 20th century and completed during wartime, the engineers continually accomplished the various projects below budget. The five miles of canal extending east from Oneida Lake was mostly sand, which allowed for the use of hydraulic dredges. That section of the new canal included several steel bridges and a breakwater extending out into Oneida Lake. However, the contract for completing the job was $86,000 under the official figures given by the Empire Engineering Corporation. Pictured is the construction on the new Barge Canal through Sylvan Beach nearing completion. Cribbing is in place as they prepare to pour concrete, used to protect the sides of the canal and to construct the pier out into Oneida Lake. The pier provided a breakwater for boats, barges, and ships using the canal.

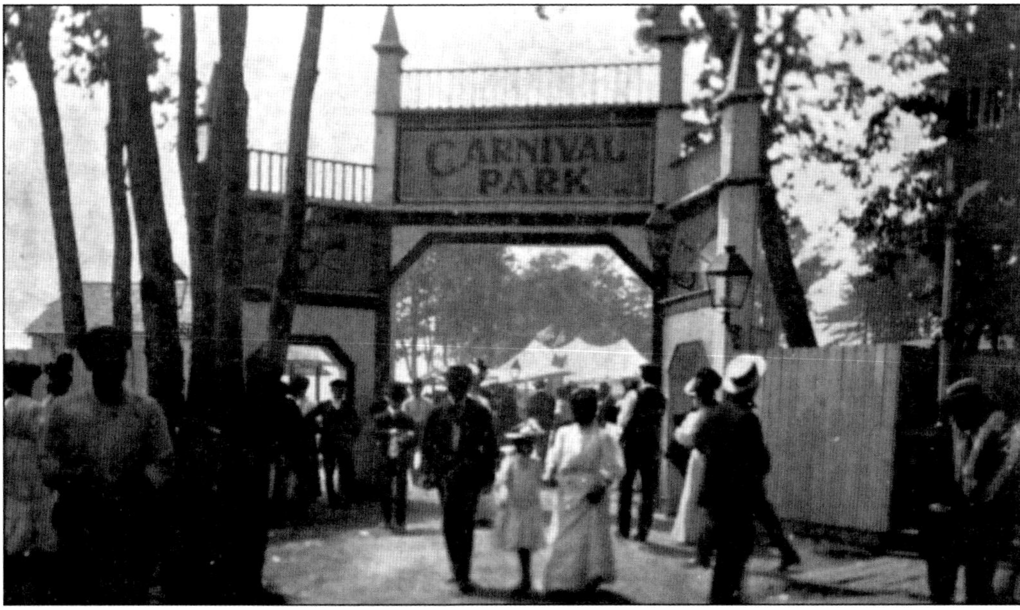

In 1902, Dr. Martin Cavana acquired ownership of Carnival Park. His innovations and improvements added a diversity of thrills and fun for vacationers. The eastern entrance to Carnival Park was located at the end of Park Avenue. As visitors entered the midway, anticipation built for both young and old. Screams from the roller coaster filled the air balanced by a merry melody from the carousel and the sounds of laughter.

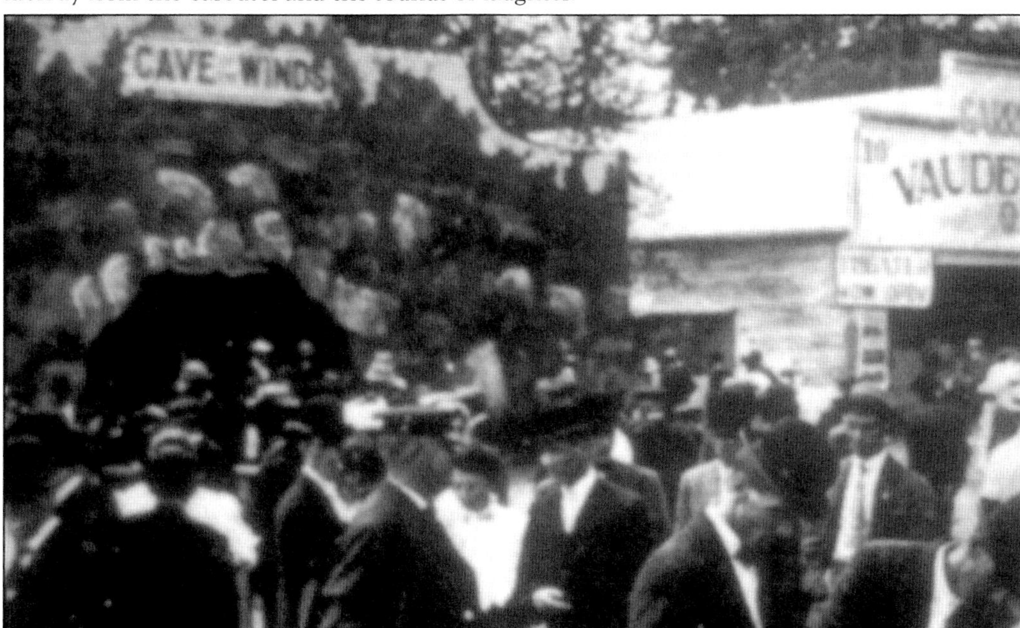

Garrka's Vaudeville and the Cave of Winds were just two of the attractions in Carnival Park. Sylvan Beach is a small village; however, during the summer season, visitors often outnumbered residents 20 to 1. There were seldom any problems. Here a police officer mingles with the crowd; the officers and residents of Sylvan Beach are known for their friendliness and willingness to help a stranger.

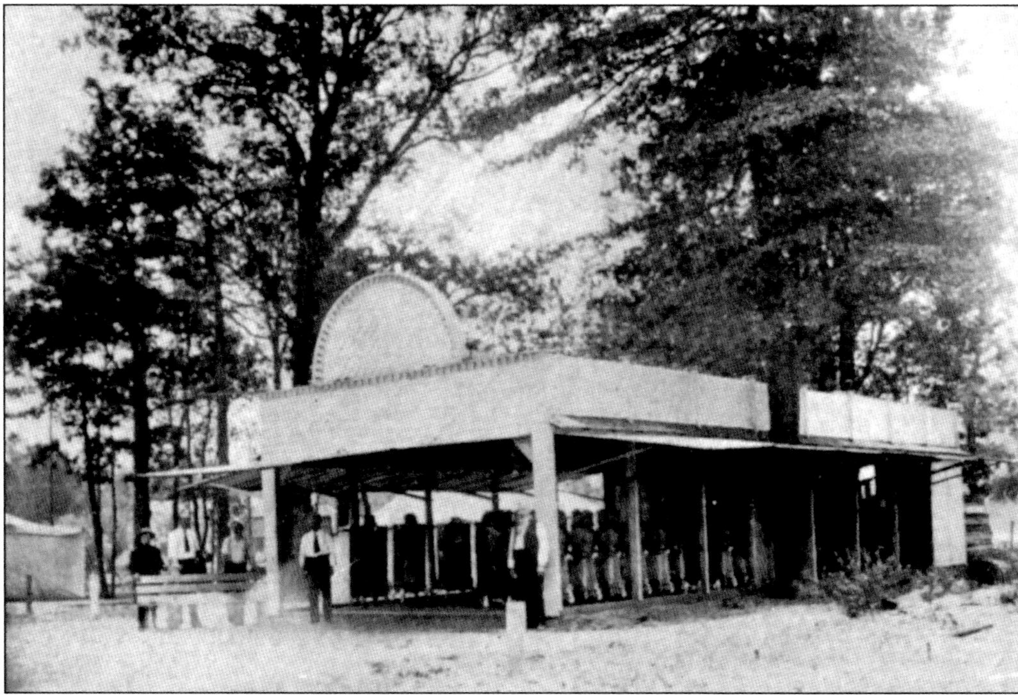

During the Cavana years, the Marcellus Brothers built the amusement halls in Carnival Park. They advertised "all the fun you want." A guy was a hero to his girl when he spent a dime to win her a nickel prize. Shooting galleries and games of chance lined the streets of Carnival Park.

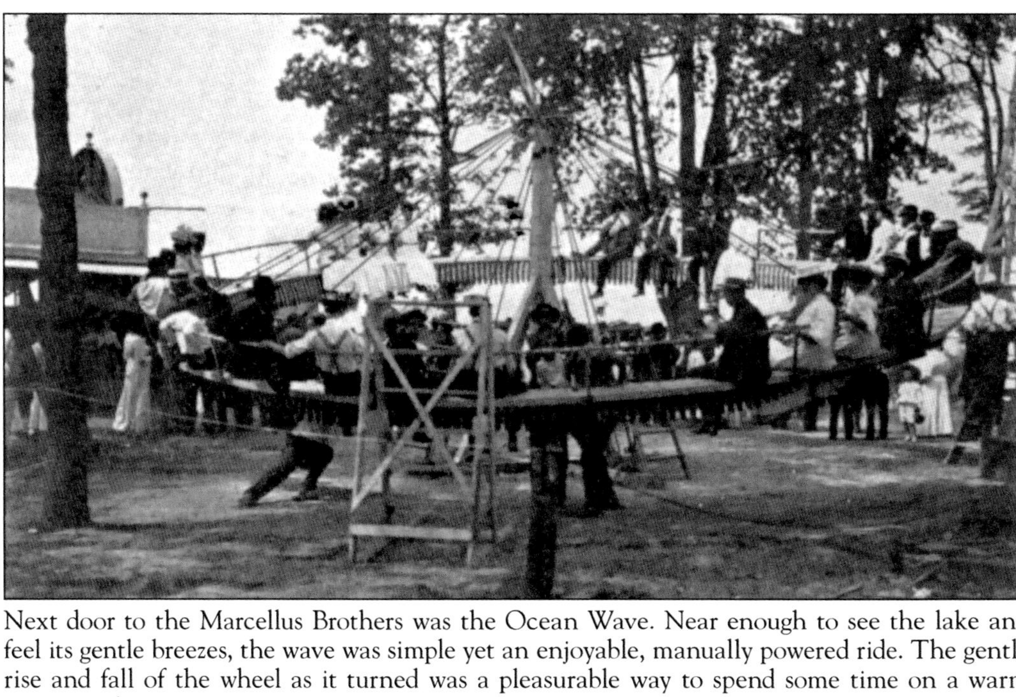

Next door to the Marcellus Brothers was the Ocean Wave. Near enough to see the lake and feel its gentle breezes, the wave was simple yet an enjoyable, manually powered ride. The gentle rise and fall of the wheel as it turned was a pleasurable way to spend some time on a warm summer's day.

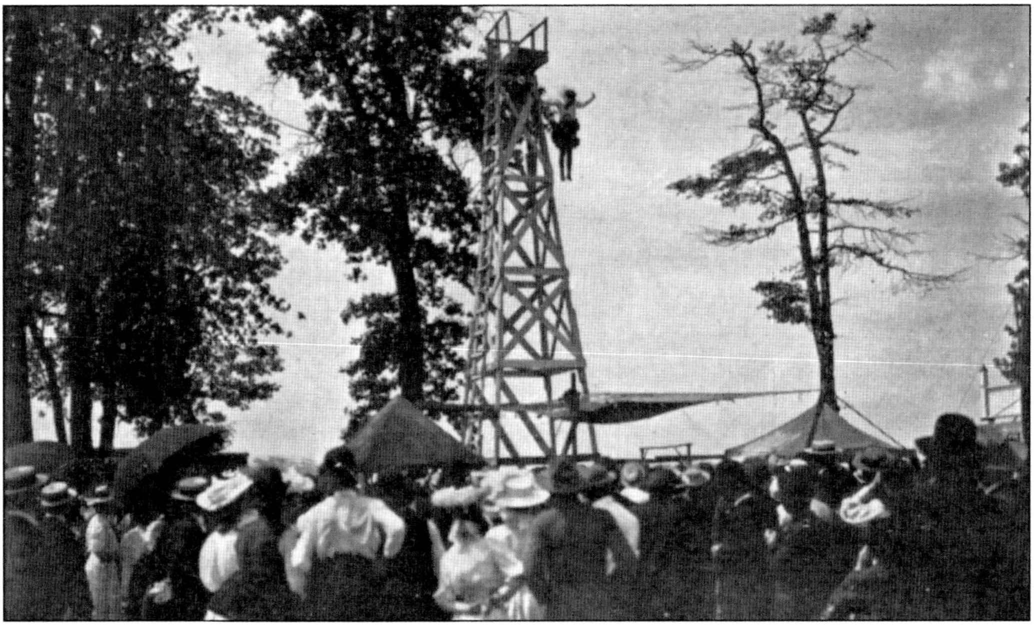

To the right of the Ocean Wave, crowds gathered to watch a young lady falling toward a tarp stretched beneath her. A wide variety of entertainment was presented each day throughout the season. When Dr. Martin Cavana expanded the midway, he imported clowns, acrobats, and high divers of both sexes. Here vacationers are thrilled by the daring feats of a young lady high diver.

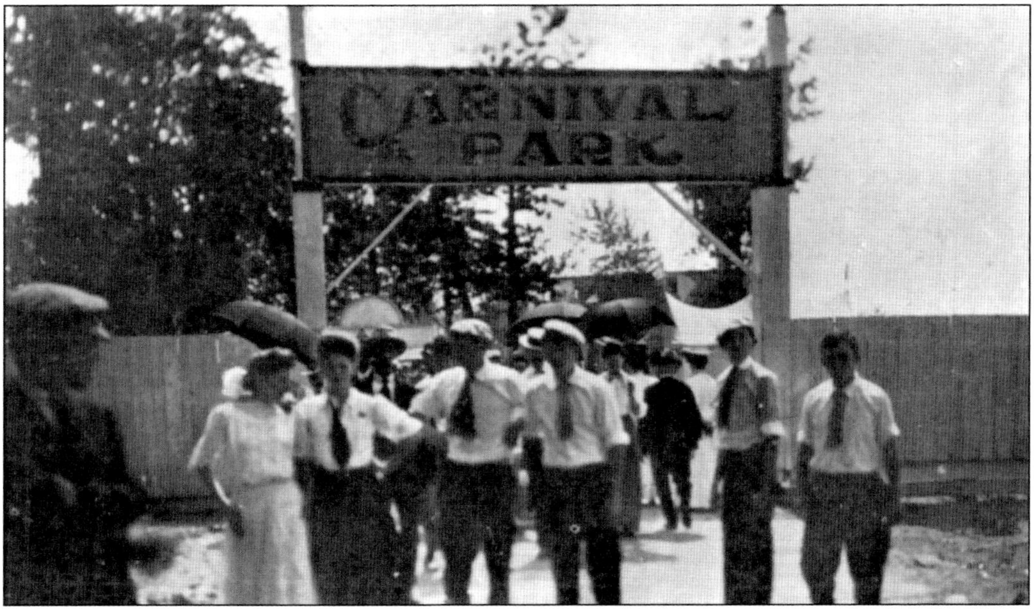

Leaving Carnival Park by way of the west gate, vacationers left the pleasure of a Ferris wheel and a miniature train ride for children behind as they approached a facade of white sands and shallow water. The beach spread out before them for nearly five miles, and the shores were cluttered with hotels, camps, and concessions. Oneida Lake offered a whole new way to experience pleasure on a summer's day.

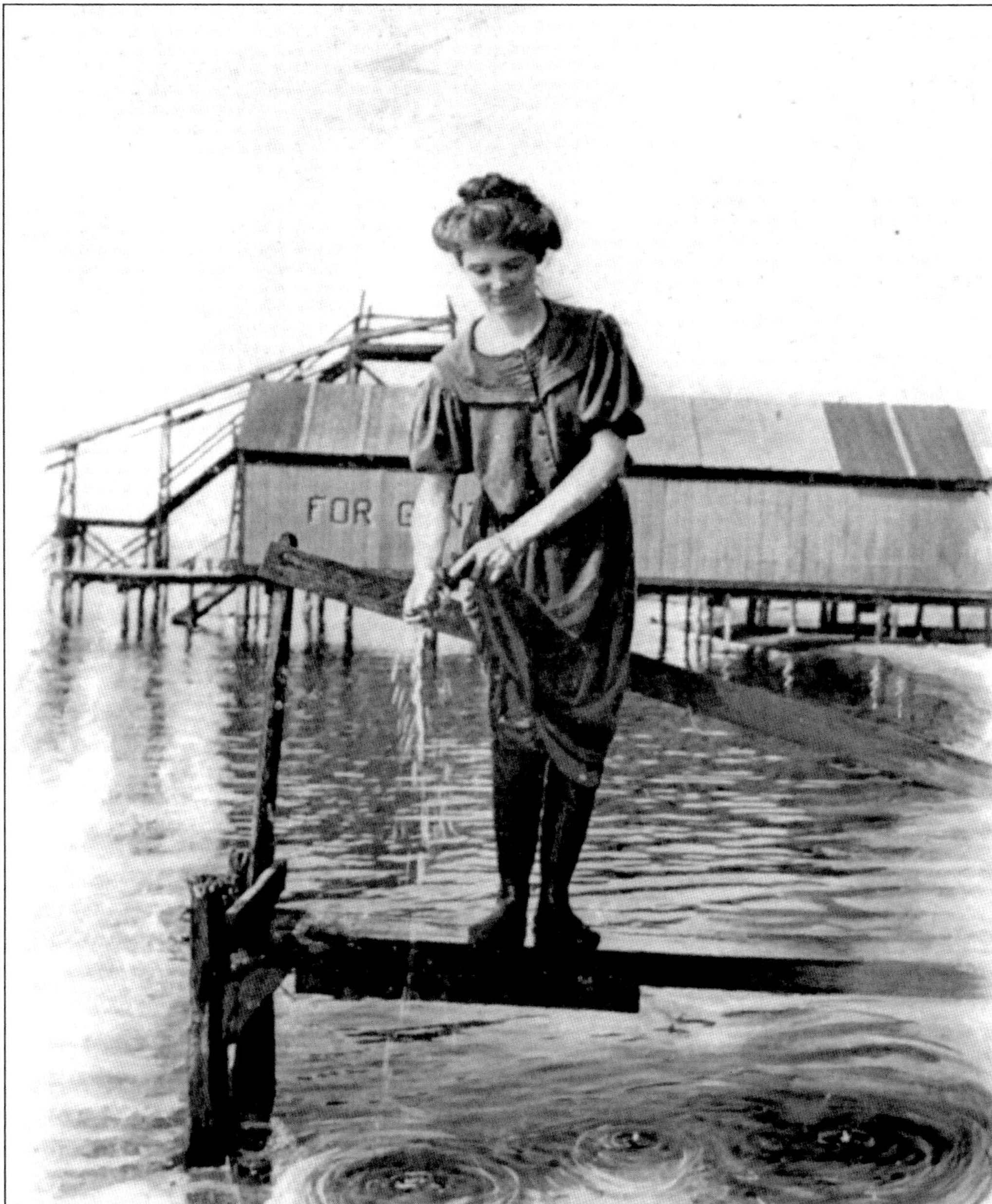

The early pioneers that explored the area named Oneida Lake after the Oneida Indians, a tribe that lived on the shores and fished the waters. It is not known if the pioneers chose that name because of their friendship with the Native Americans or because, like the Oneida Indians, the lake was most often calm and gentle. Sylvan Beach, located centrally in New York State, was acknowledged to be unsurpassed as a freshwater bathing area. Many visitors considered the beaches in Sylvan Beach far superior to those of the famous bathing beaches at Coney Island. The freshwater lake was fed by many springs, rivers, and creeks, and the white, sandy beaches at Sylvan Beach gave way to shallow, cool, clean water, most enjoyable on a hot summer's day. The lake teemed with many varieties of fish that included northern pike, Atlantic salmon, catfish, and perch, providing employment for residents as well as sport for visitors.

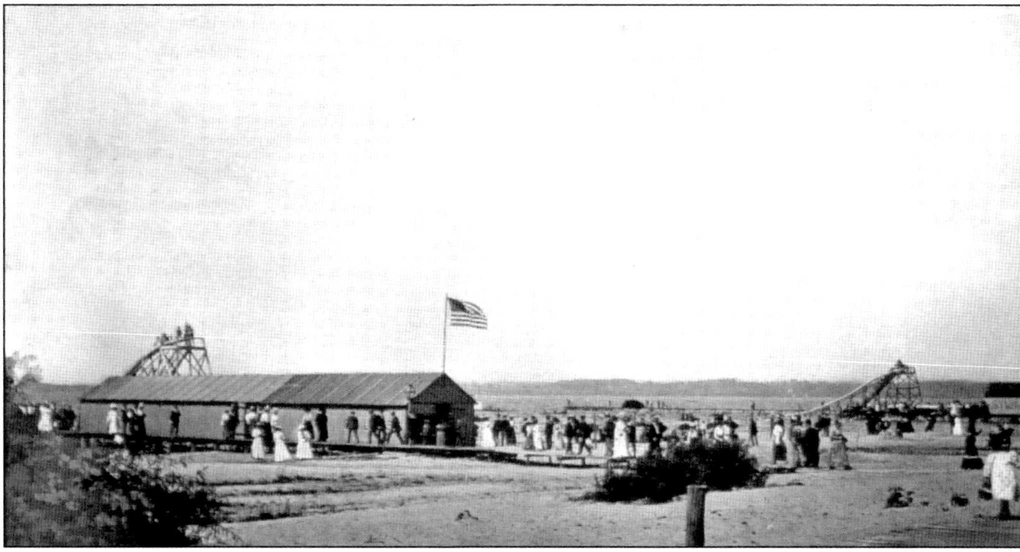

The Rowe Brothers bathhouse and toboggan slide, seen on the far right, were erected by George Delong in 1893. Ladies' and gentlemen's sections of the bathhouse were well marked, with the ladies' most often located nearest to the shore. Holes in the floor were provided for personal necessities; remember this was a time in history when outhouses were the norm.

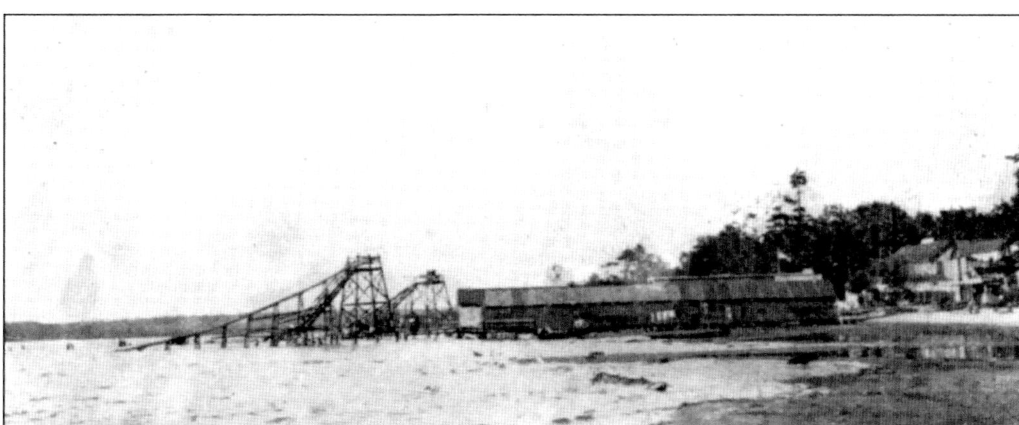

Several toboggans and additional bathhouses appeared over the years. Here are just two of the bathhouses and toboggans known to exist, one of which belonged to Rosco and Eva Cook, relatives of local centenarian George Cook. A popular attraction, the toboggan slide was the subject of a great many of the postcards produced during the era and also today.

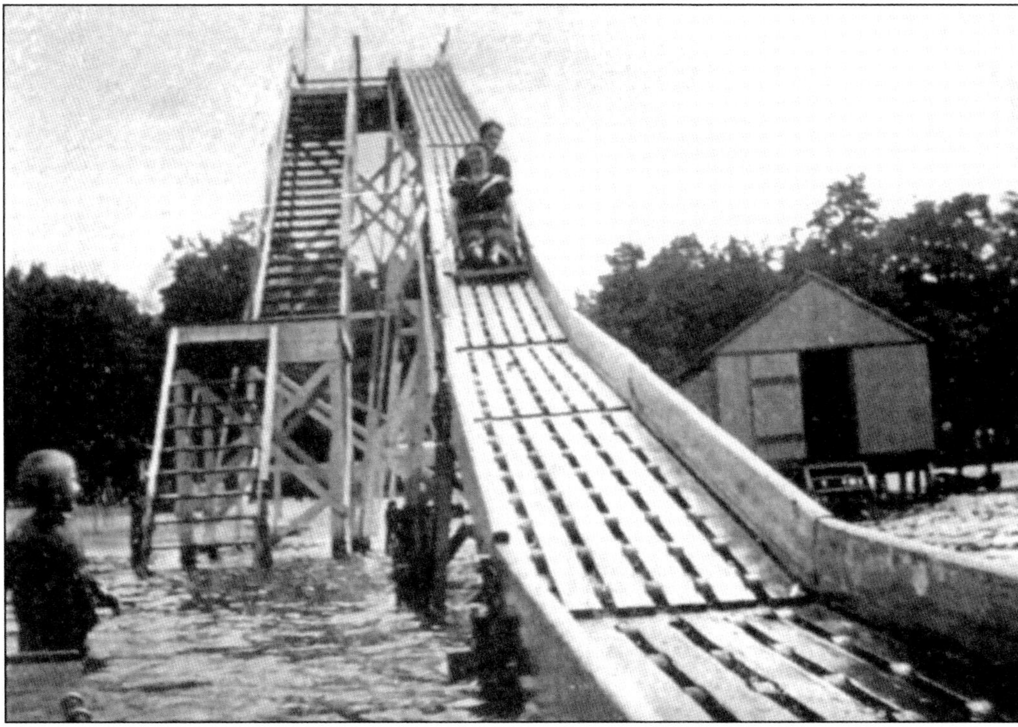

The regular thump of the toboggan as it slid from one section to the next going ever faster toward the water added to the thrill of the ride. The toboggans and bathhouses appeared in different locations, because after the warm season each year, they were placed onshore, keeping them safe from damage by the lake ice. So their positions were moved a bit each year.

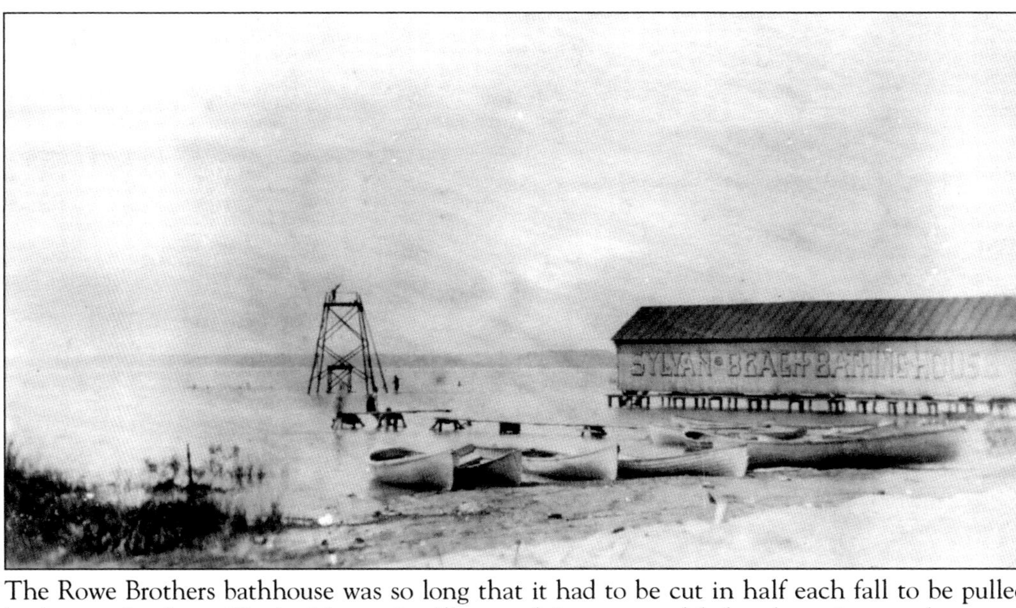

The Rowe Brothers bathhouse was so long that it had to be cut in half each fall to be pulled back onto the shore. The bathhouse is still around; it was remodeled and continues to be part of the entertainment in Sylvan Beach. Located next to the slide in the midway, the Rowe Brothers bathhouse is now Laugh Land.

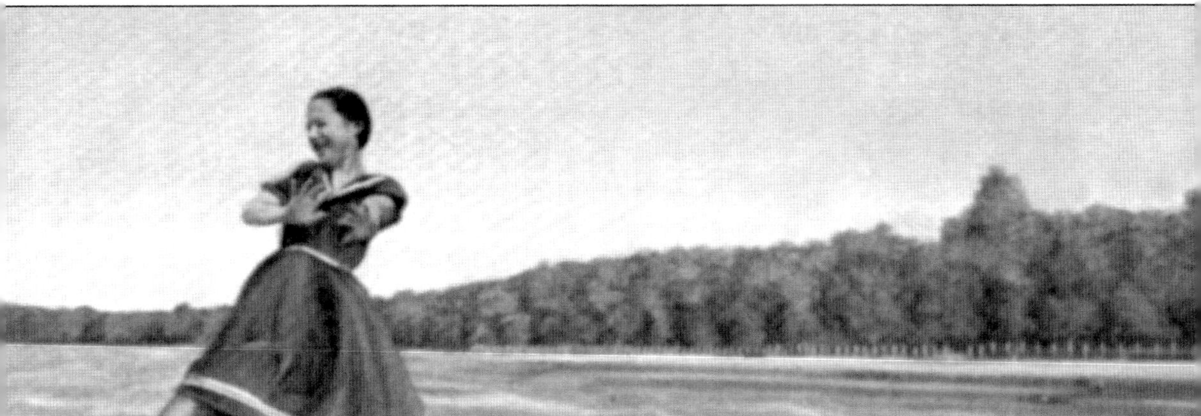

Mailed in 1907, this happy postcard carries the message, "This is the lake, up the lake about a quarter mile there's a regular summer colony—hotels, side shows, etc. The shore curves about and Wood River makes a nose shaped harbor. The lake is so shallow the bathers have to go out a long way to swim. We stocked up on plenty of food yesterday, but I lost the key!" Another card mailed on June 15, 1910, said, "I walked way out where the water came to my chin standing up straight. If I had you here I'd surely throw you in. Lois." The swimming costumes worn by women at the dawn of the 20th century often included dark stockings, hats, and slippers that laced. These young ladies seem to have dispensed with these added encumbrances and are having a great time.

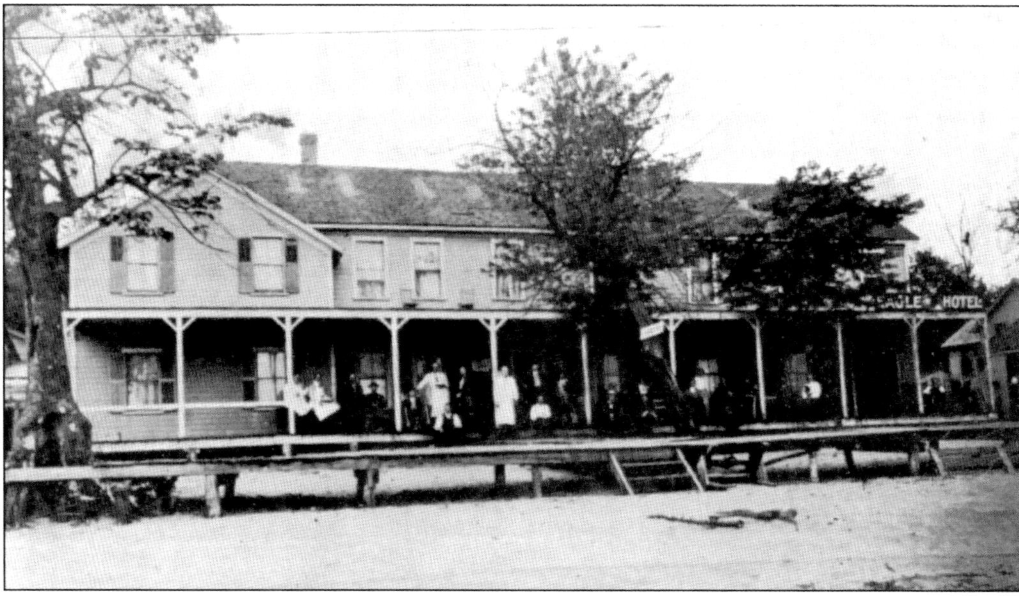

The Eagle Hotel appeared on many of the traditional postcards from Sylvan Beach. Known by the word *hotel* on its roof in huge letters, it has often been identified incorrectly. Just a two-minute walk from the New York, Ontario and Western Railway depot, proprietor J. Frank Miller offered 40 rooms in the lakefront hotel at reasonable rates. Also provided were a dance pavilion, bathhouse, and steamboat landing.

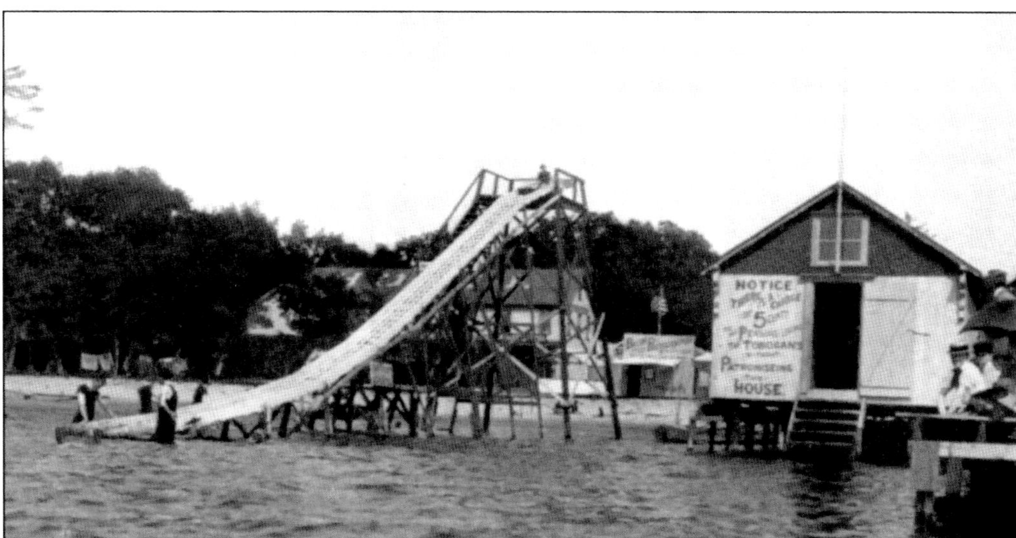

With a few steps over the boardwalk, patrons of the Eagle Hotel could take advantage of the sandy beach or experience the thrill of the toboggan slide. The sign on the bathhouse states there is a 5¢ charge to anyone using the toboggan even if they did not patronize the bathhouse. Bacon Photographer offered three pictures for 50¢; often those photographs were placed on postcards.

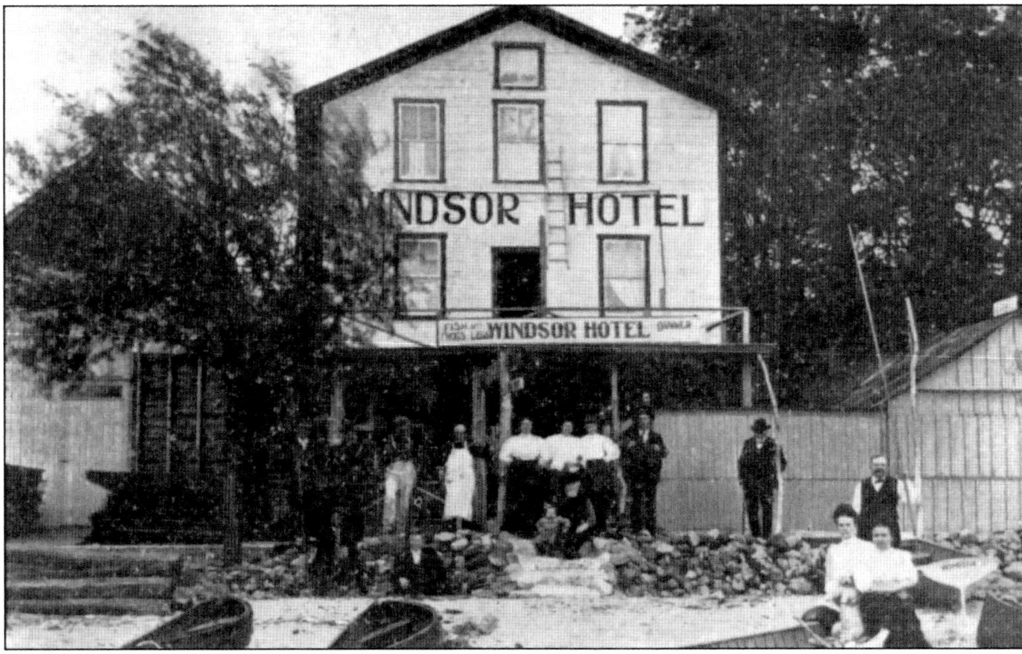

A short distance away to the south of the Eagle Hotel was the Windsor Hotel. Advertised as being only 1,000 steps from the New York, Ontario and Western Railway depot, this large hotel offered facilities for 100 guests. Proprietor D. Rosco Hart boasted his establishment as the "best location on the lake" and offered a large menu of frog legs, fish, chicken, meats, and vegetables.

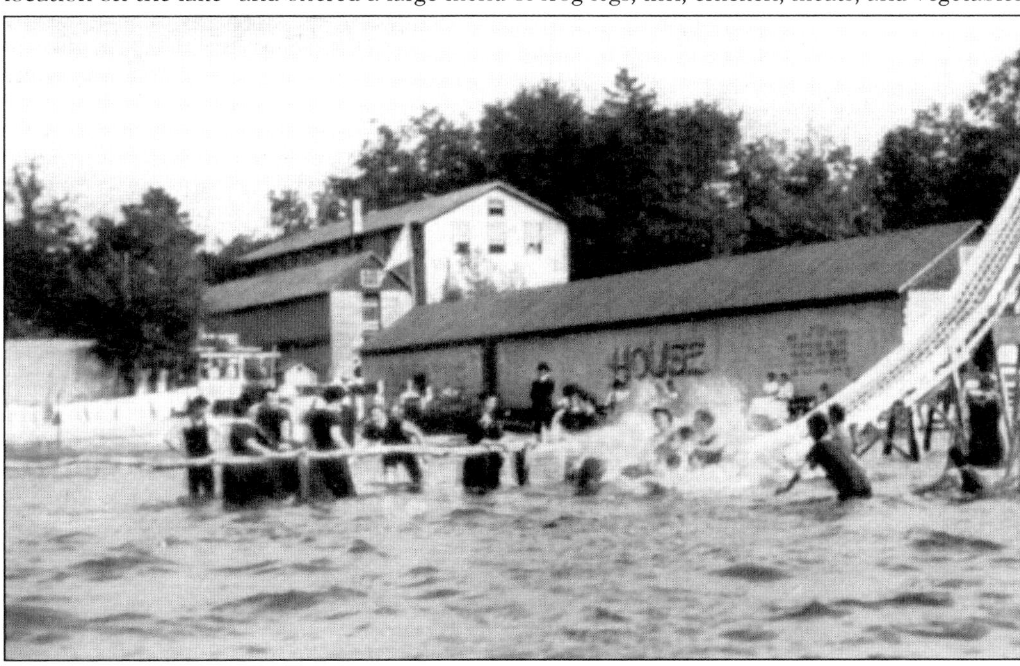

Although the major hotels stayed in the same place year after year, many of the concessions on the lakeshore changed, as did the position of the bathhouses and the toboggans, which can easily be seen in this picture. That is the Windsor Hotel peaking over the roof, but the toboggan is placed at a different angle.

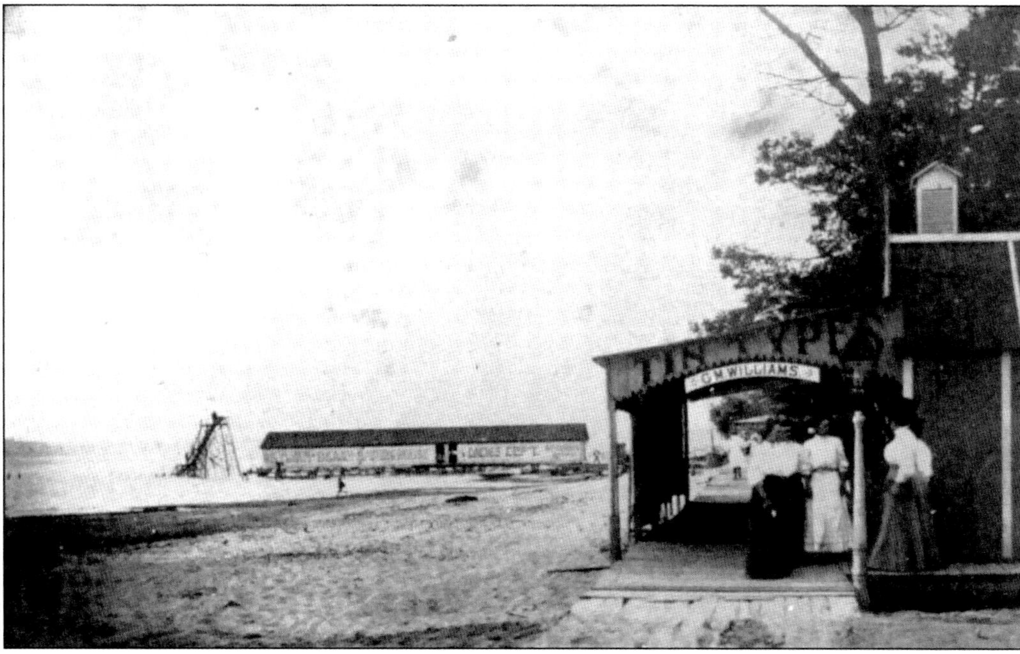

Looking north, Williams Tin Type was a regular sight and a popular stop for many of the vacationers on the beach. Located near the Rowe Brothers toboggan, the establishment advertised tintypes and postcards. A book produced around 1910 stated, "Look for the postcard man on the boardwalk, sixteen years of satisfactory work."

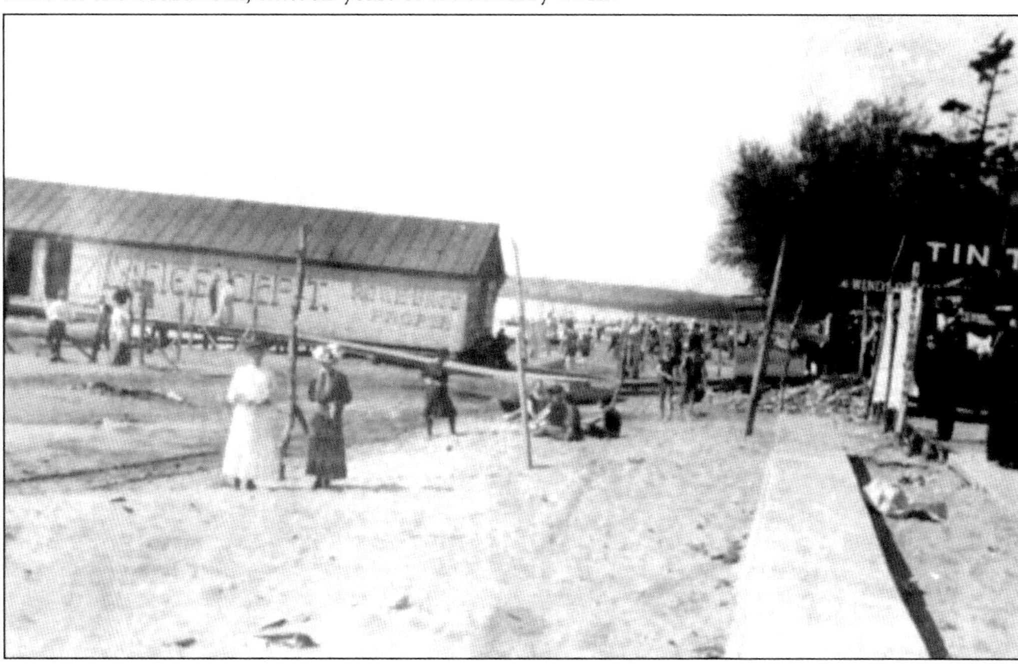

Tintypes were made by taking a photograph directly onto a sensitized plate of enameled tin or iron. Also called a ferrotype, they were very popular in the late 1800s. The boardwalk is very narrow at the south end of the beach in this photograph from around 1910. Evidence shows most all the boardwalks were replaced with concrete walks by 1913.

This tintype was produced on August 11, 1898. The first names of these young ladies are not known; however, one is a Haskins, and one is a Cook. Tintype establishments sprang up all over Sylvan Beach. Relatively inexpensive, tintypes were a pleasant reminder of a happy vacation or a great gift for friends and loved ones.

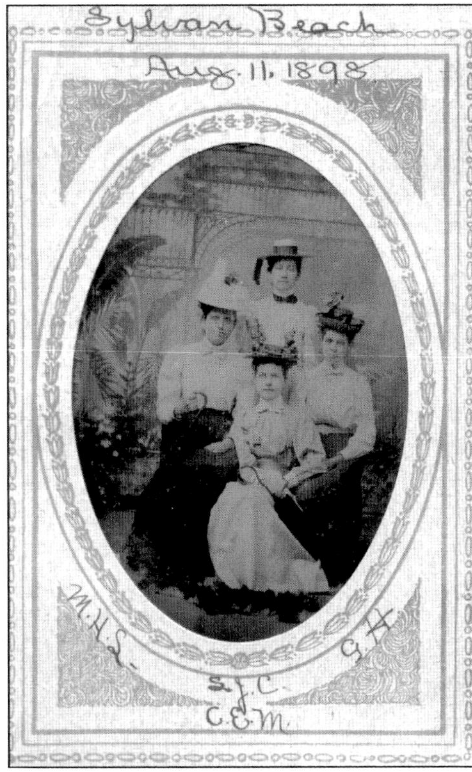

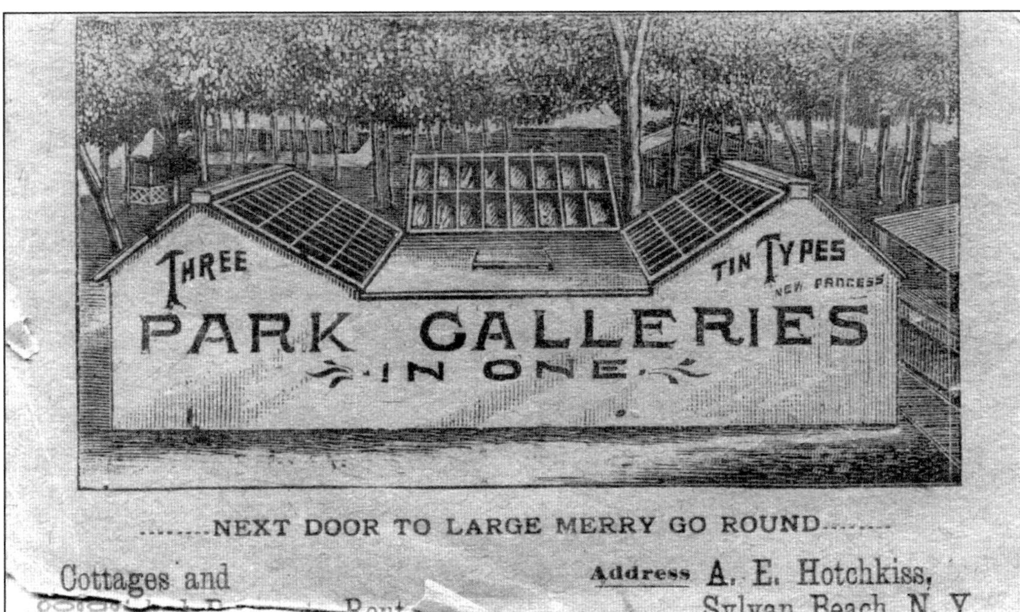

Several of the hotels in Sylvan Beach housed tintype studios. The Bon-Ton Studio, run by W. H. Pearce, was based in the Forest Home Hotel. The above tintype was produced at the Park Galleries, which advertised the new photography process as three tintypes in one. It was conveniently located near the "large merry go round." The folder also advertises cottages and rooms to let from A. E. Hotchkiss.

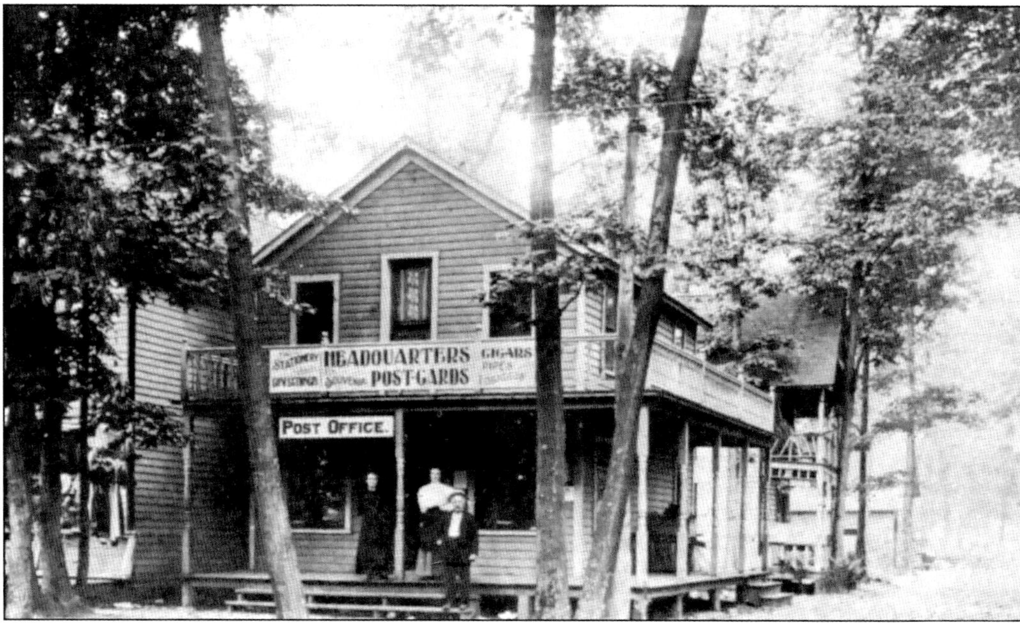

In this photograph taken in Sylvan Beach around 1910, the sign says, "headquarters for souvenir postcards." A small tobacco and stationery store also housed the post office. Years ago, almost all postal facilities in these small hamlets were housed in some type of store and were only a sideline for the store owners.

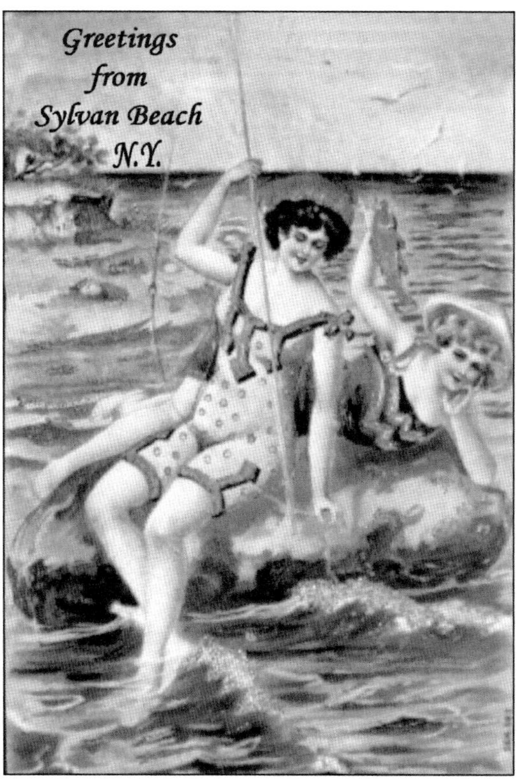

This Victorian-style postcard is a good representation of the whimsical type of pictures used to advertise the wonderland that was Sylvan Beach. It was a place to go to enjoy and leave the toil of making a living behind. The back of this card is not divided, with one side for the address and one side for the message, as later cards were. It cost just 1¢ to mail.

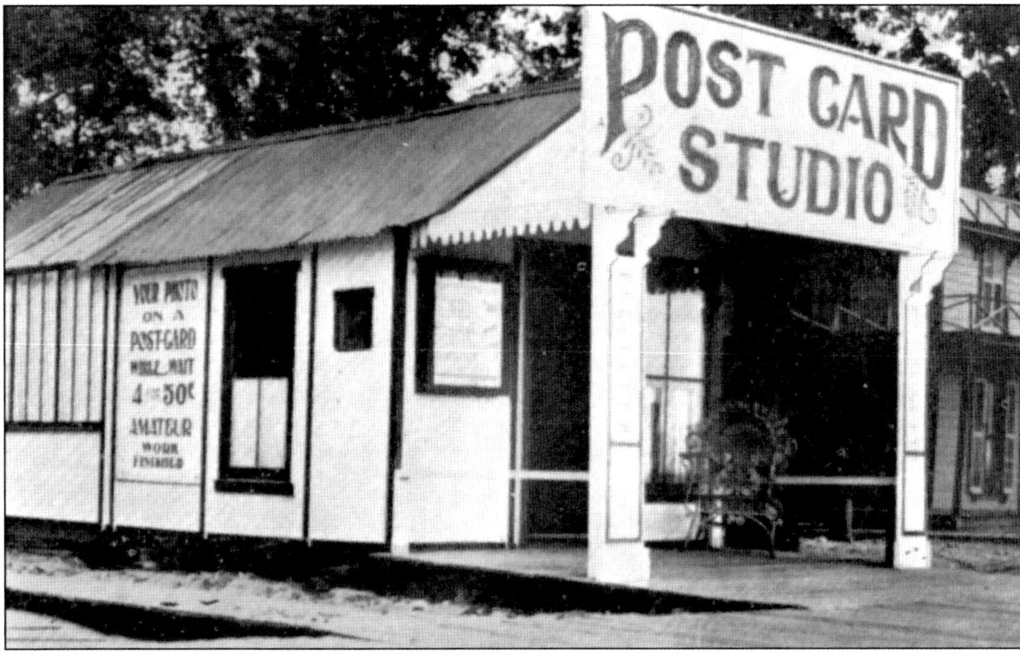

With the invention of photographic paper, photographs were easier to produce. Personal postcards showing one person or a group on vacation were soon to follow. Around 1910, C. N. Dutton describes himself as the pioneer of postcards. His sign advertised four cards for 50¢, and he would put a customer's picture on a postcard while the customer waited.

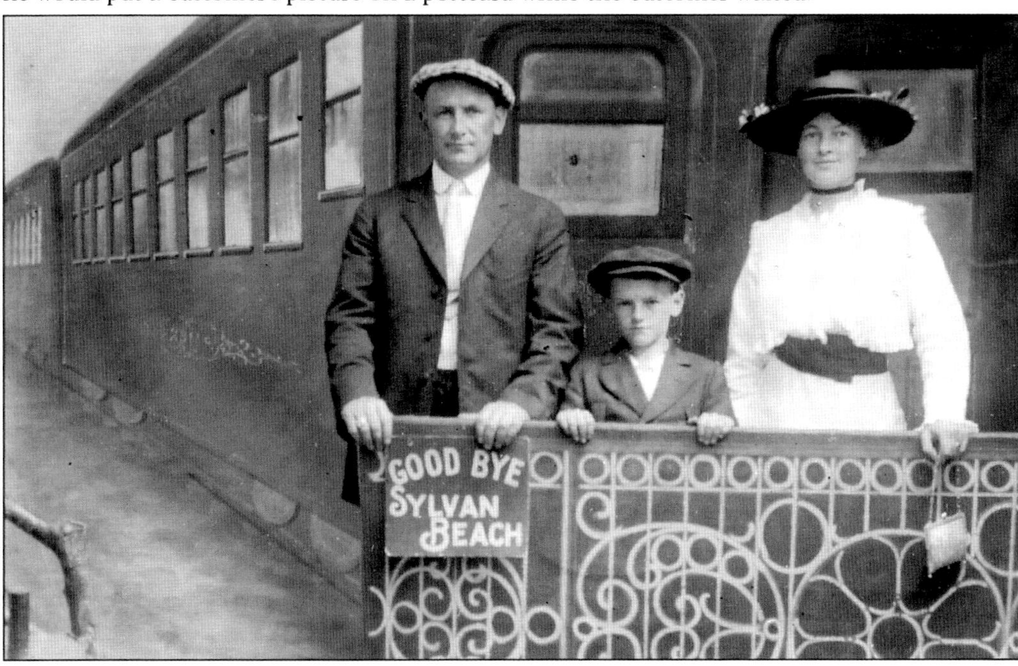

It appears that Oneida residents William and May Rogers Woglum and their son Cornelius are aboard a railroad car leaving Sylvan Beach. However, things are not always as they seem. This photograph was taken in a photographer's studio and placed on a postcard. The railroad car was a popular background used over and over again. May was one of Walton Rogers's daughters.

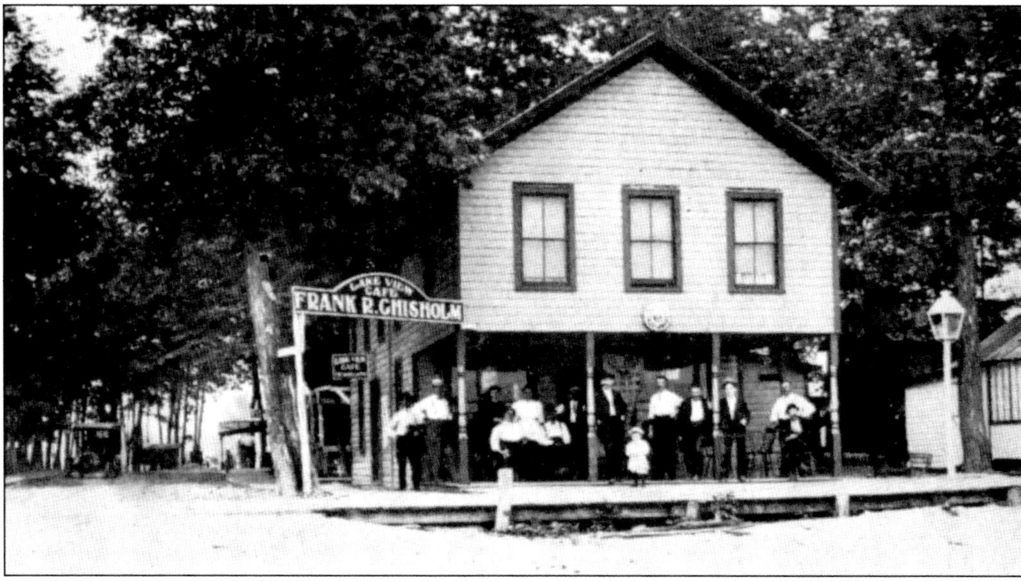

The Park View Hotel, located near Wood River across from Spencer's Park, was a victim of progress. It was torn down in the 1960s to make room for a new highway bridge across the Barge Canal. Sylvan Beach was built by a cross section of society; at one time, this local hangout was owned by people who came from Spain.

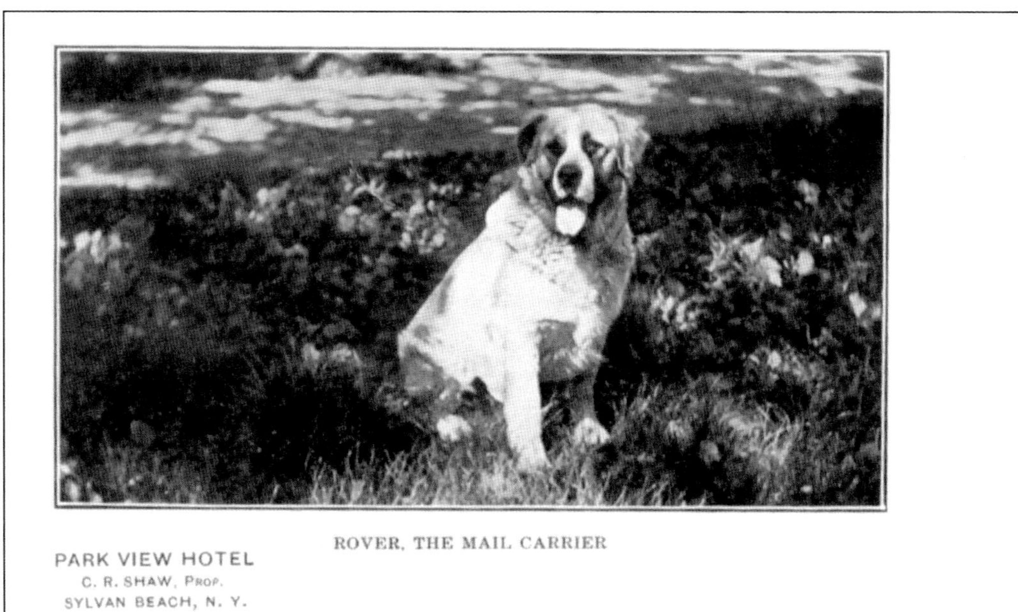

When C. R. Shaw was the proprietor of the Park View Hotel, he featured Rover the mail dog on souvenir postcards from the hotel. Inside the hotel were mirrors similar to those in the fun house in the midway. Some made patrons look tall and skinny or short and fat, and a few even left them feeling dizzy.

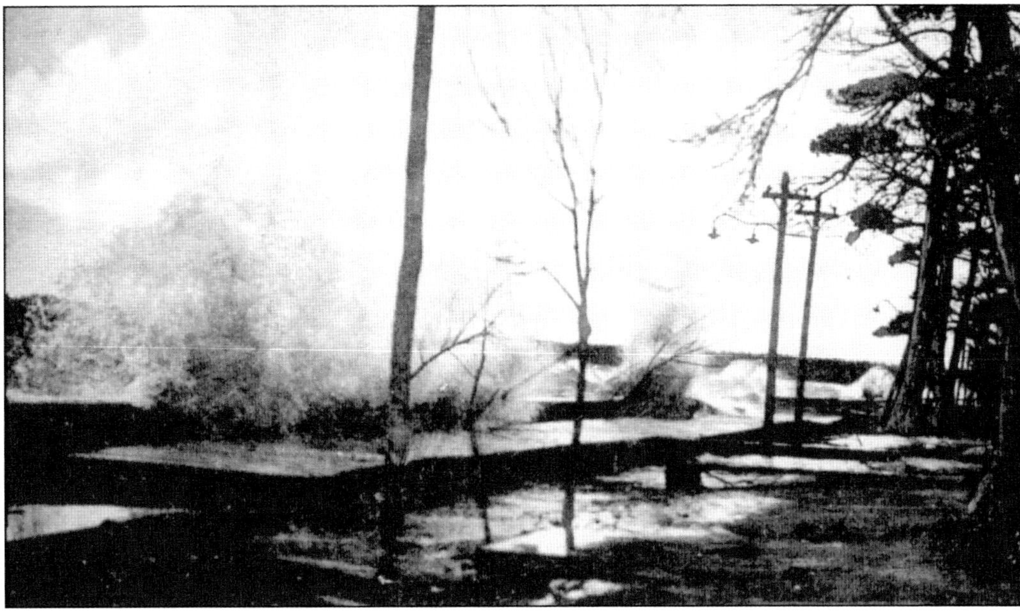

A particularly destructive windstorm hit Sylvan Beach on April 23, 1912. A photographer caught the spray from the breaking waves as they whipped over the lampposts lining the boardwalk along the beachfront. Eventually sections of the boardwalk were undermined and washed away. It was not the wind but the forces of water that caused the greatest amount of property damage over the years.

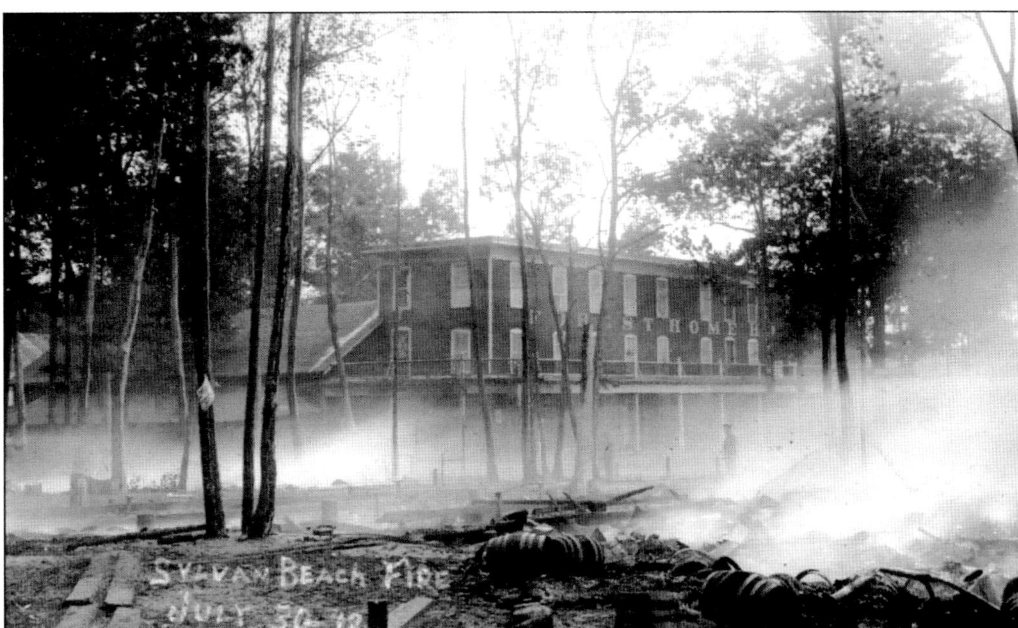

The remnants of hotels and taverns are seen here on July 30, 1912. A fire consumed many of the buildings in the area, but the Forest Home Hotel survived. Often a lightning strike started a fire, and the fire department of the time was nearly powerless to stop the destruction. Many times, firemen helped to remove the contents from the buildings nearby in case they caught fire too.

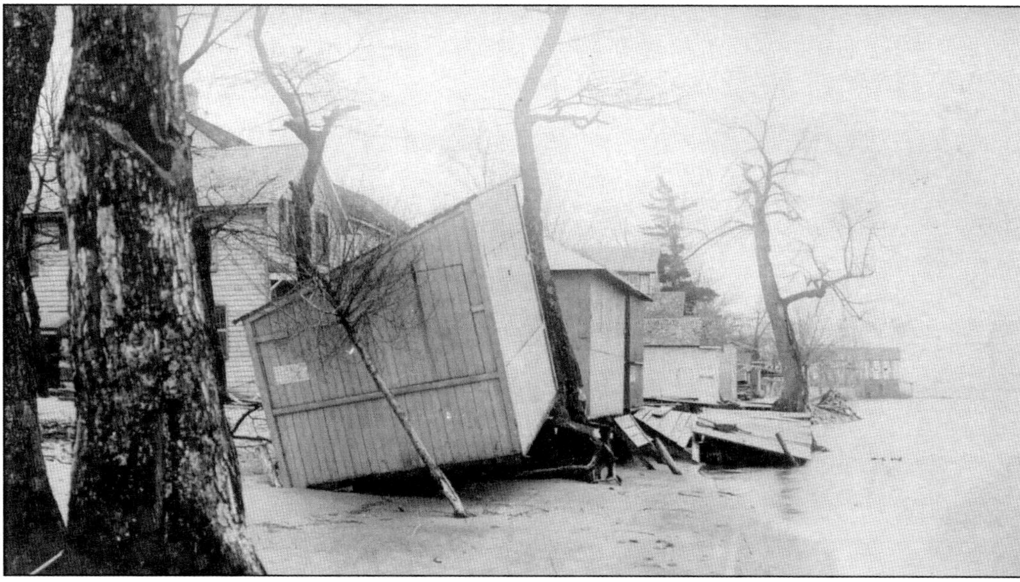

On a gray day for Sylvan Beach, wind and water tossed concession stands about like so many empty boxes. A toboggan lies on its side by the bathhouse in front of the Windsor Hotel. The awning on Williams Tin Type was still there, and so were the people determined to make things right. Sylvan Beach has cleaned up, straightened up, rebuilt, and refurbished so many times, it is just another day to them.

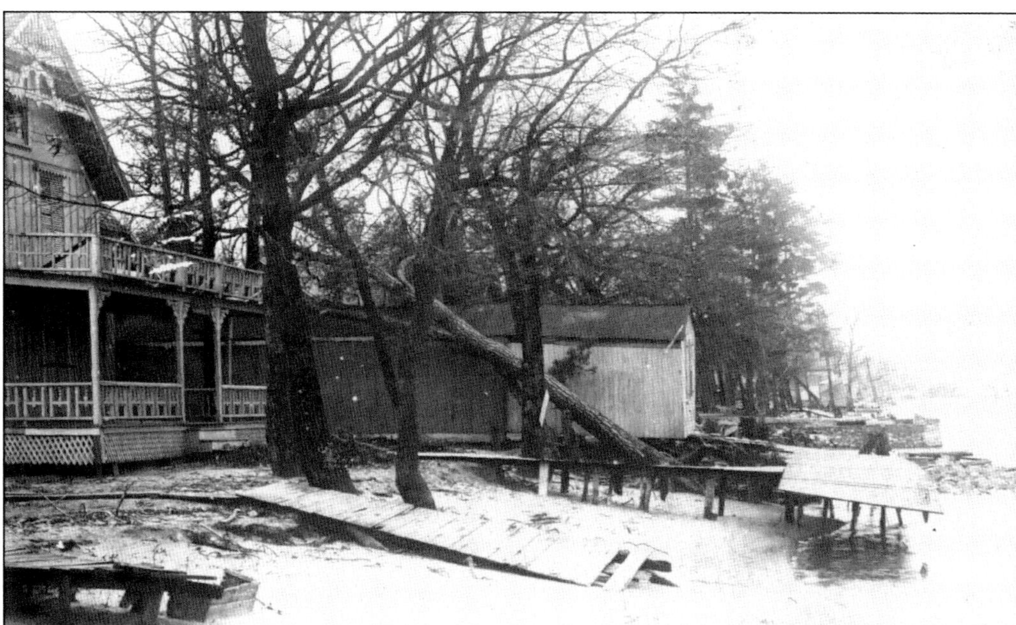

There is no better place to be than Oneida Lake on a calm, peaceful day with the blue skies above and birds gliding gracefully to and fro. However, when a west wind picks up, it is an entirely different matter. As a shallow lake, it quickly builds great waves, steep and choppy; they are hazardous to boats on the lake and to the shoreline.

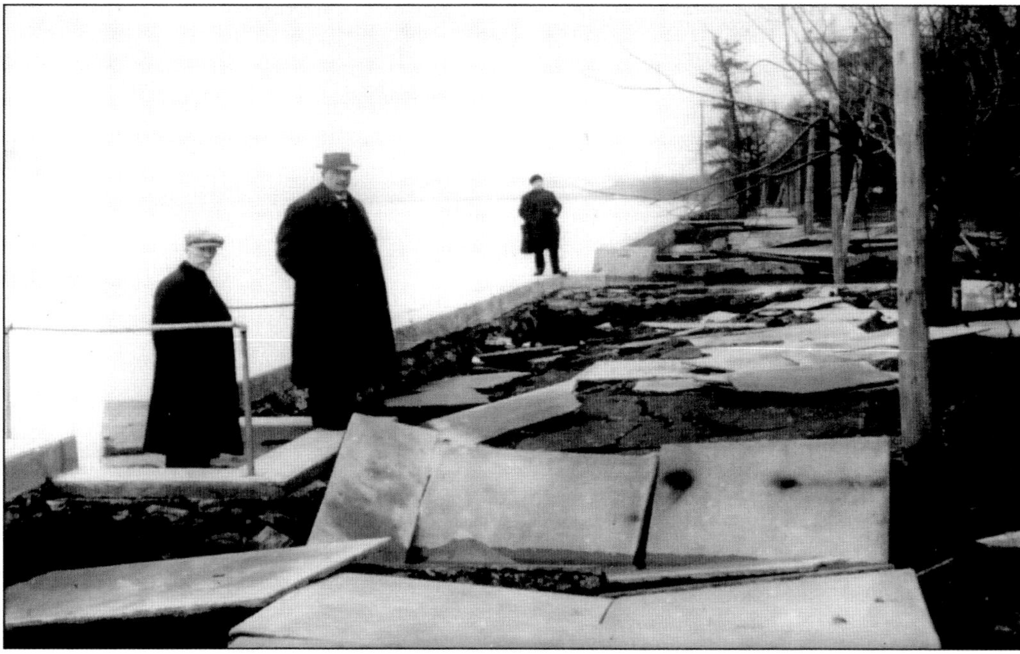

William O'Brien (center), superintendent of the central division of the Erie Canal, inspects the damage caused by a storm in 1913. Storms on Oneida Lake can pass as quickly as they arrive. Within minutes, the frightening ferocity of giant waves and flying objects is replaced by an eerie peace on a calm lake belied by a shattered concrete promenade haphazardly strewn about.

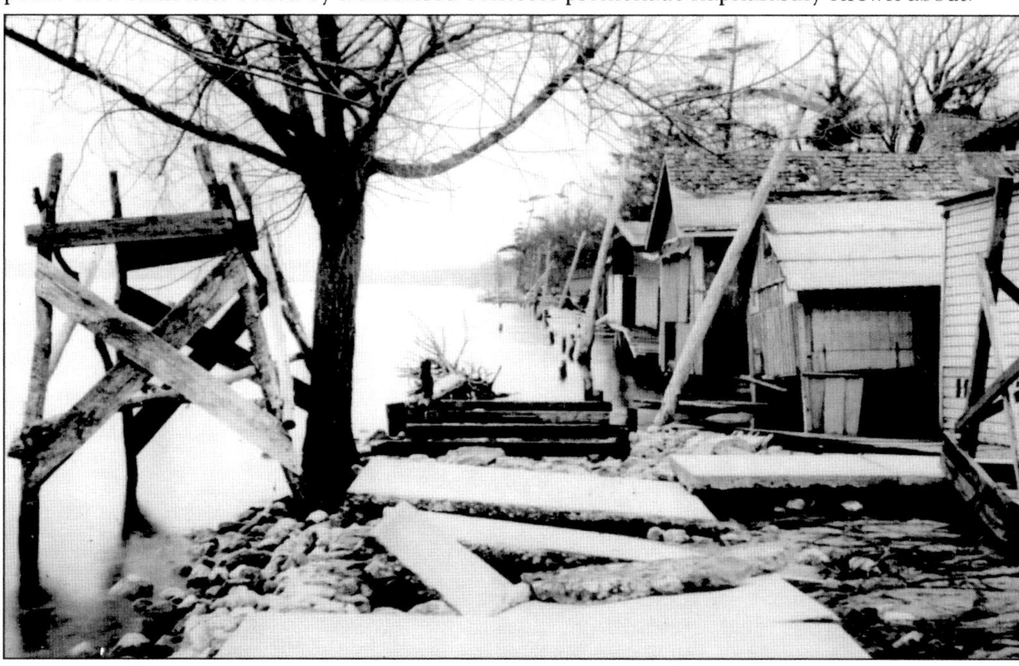

Remnants of the storm of 1913 continue to litter the shoreline in this photograph. A portion of the high-diving platform from Carnival Park has somehow ended up sitting in the lake. The broken concrete slabs of a lakeshore sidewalk led to no sidewalk at all, where water has replaced the avenue that once lay in front of these cottages.

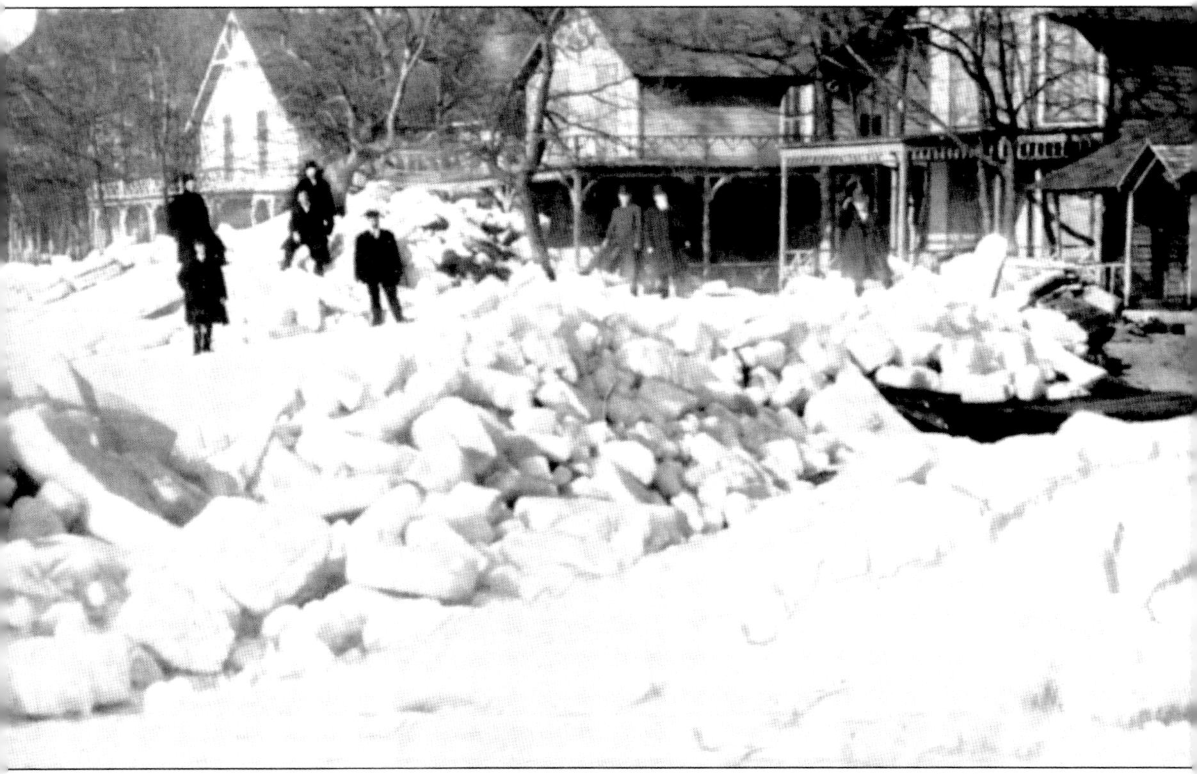

A deep thunder fills the night, a rumble that can be heard from miles away. Children were told it was the spirit of Paul Bunyan, who was bowling to pass the time away. However, they learned at a very early age that it was the ice breaking up on the great Oneida Lake. Wind and currents pile the ice, sometimes to unbelievable heights, as seen here. Dr. Martin Cavana is pictured in front to the right. Oneida Lake is 22 miles long and encompasses an area of nearly 80 square miles. With 65 miles of shoreline, it is the largest freshwater lake contained within the boundaries of one state and also the largest in its class within the continental United States. It cools local residents in summer, and warmth from the water affects the winter. It has fed the people and provided them with sport and, at times, has been the cause of great sadness. Always it has been there, Oneida Lake, the reason for it all.

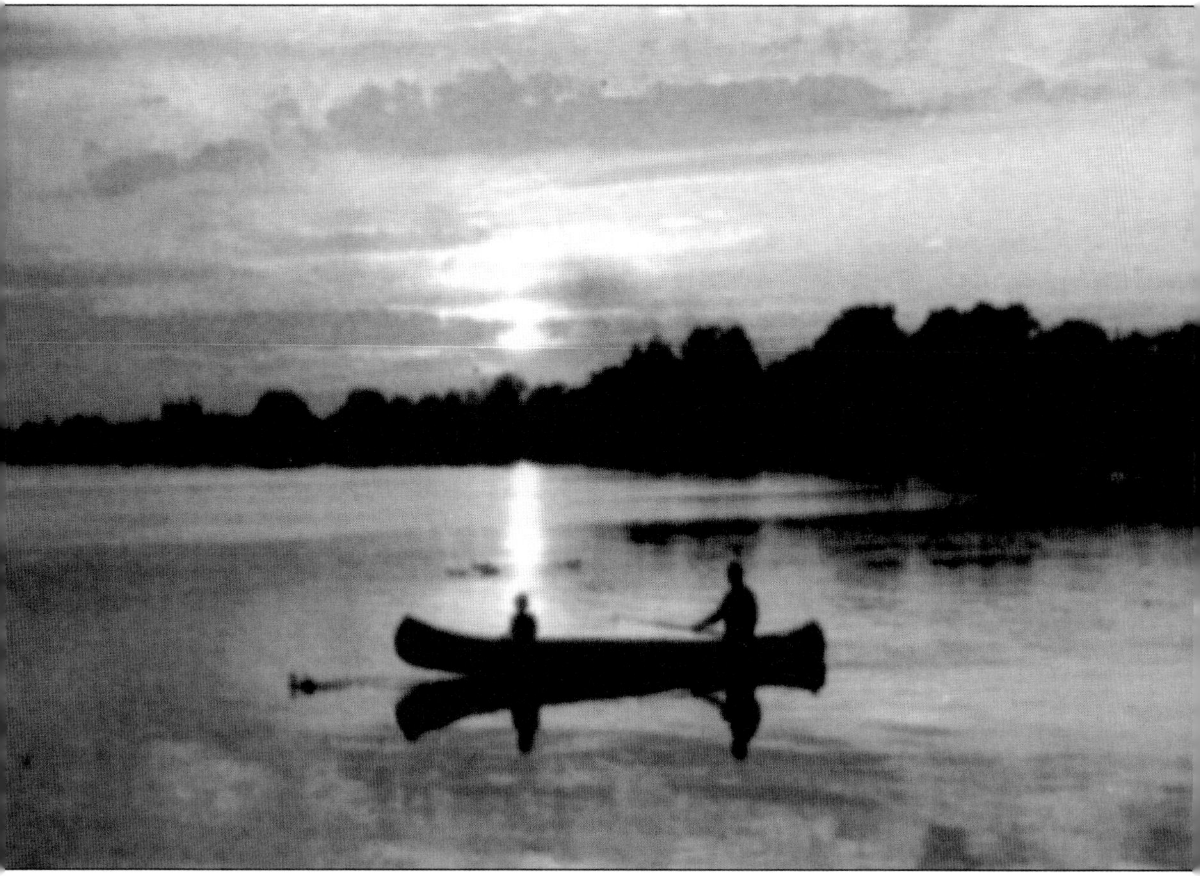

Life is easier today with all the modern inventions, but it seems to be moving so fast. In the early days, people came to Sylvan Beach seeking the peace and seclusion offered by a quiet river and a shallow blue lake. First the railroad invaded, and then the Barge Canal cut through Wood River. Luna Park was lost to progress, and finally the automobile appeared. Sylvan Beach has worked hard to survive and capture some of the magic of the golden years. It must have been a much gentler time, a time worth remembering. It took many families to build Sylvan Beach and North Bay. It was not just the elite but also the people that labored daily: the farmers, fishermen, store owners, and the people that worked for them. It was the people that worked day after day with their friends and neighbors to survive that made a difference. It is for them that this history is written. Good night Sylvan Beach, live long and prosper.